AF608747

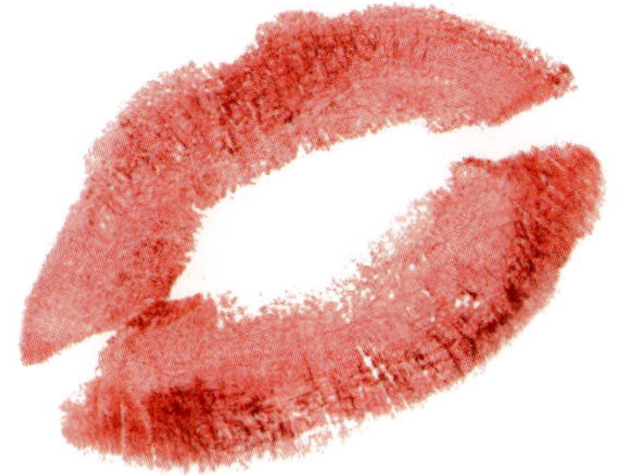

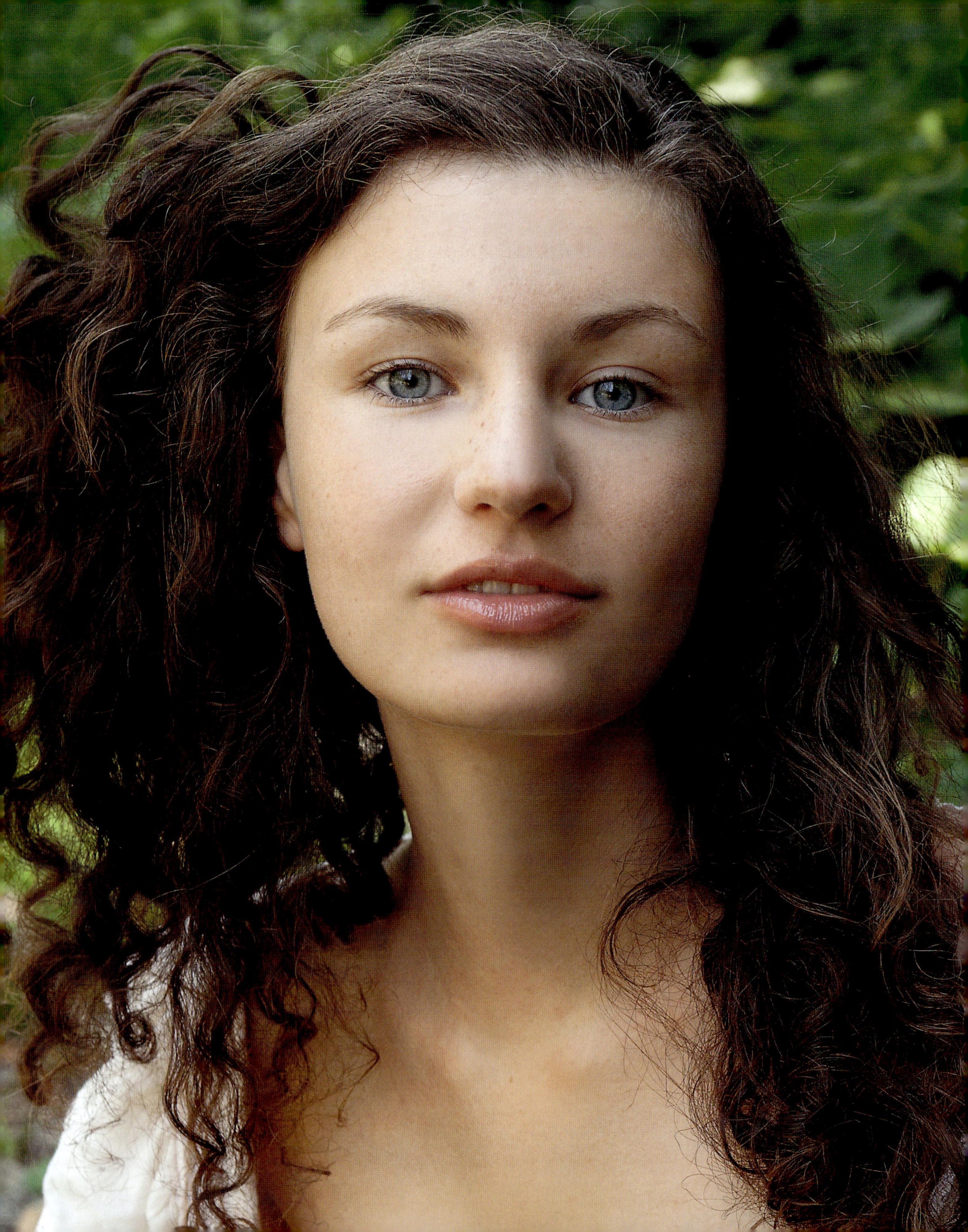

STEFAN SOELL

SUSANN

MY ALL TIME FAVOURITE MODEL

EDITION Skylight

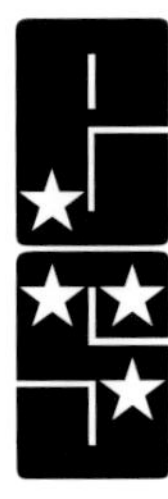

First Edition 2024

EDITION SKYLIGHT
Rosengartenstr. 13B
CH-8608 Bubikon/Zürich
Switzerland
info@edition-skylight.com
www.edition-skylight.com

ISBN 978-3-03766-698-2

Bibliographic information published by Die Deutsche Bibliothek
Die Deutsche Bibliothek lists this publication in the Deutsche Nationalbibliografie; detailed bibliographic data are available in the Internet at http://dnb.ddb.de.

www.stefansoell.de
English text editing: Eugene Edwards

Printed in Czech Republik

SUSANN

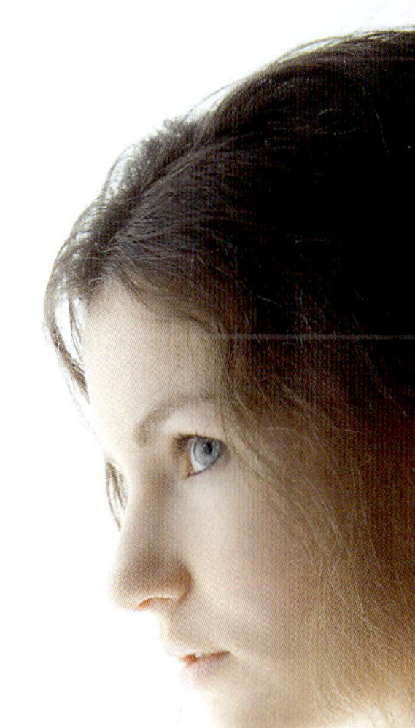

Damals, ich weiß es noch ganz genau, das erste Shooting im lauwarmen Wasser des Bodensees. Bis zur Hüfte hoch umschmeichelte es zart meine Beine an diesem heißen Sommerabend. Als ich meinen Blick nach unten richtete, konnte ich die Fische beobachten und die Fische mich – wahrscheinlich völlig irritiert von den zwei strampelnden, nackten Beinen unter Wasser. HIIILFFE!! Dieses lebhafte Gewusel unter Wasser jagte mir doch einen «leichten» Schrecken ein. Schnell schwamm ich zu einem kleinen Rettungsfelsen, der aber unter der Wasseroberfläche lag. Ich stellte mich darauf und siehe da, es machte den Anschein, als würde ich auf dem Wasser stehen. Und Stefan rief völlig außer sich vor Begeisterung: «Susann bleib so! Ja genau so! Ohh man, sieht das irre gut aus!» Darauf folgten ein paar sehr gelungene Bilder und das, ohne von den Fischen «angeknabbert» zu werden. (→ S. 106)

Ein grandioses Erlebnis hatte ich oben in den Bergen auf 2000 Metern Höhe. Die Sonne stand tief und verschwand fast hinter den Gipfeln. Perfekte Lichtverhältnisse! Ein See! Drumherum verwachsen mit Moos und Gräsern. Optimal um ein paar Bilder zu schießen. Obwohl es hundselends-kalt war, zog ich mir die Kleider aus. Solidarisch wie Stefan ist, entledigte auch er sich seiner dicken Jacke und fotografierte nur in dünner Hose und T-Shirt. Ein Traum von See war das. Es erinnerte ein bisschen

I still remember it very well, my very first photo shoot, it was in the lukewarm water of Lake Constance. It caressed my legs up to the waist on a hot summer evening. Looking down I could watch the fish and the fish watched me – probably totally irritated by the two poking bare legs. «Help!» This lively hustle and bustle under water gave me quite a fright. I quickly ran to a small rock that was just below the surface of the water. Behold, I stood on it and it seemed like I was standing on the water. And Stefan, completely beside himself with enthusiasm, shouted: «Susann stay like that! Yes exactly! Oh man, that looks crazy good!» This was followed by a couple of very successful pictures without being nibbled by the fish. (→ p. 106)

I had a unique experience in the mountains at 2000 meters above sea level. The sun was low and almost disappeared behind the peaks. Perfect lighting conditions, a mountain lake on the shore overgrown with moss and grass, ideal for taking photos. Although it was very cold, I stripped off my clothes. Showing solidarity like Stefan, who also took off his thick jacket and only took the picture in thin pants and a T-shirt. It was a dreamy mountain lake. The scene was somewhat reminiscent of Scotland – and best of all, without frogs and other creepy crawlies at this altitude. The temperature was just 10 °C, but the breathtaking pictures made it worth it. Completely frozen, we finally started heading back and

an Schottland – und das Beste, ohne Frösche und anderer Krabbelviecher. Die Temperatur betrug gerade einmal 10 Grad, doch hat sich das Zittern gelohnt für ein paar atemberaubende Bilder. Endlich den Rückweg angetreten und völlig durchgefroren sahen wir von weitem eine Hütte. Da kam uns gleich der Gedanke einen Almkäse mitzunehmen. Also machten wir uns auf den Weg zur einsamen Hütte, gelegen auf der Hochebene des Bergrückens. Dort angekommen, wurden wir herzlich vom Almöhi und seiner Frau empfangen, die tatsächlich auch einen Käse für uns hatten. Als die beiden merkten, wie durchfroren wir waren, luden sie uns in die Holzhütte ein, auf eine heiße Tasse Tee. Gemütlich knisterte der Ofen in der Ecke, an dem wir unsere starren Glieder aufwärmten. Während Stefan sich angeregt mit unseren Gastgebern unterhielt, versuchte ich der Konversation zu folgen, welches mir jedoch nicht gelang, da die einheimische Sprache für Außenstehende nicht leicht verständlich ist. Glücklicherweise sprach Stefan hervorragend die «Sprache der Alpen». Da die Verständigung gut lief, lehnte ich mich entspannt zurück, mit meiner heißen Tasse Tee in den Händen und nickte lächelnd dem Almöhipärchen zu. (→ S. 110)

Eine duftende Kuhweide behielt ich tatsächlich in guter Erinnerung, auch wenn hin und wieder ein Füsschen in dem ein oder anderen Häufchen landete. IHHH! Bestimmt hatten die Kühe auch ihren Spaß daran gefunden, eine splitternackte Susann durch die Wiese hüpfen zu sehen. Eine der Kühe war wohl ganz besonders angetan und wollte mich gleich von hinten abschlecken. Und alle Kühleins muhhhhten im Akkord. Ohne diese sympathischen Tiere wären die Alpen nicht mehr dieselben. Von weitem hörte man sie laut rufen «muuhhh» und ihre Glocken, die sie um den Hals trugen, erklangen in einer wundervollen Melodie. Wenn man den Klängen des Glockenspiels folgt weiß man genau, Käs' und Almmilch sind nicht weit entfernt. Und so wurden wir nach dem Kuhweiden-Shooting mit einem Glas frischer Milch auf der Almhütte belohnt. (→ S. 112)

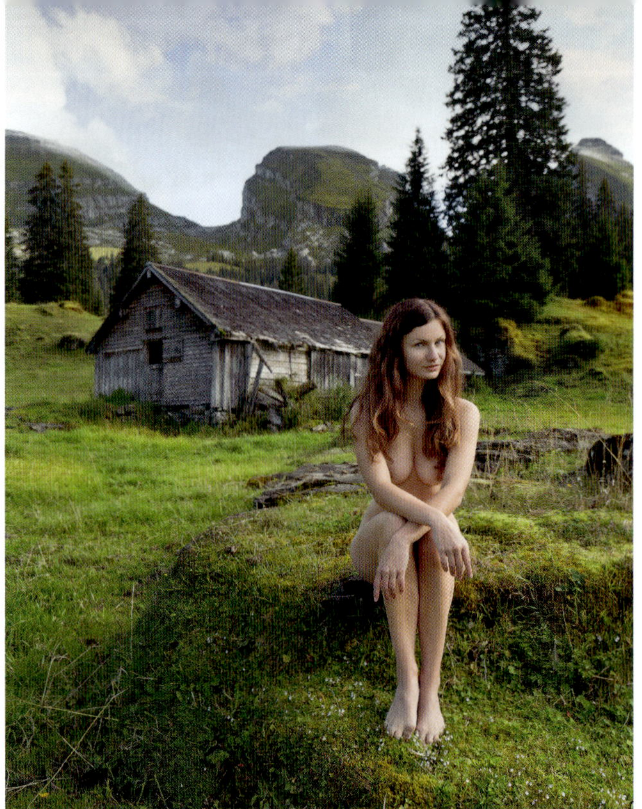

from afar we saw a hut. We immediately had the idea of buying mountain cheese. So we made our way to the lonely hut, located on a plateau. When we got there, we were warmly welcomed by Almöi and his wife, who actually had some cheese for us. When the two noticed how cold we were, they invited us into the wooden hut for a hot cup of tea. We happily warmed up our stiff limbs on the stove that crackled cozily in the corner. While Stefan was chatting with our hosts, I tried to follow the conversation. However, I didn't succeed because the local language and dialect are very difficult to understand for those not from this area. Luckily Stefan speaks the language of the Alps very well. Since the communication went well, I leaned back, relaxed, with my hot cup of tea in my hands and nodded to the Almöi couple with a smile, pretending that I understood everything. (→ p. 110)

I also have fond memories of a cow pasture smelling of flowers and herbs, even though my foot occasionally landed in one or the other pile of cow poo, ehhhh!

The cattle found it amusing to see a stark naked Susann hopping across the alpine meadow. One of the cows was particularly fond of me and wanted

Ich weiß es noch wie heute. Auf dem Weg zu einer phänomenalen Location stoppten wir kurz um ein paar traditionelle Dirndl bei einem Verleih abzuholen. Aufgeregt, wie ich war, hüpfte ich aus dem Auto und lief zu Stefan hinüber. Aber halt – hatte ich nicht in all meiner Eile etwas Wichtiges vergessen? Natürlich, der Autoschlüssel! Oh nein – der Autoschlüssel, ich habe ihn auf dem Beifahrersitz liegen gelassen. Welch prekäre Situation. Stefans Gesichtsausdruck werde ich bis heute nicht vergessen. Doch pfiffig wie er ist, hatte er schon die rettende Idee. Die Lösung war ein Drahtseil, aus dem er sich eine Art Angel bastelte und sich über den kleinen Spalt der geöffnete Fensterscheibe ins innere des Autos hangelte und dabei den auf dem Beifahrersitz liegenden Schlüssel heraus fischte. Geschafft! Dank Stefans Einfallsreichtum und seinen geschickten Fingern. Nach dieser aufregenden Autoschlüssel-Angel-Aktion ging es nun endlich auf zum Fotoshooting. (→ S. 136/137)

Rund um den Bodensee gibt es wundervolle Locations, wie zum Bespiel ein riesiger Findling, auf dem ich es mir natürlich erstmal gemütlich machte. Und nicht nur ich, sondern auch viele kleine, nackte Frösche wollten unbedingt bei dem Shooting dabei sein. Einer der frechen, glitschigen Gesellen hüpfte mich fast an. Hilfe suchend schreckte ich zurück. Hier wimmelte es nur so von Kröten. Was wenn die mich alle anhüpfen? Ein scheußlicher Gedanke. Dann kam aber Stefan in rettender Eile herbei, schließlich konnte er es nicht zulassen mit einer völlig demotivierten und ängstlichen Susann weiter zu fotografieren. Es gelang ihm, alle Frösche waren ganz und gar verschreckt, so dass ich mich am Ende sogar traute auf dem Fels zu liegen. (→ S. 145)

An einem angenehmen Nachmittag Ende August, radelten Stefan und ich durch die Gegend auf der Suche nach einem schönen Plätzchen für ein Shooting. Nach einer längeren aber abwechslungsreichen Radtour entdeckten wir eine traumhafte Stelle direkt am See. Oder besser gesagt im See. Fast knietief in den Wellen versunken, fühle ich mich ein biss-

to lick me from behind with her huge, wet tongue. And all them moo-ed in unison. The Alps would not be the same without these friendly animals. They could be heard shouting «moo» and their bells, worn around their necks, rang out in a wonderful melody from afar. If you follow the sounds of the bells, you know for sure that cheese and alpine milk are not far away. After this cow pasture photo shoot, we were rewarded with a cool glass of fresh milk at the alpine hut. (→ p. 112)

I remember it as if it only happened yesterday. On the way to a phenomenal location, we stopped briefly to pick up a pair of traditional dirndls from a rental shop.
Excited as I was, I hopped out of the car, slammed the car door behind me and ran over to Stefan! But wait – in all my haste, hadn't I forgotten something important? Of course, the car key! Oh no – the car key, I left it on the passenger seat. What a tricky situation! I will never forget Stefan's facial expression to this day. But as clever as he is, he already had an idea that would save us. The solution was a wire from the nearby gas station. He made a kind of a fishing rod from the wire, which he then shimmied through the small gap in the open window and fished out the key lying on the passenger seat. We made it! After this exciting action time, it was finally time for the photo shoot! (→ p. 136/137)

There are wonderful locations around Lake Constance, such as a huge boulder on a lonely mountain river, where I of course made myself comfortable immediately. And not only me, but also many small frogs around the stone wanted to be part of the photo shoot. One of the cheeky, curious, slippery fellows almost jumped on me. I flinched, seeking help and suddenly noticed that it was teeming with frogs. What if they all jump at me? A terrible thought. But then Stefan came in a hurry to save the situation and chased away the frogs – after all, he couldn't allow himself to continue working with a completely unmotivated and anxious Susann. It worked – all the frogs had disappeared,

chen wie der griechische Wassergott Neptun, nur in weiblicher Form und statt des Dreizacks eine hellblaue Fahne in der Hand. Am Himmel zogen dunkle Wolken auf, welche sich zu einem Gewitter auftürmten. Dramatischer ging es nicht, Weltuntergangsstimmung! Wind, Regen, Donner, Blitze und Stefan und ich mittendrin. Als hätte ich quasi den Sturm herbei gerufen mit meiner magischen Götterfahne. Bis auf die letzte Minute fotografierten wir, dann kam der Platzregen. Schnell holten wir unsere Räder und radelten im strömenden Regen zurück nach Hause. Klitschnass bis auf die Haut kamen wir an und ich erfreute mich einer heißen Dusche. (→ S. 158)

Zwei Eier, Mehl, etwas Butter, Zucker und ein paar säuerliche Äpfel – Was ergibt das? Na klar, einen Apfelkuchen à la Susann! Was für eine Idee einen Apfelkuchen zu backen, in der eigenen Model-Studentenküche und das in Form eines Shootings festzuhalten! So ein grandioser Einfall kann auch nur von Stefan kommen. Natürlich hatten alle Beteiligten (Model, Fotograf und Assistent) jede Menge Spaß dabei. Vor allem, den mit so viel Sorgfalt und Liebe gebackenen Kuchen am Ende zu vernaschen! Und dabei ganz zu vergessen noch ein Foto zu machen, bevor das große Naschen begann. Deshalb durfte Stefan den Kuchen zuhause noch einmal backen, um diesmal ein Foto davon zu machen. Das Gute ist, er durfte gleich zweimal in den unvergleichlichen Genuss kommen! (→ S. 154)

Ich konnte so richtig meine Gedanken schweifen lassen, als ich mich an einem lauen Tag im Februar bei angenehmen 24° C im schwarzen Sand eines Vulkanstrandes auf Lanzarote räkelte. Es war ein wunderschönes Gefühl den rauen, warmen Sand über meine Schenkel gleiten zu lassen. Fast wie in Trance spielte ich mit dem Sand und genoss die umwerfende Natur, die sich durch märchenhafte Strände prägte. Durch die Abgelegenheit des Strandes konnte man ganz für sich allein sein und abgesehen von ein paar Kakteen unbeobachtet vor sich hin träumen. Aber nicht nur dieser Strand

so that in the end I even dared to lie down on the big rock. (→ p. 145)

On a warm afternoon in late August, Stefan and I were cycling around looking for a nice location for a photo shoot. After a long but pleasant bike ride, we discovered a fantastic spot right on Lake Constance. Or rather in the lake. Almost knee-deep in the big waves, I felt a bit like Neptune, the Greek god of water, in female form and holding a light blue flag in my hand instead of a trident. Dark clouds were gathering in the sky, which quickly turned into a thunderstorm. It could not have been a more dramatic, doomsday mood! Wind, rain, thunder, lightning and Stefan and I right in the middle of it all. As if I summoned the storm with my magical blue god flag. We took pictures up to the last minute, then the downpour came. We quickly got our bikes and cycled back home in heavy rain. Soaking wet we arrived and I really enjoyed a hot shower. (→ p. 158)

Two eggs, flour, some butter, sugar and some tart apples – what does that make?
Of course, an apple pie a lá Susann! What a great idea to bake an apple pie in my own student kitchen and capture it in the form of a shoot. Everyone involved (model, photographer and assistant) had a lot of fun. Above all, to eat the cake that was baked with so much care and love at the end! And forgetting to take a photo of the finished cake before the big snacking began. So Stefan had to bake the cake again at home to take a picture of it this time. The good thing is that he was able to enjoy the incomparable pleasure twice! (→ p. 154)

I could really let my thoughts wander as I lounged on the black sand of a volcanic beach on the island of Lanzarote, on a balmy February day in a pleasant 24°C. It was a wonderful feeling to let the rough, warm sand slide over my thighs. Almost like in a trance, I played with the sand and enjoyed the stunning nature with its beautiful beaches. The remoteness of the beach made it feel like you could have

erhöhte meine Glücksgefühle. Auch zwischen den Steinburgen am hellen Muschelstrand, bei Sonne und Meer, Wind und Wellen schien der Stress des Fotoshootings fast vergessen. Ein solch schönes Setting erleichterte die Arbeit doch um ein Vielfaches. Als die Fotos geschossen waren, kehrten wir vom Hunger getrieben in einer altertümlichen Finka ein und versorgten uns mit den regionalen Köstlichkeiten und einem genüsslichen Gläschen Roséwein. So ließen wir den erlebnisreichen Tag ausklingen, bis zum nächsten, wenn es wieder auf Strand-Entdeckungstour ging auf Lanzarote. (→ S. 60/61)

it all to yourself and daydream unobserved. But not only this beach increased my feelings of happiness. Even between the stone castles on the bright shell beach, with sun and sea, wind and waves, the stress of the photo shoot seemed almost forgotten. Such beautiful locations made the work a lot easier. When we were taking photos, we always went to this old-fashioned finca, driven by hunger we stocked up on regional delicacies and a delicious glass of wine. And so we let the eventful day end until the next, when we went on a beach discovery tour in Lanzarote with many unforgettable experiences. (→ p. 60/61)

Susann

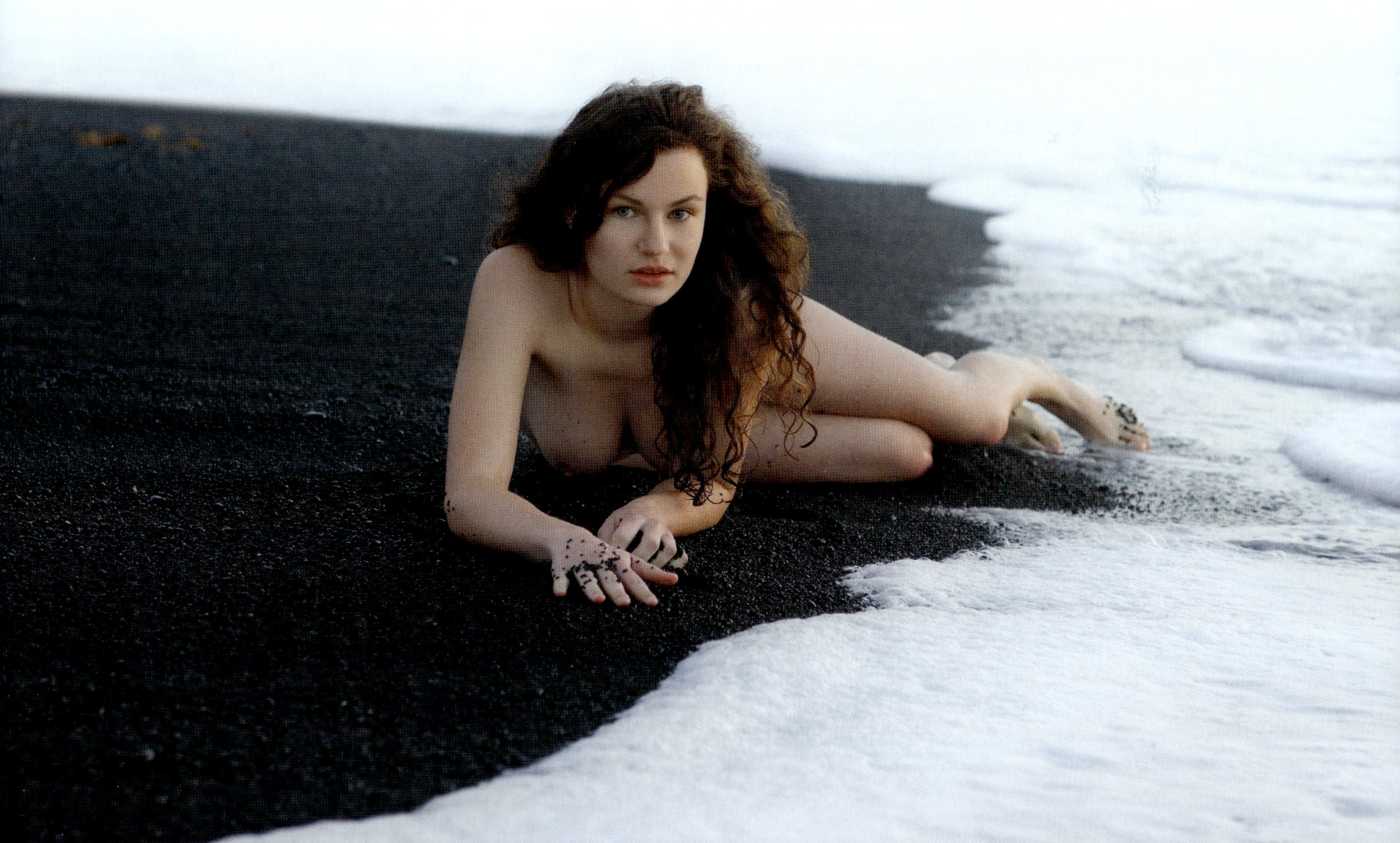

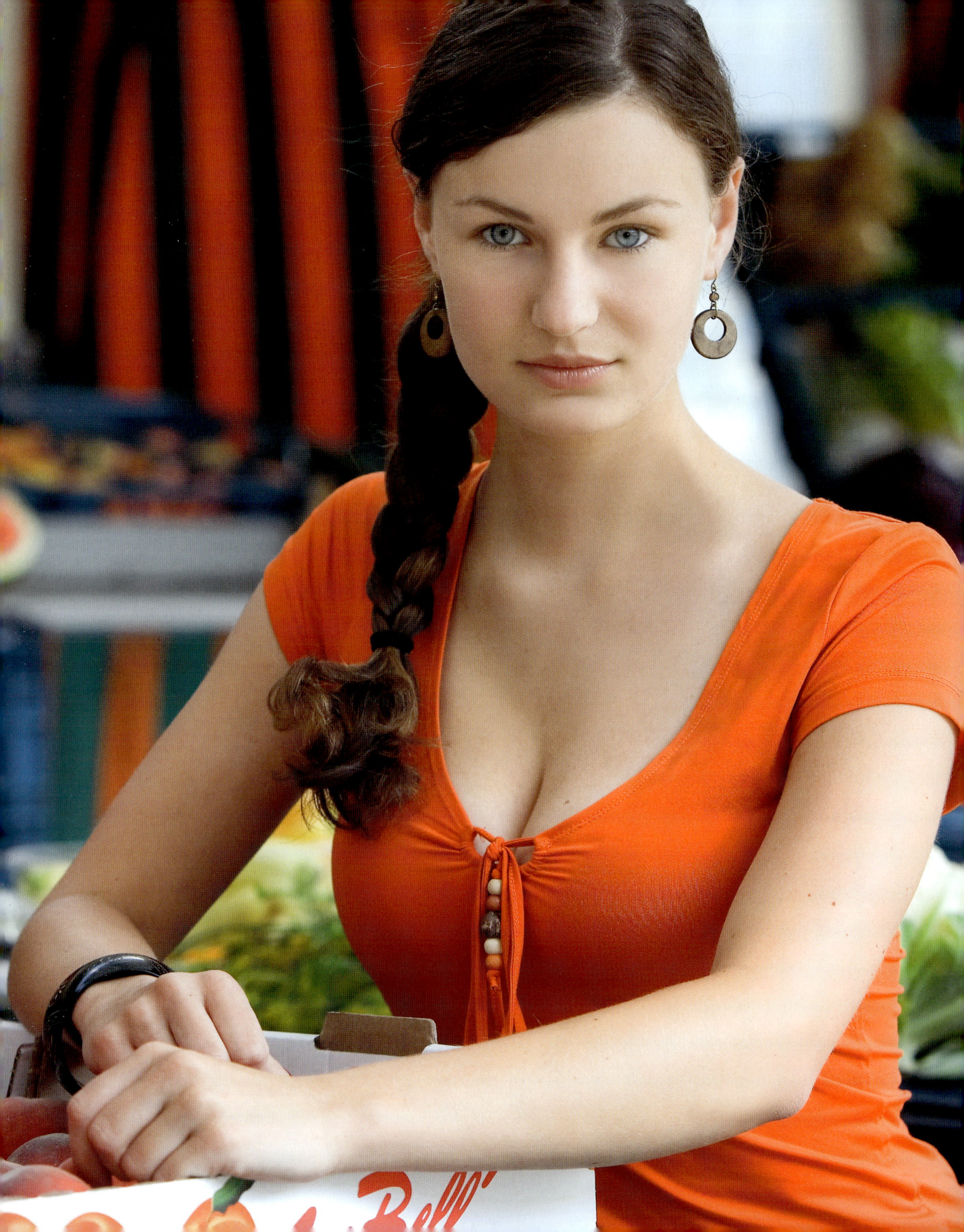

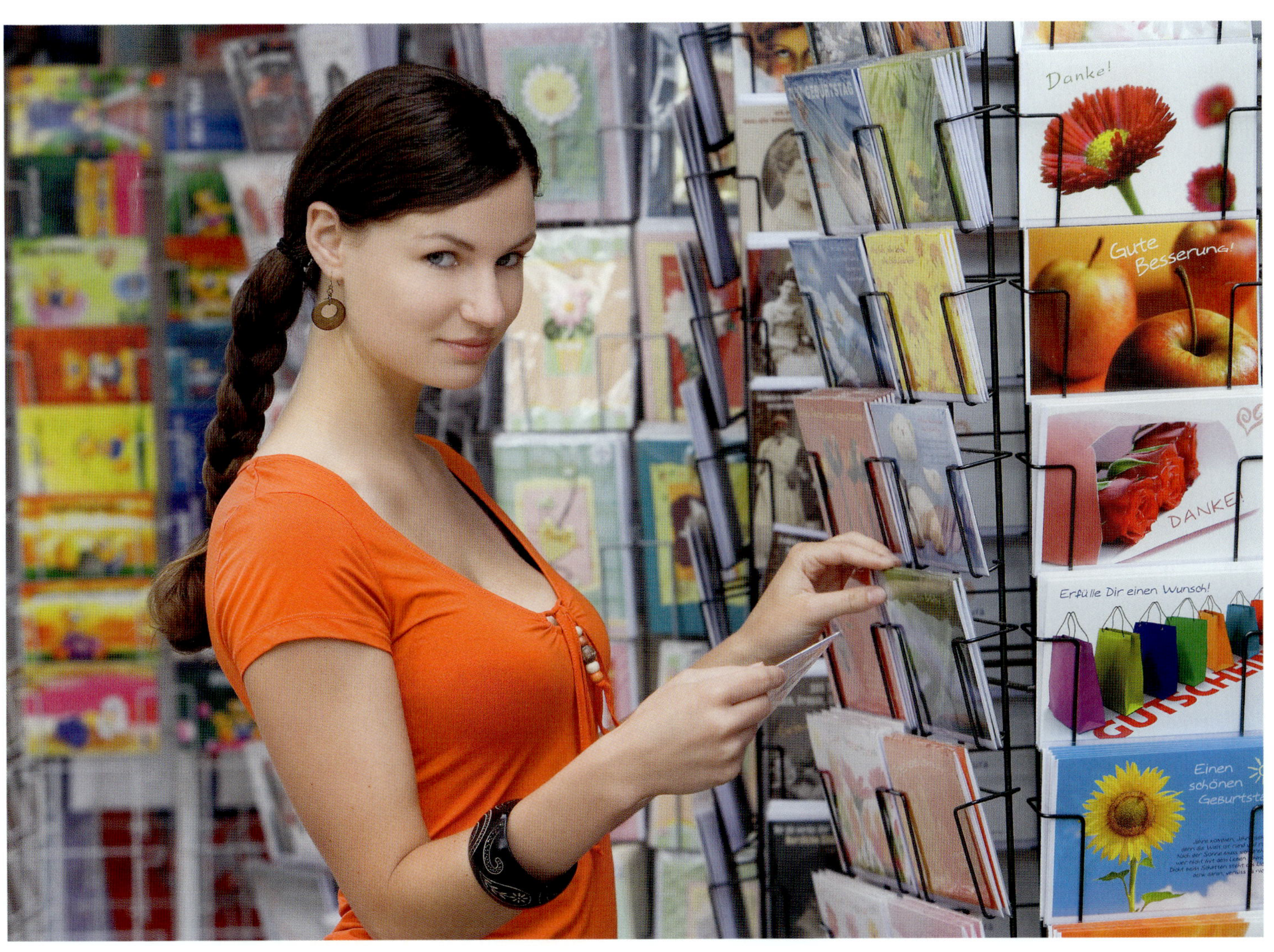
Danke!
Gute Besserung!
DANKE
Erfülle Dir einen Wunsch!
Einen schönen

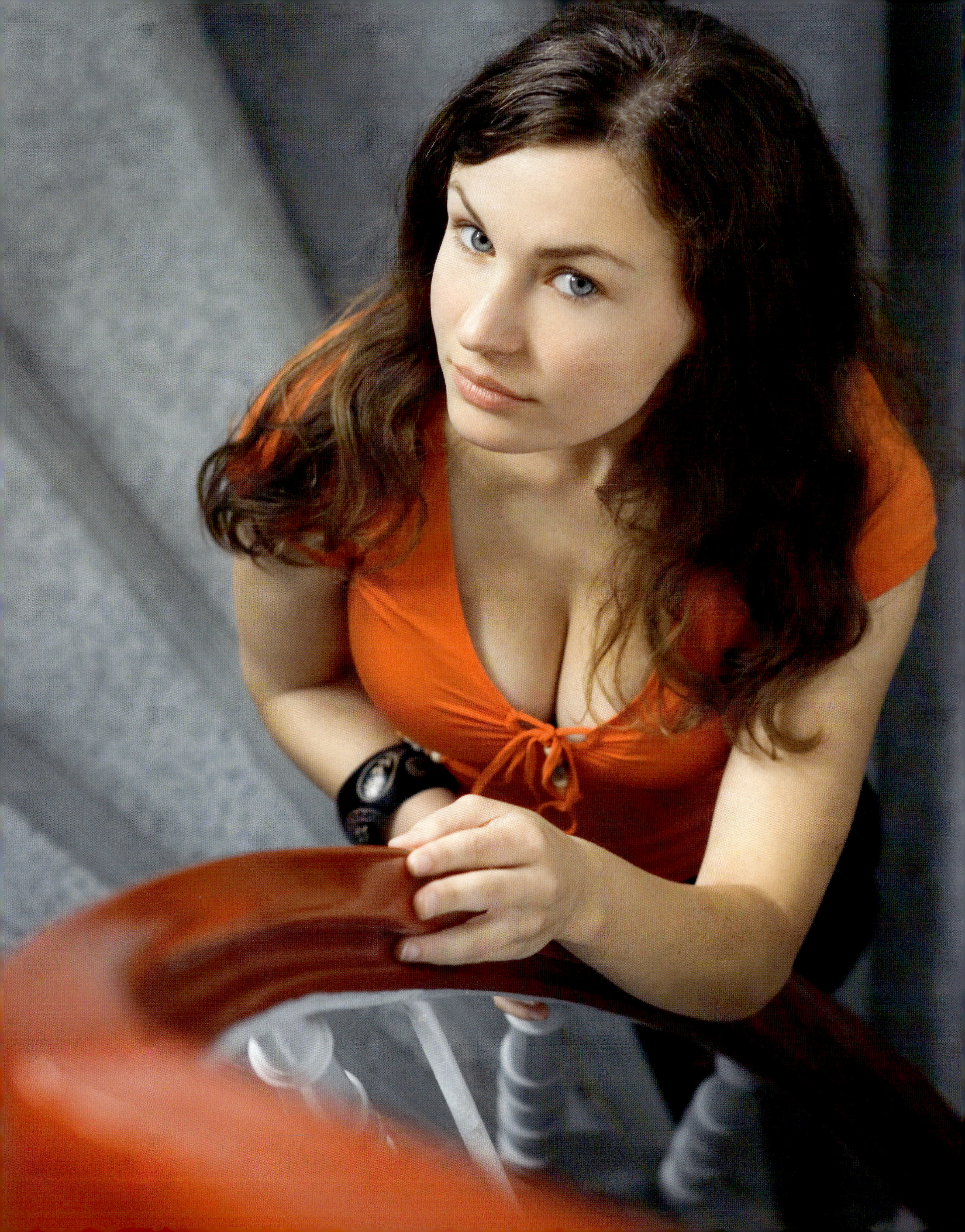

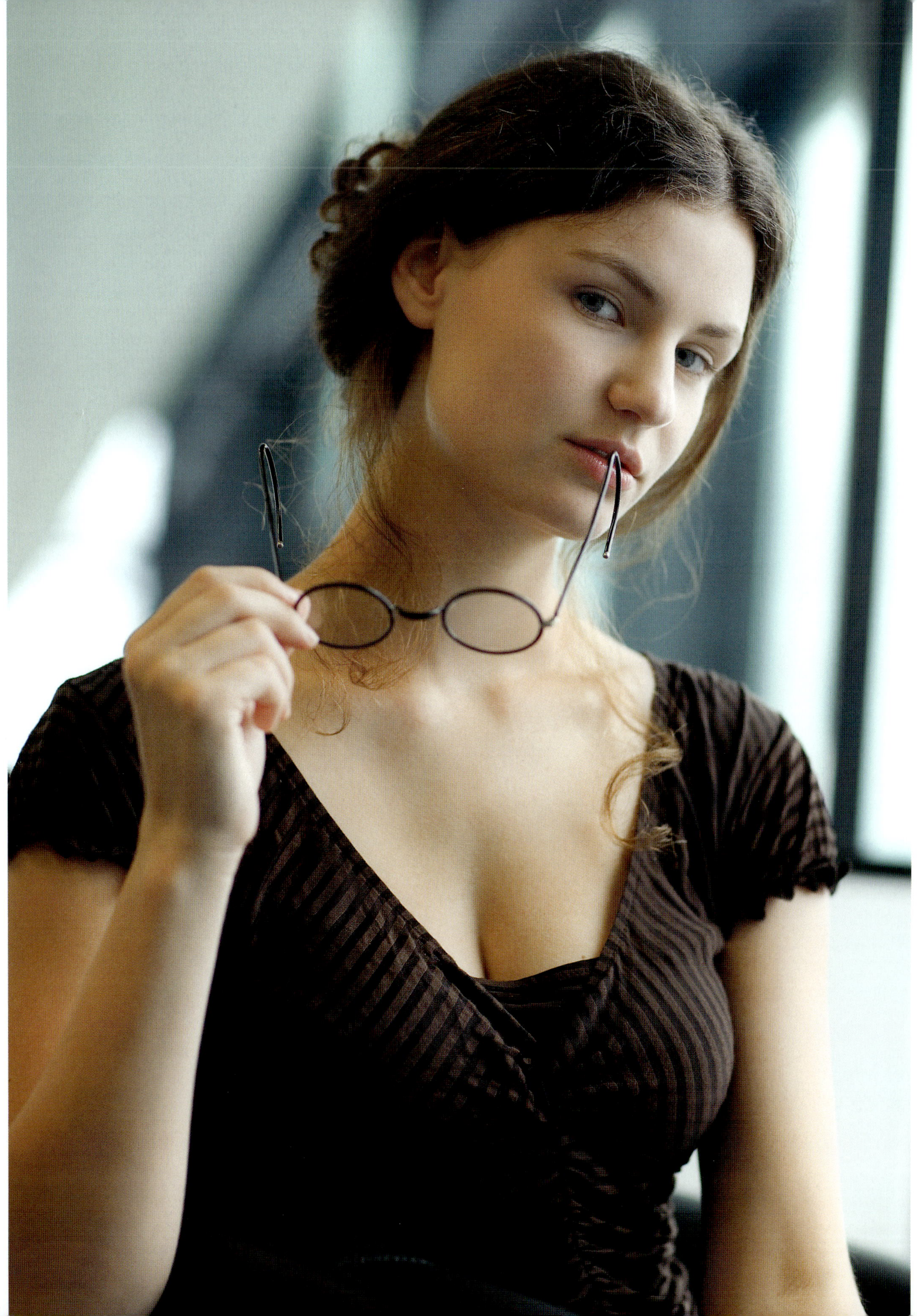

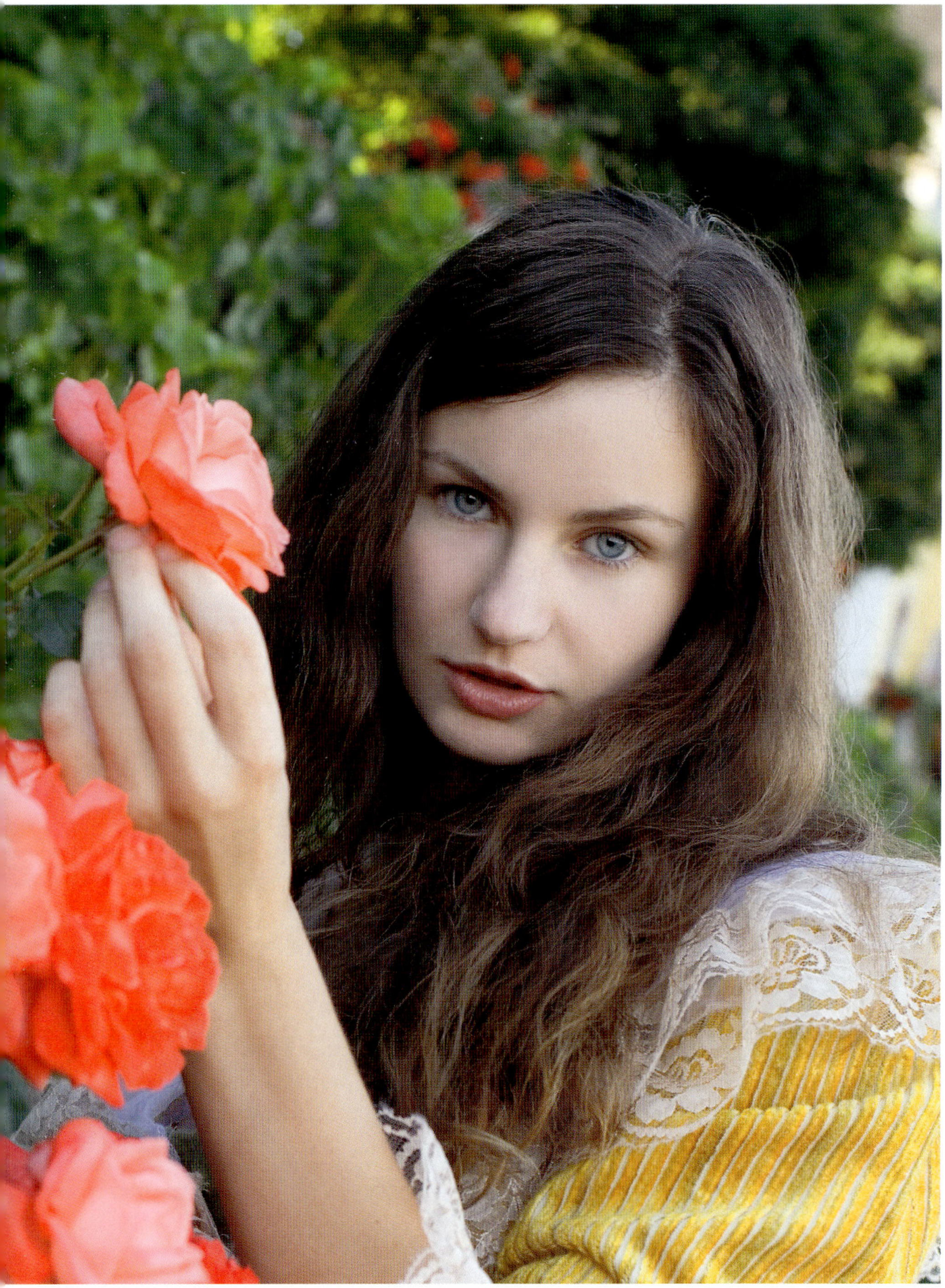

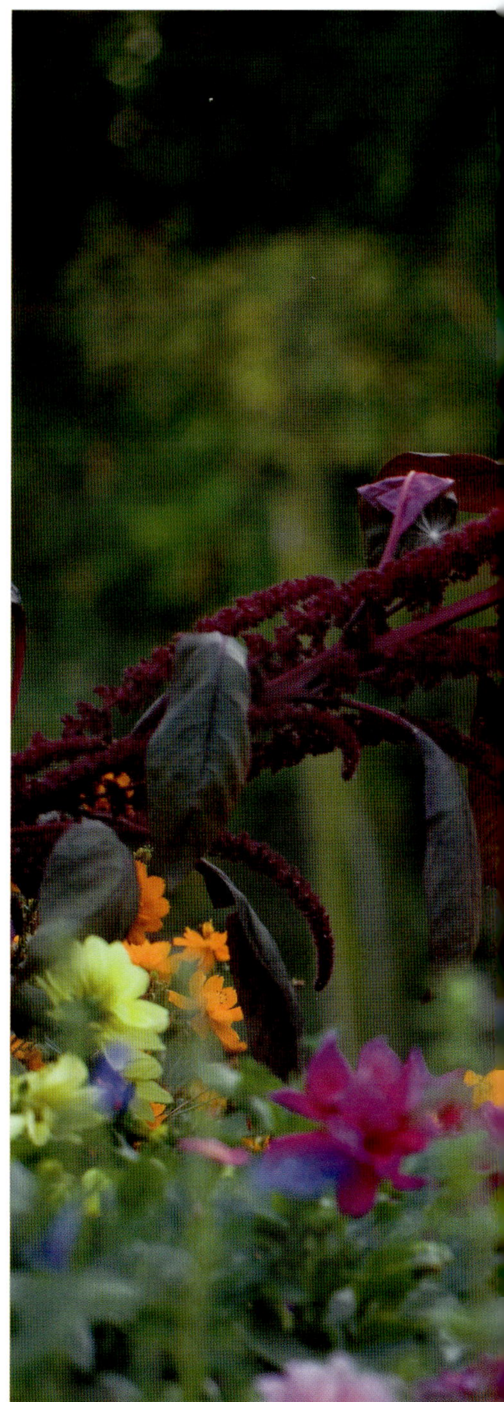

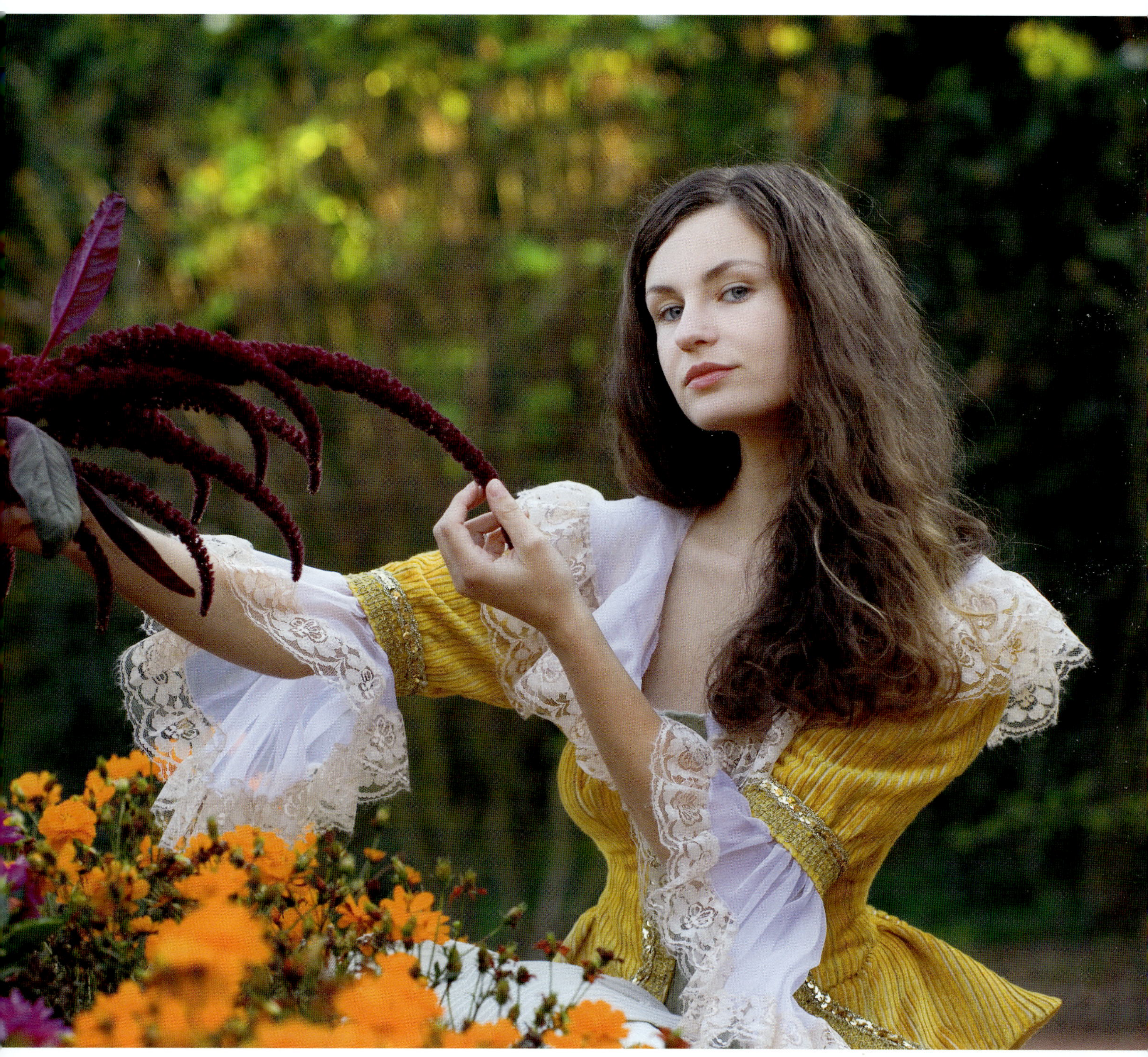

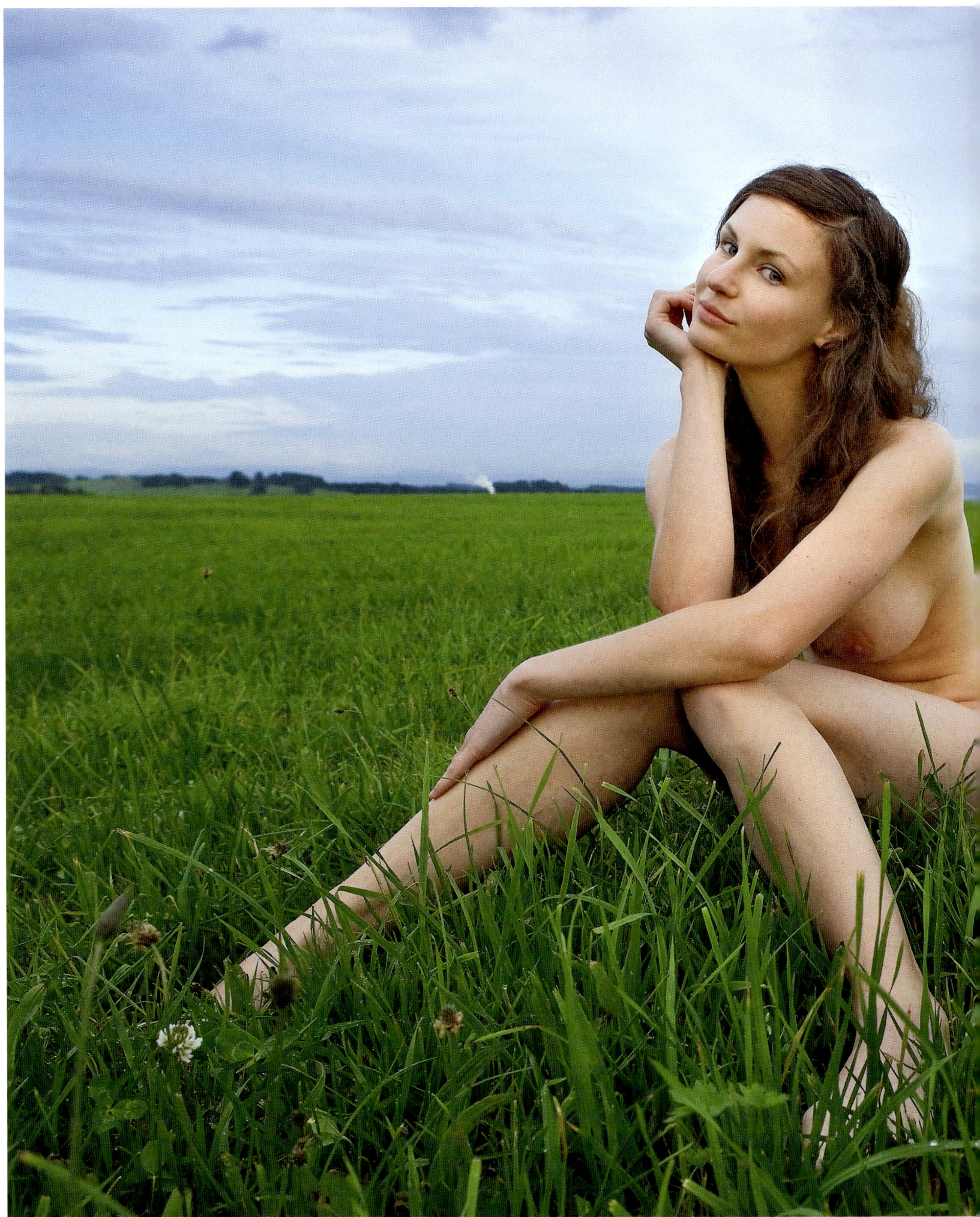

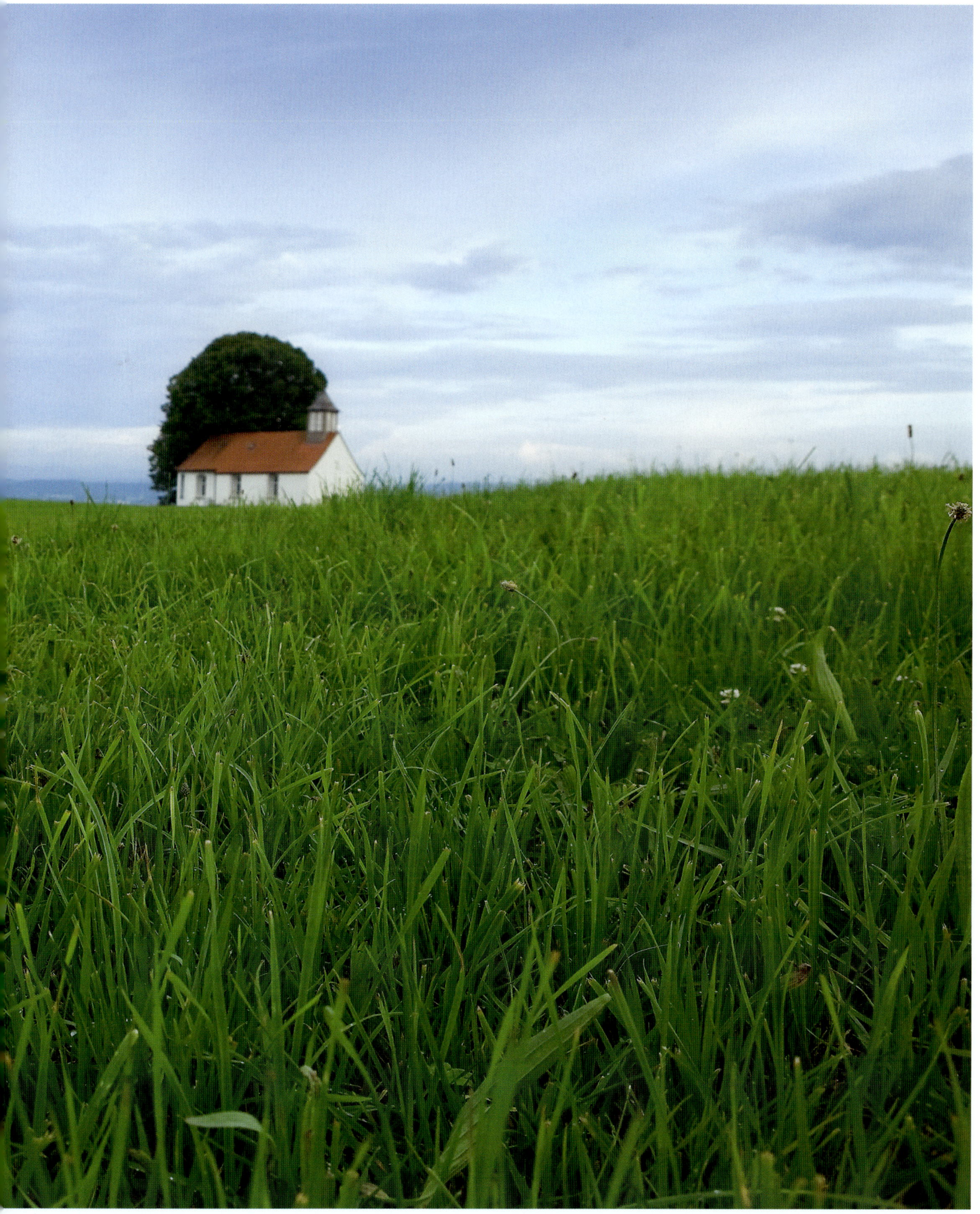

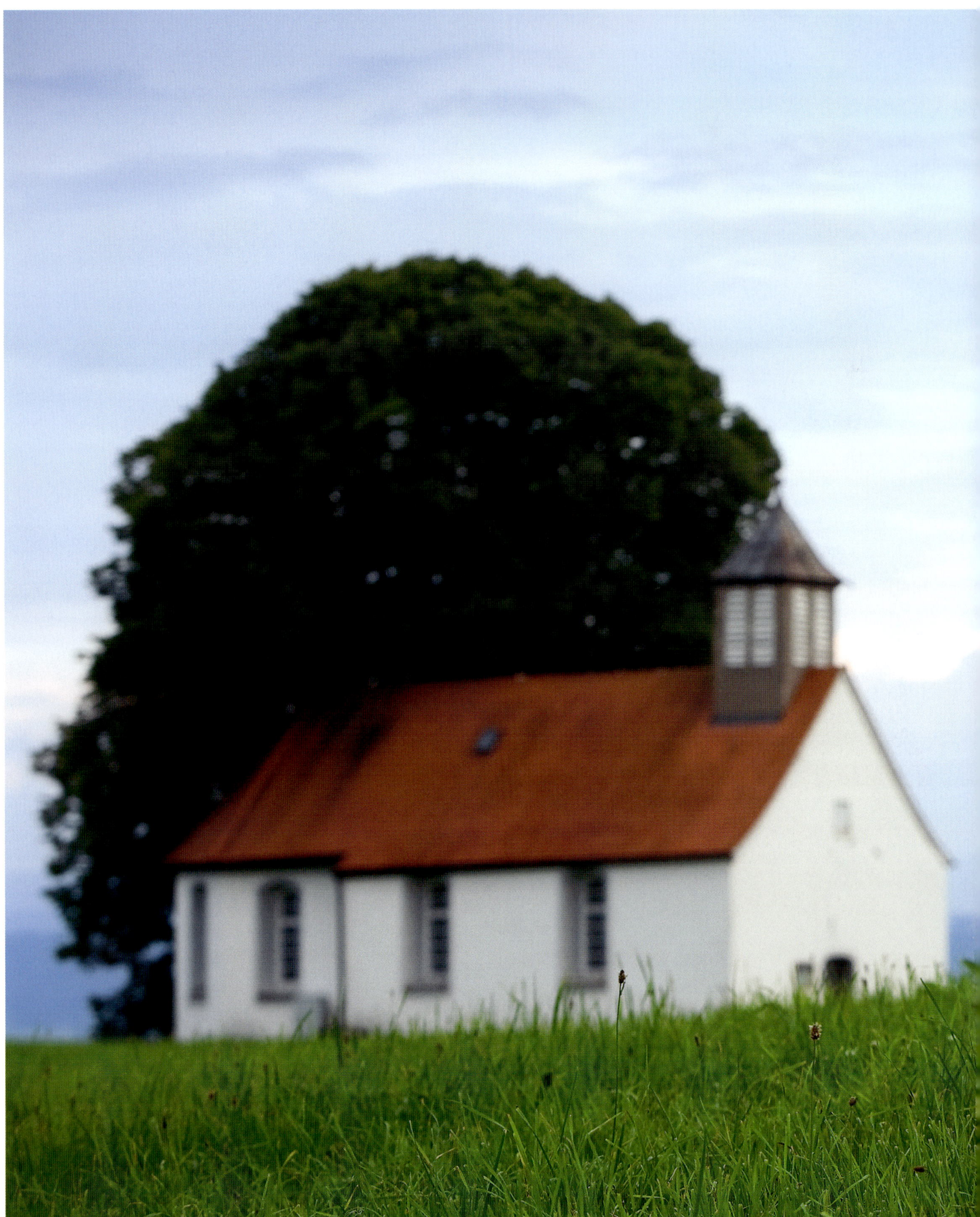

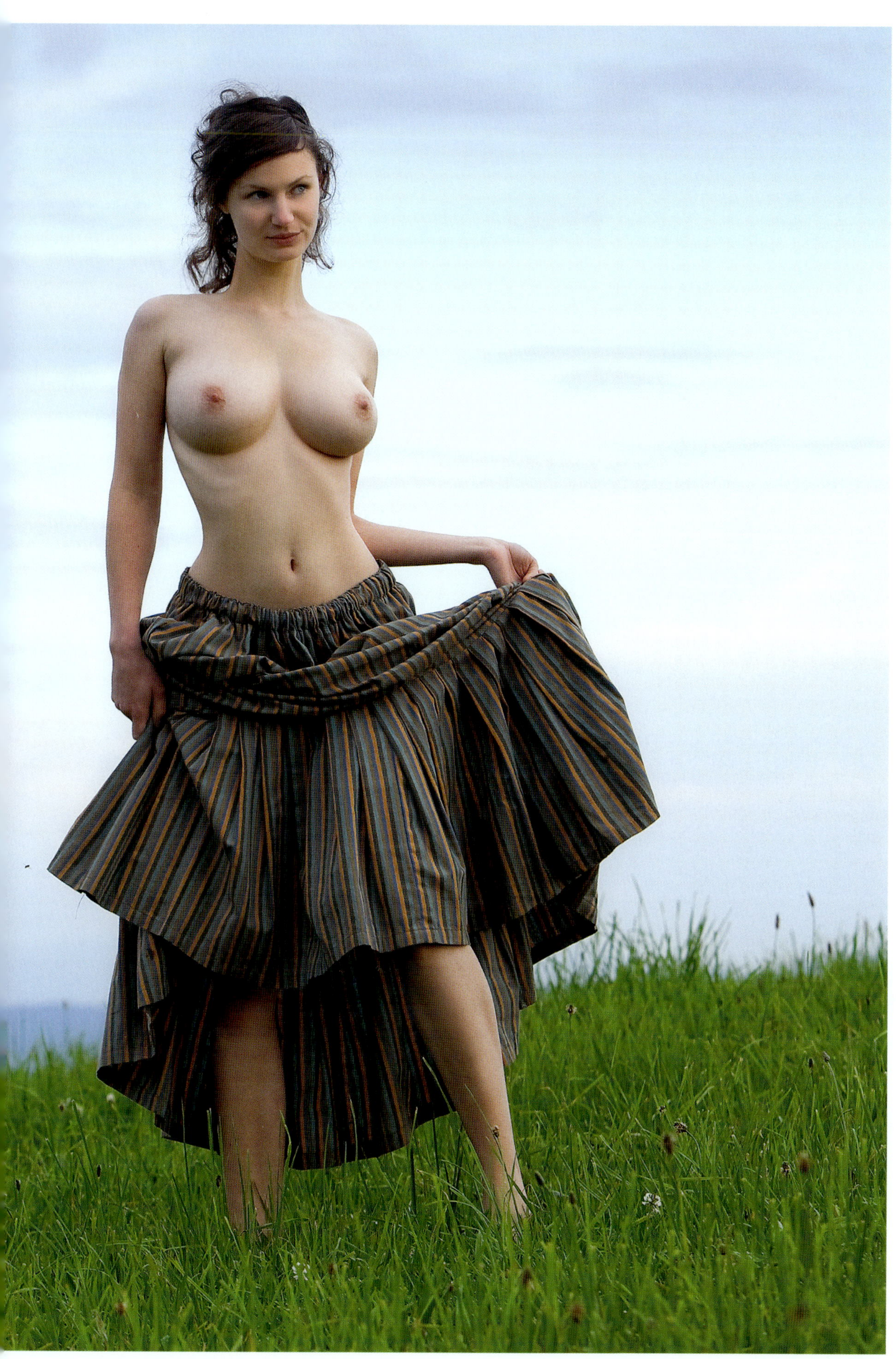

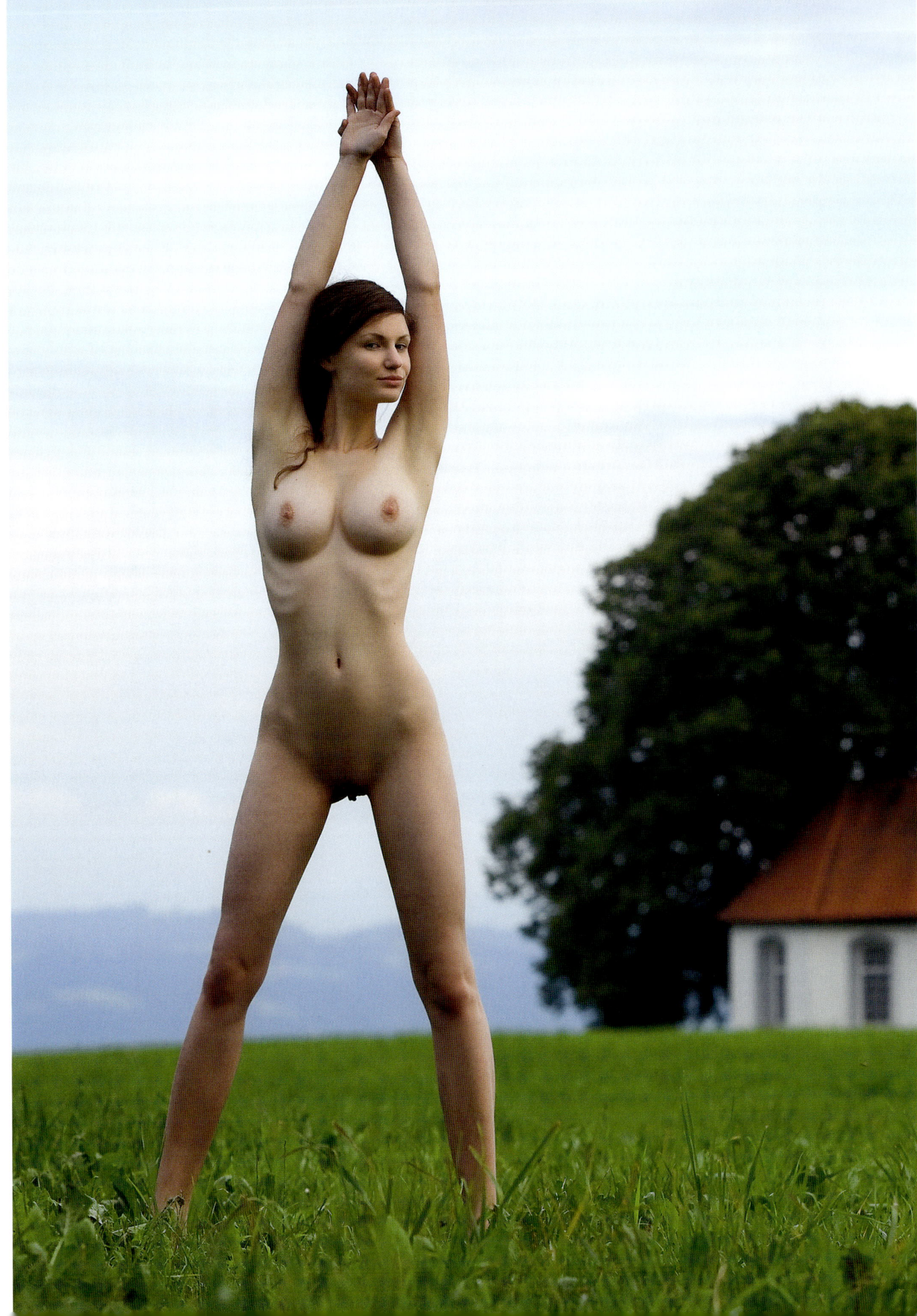

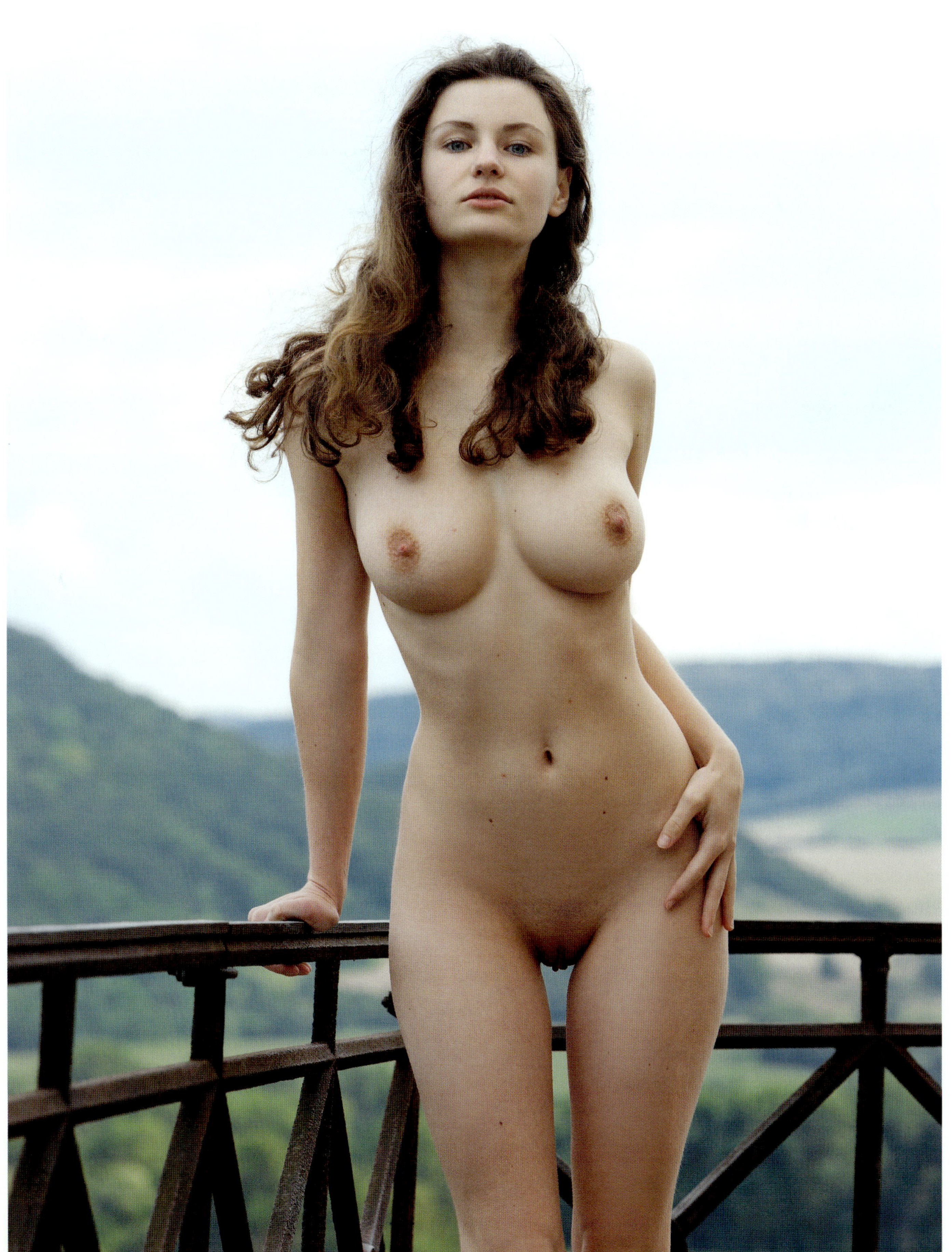

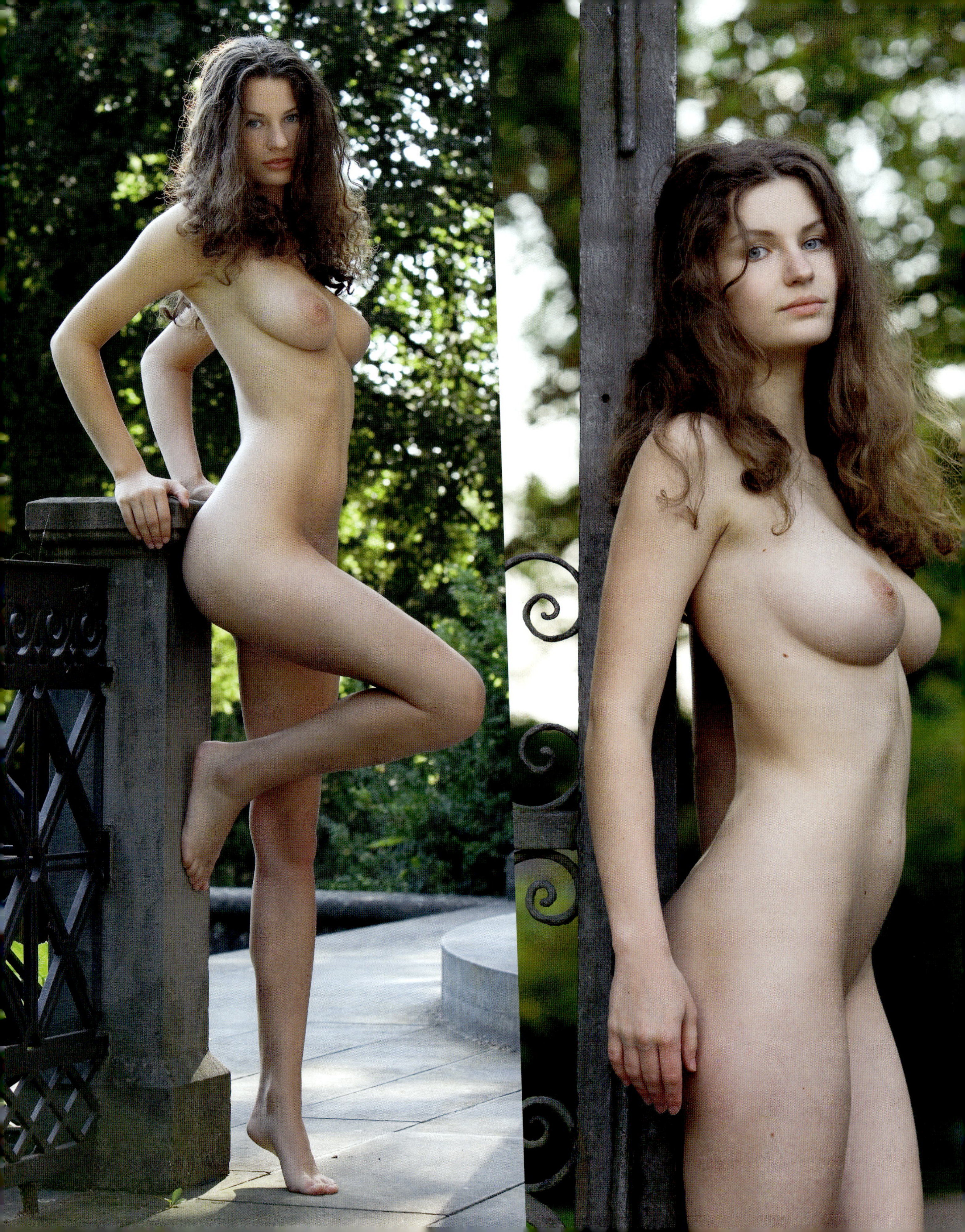

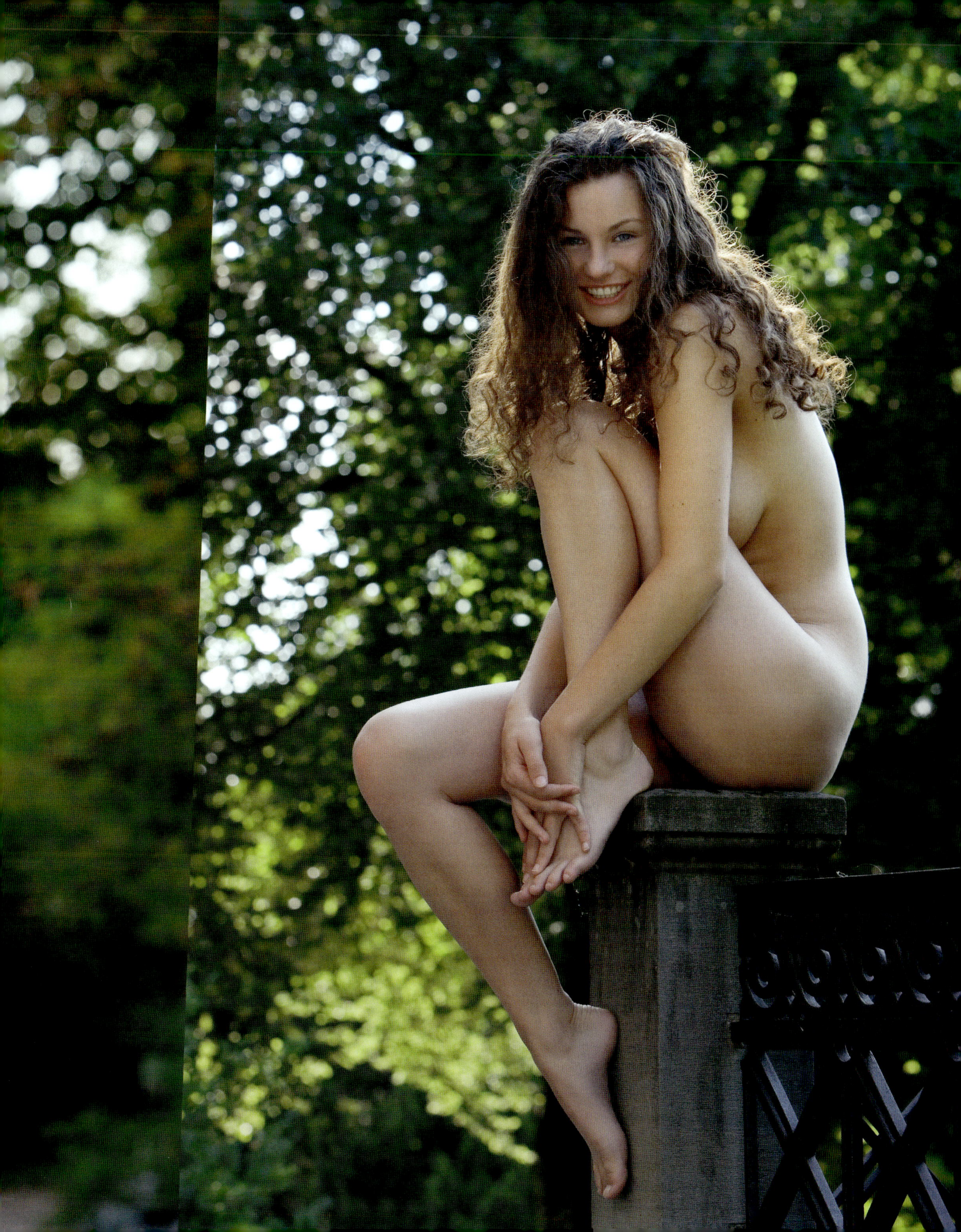

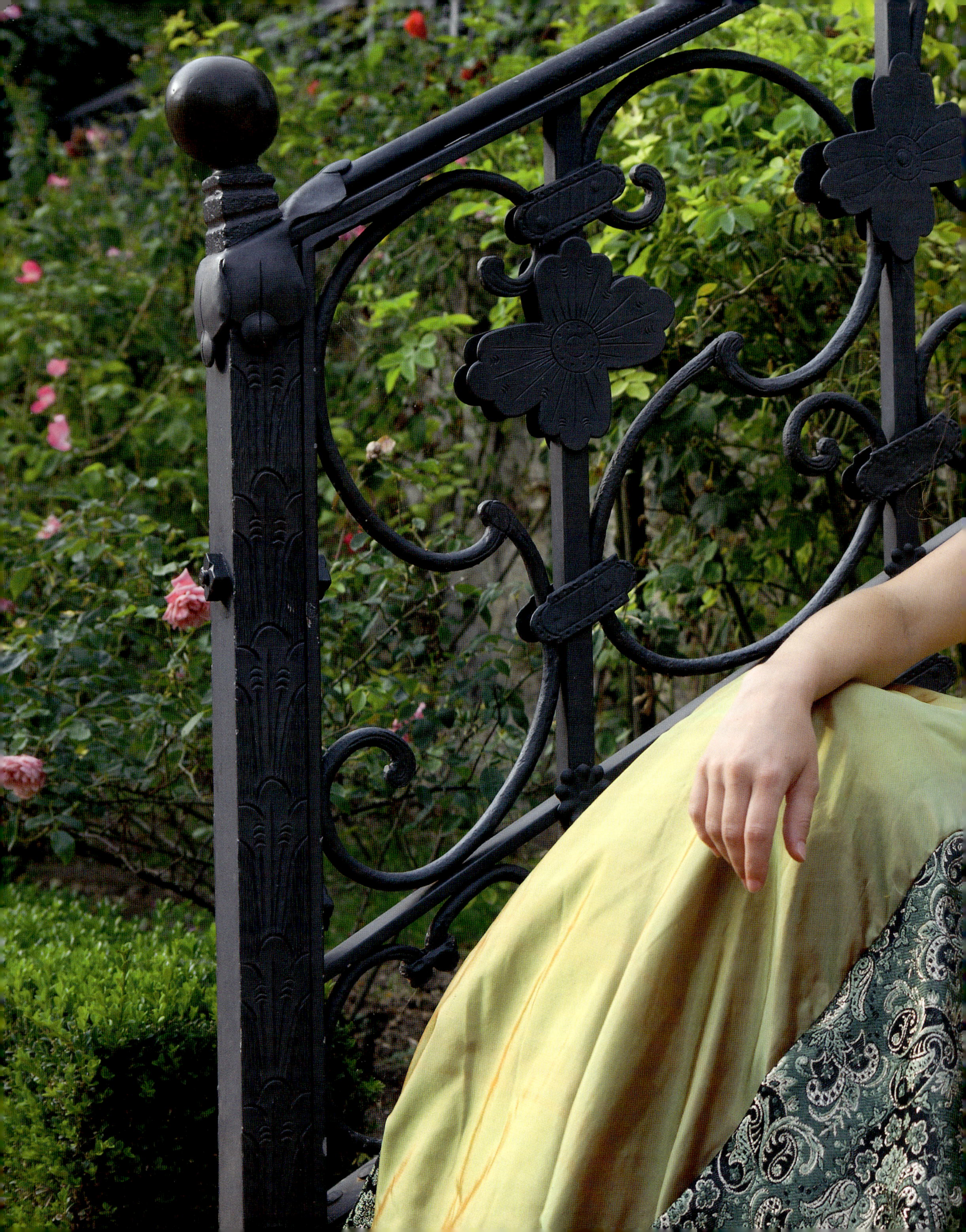

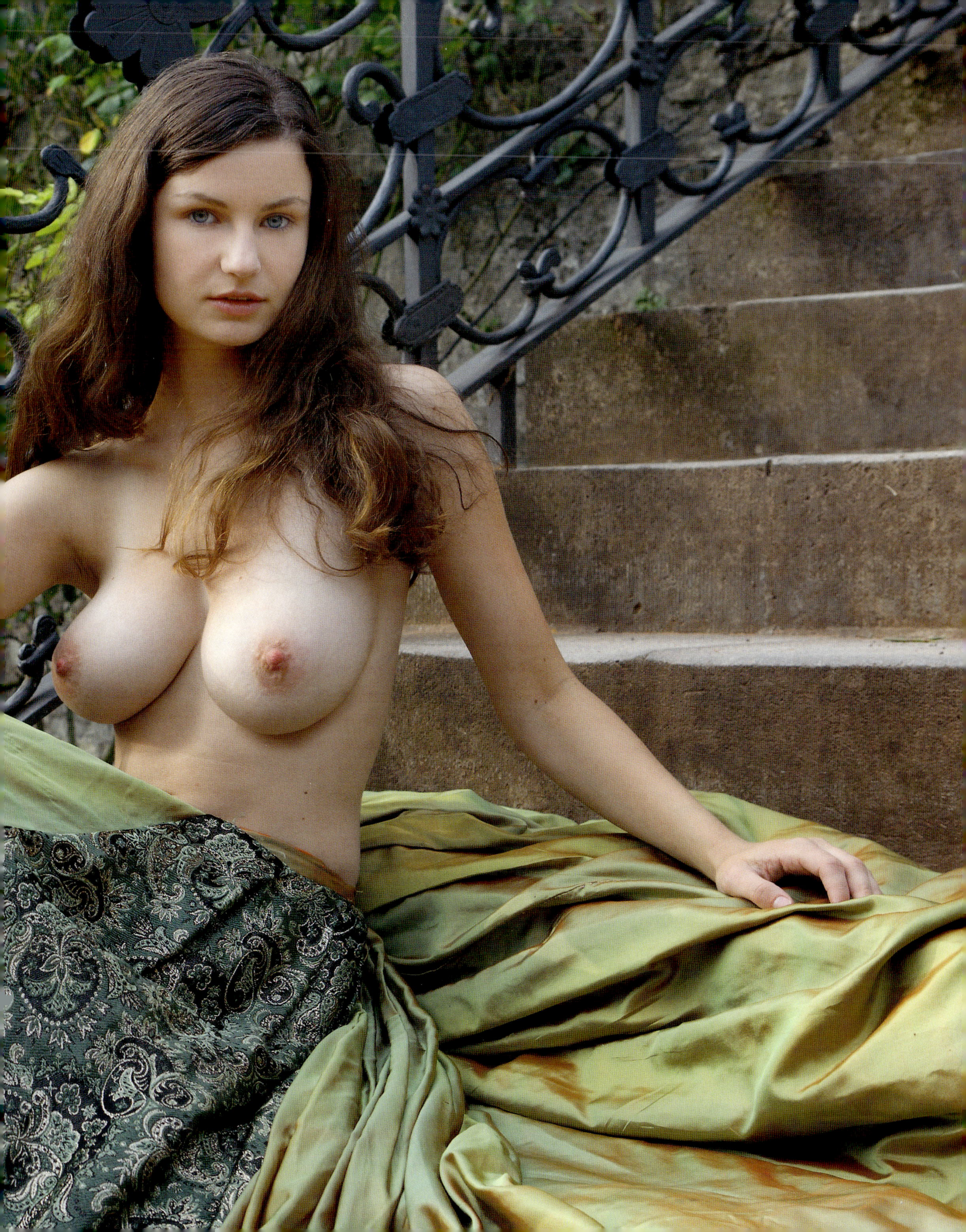

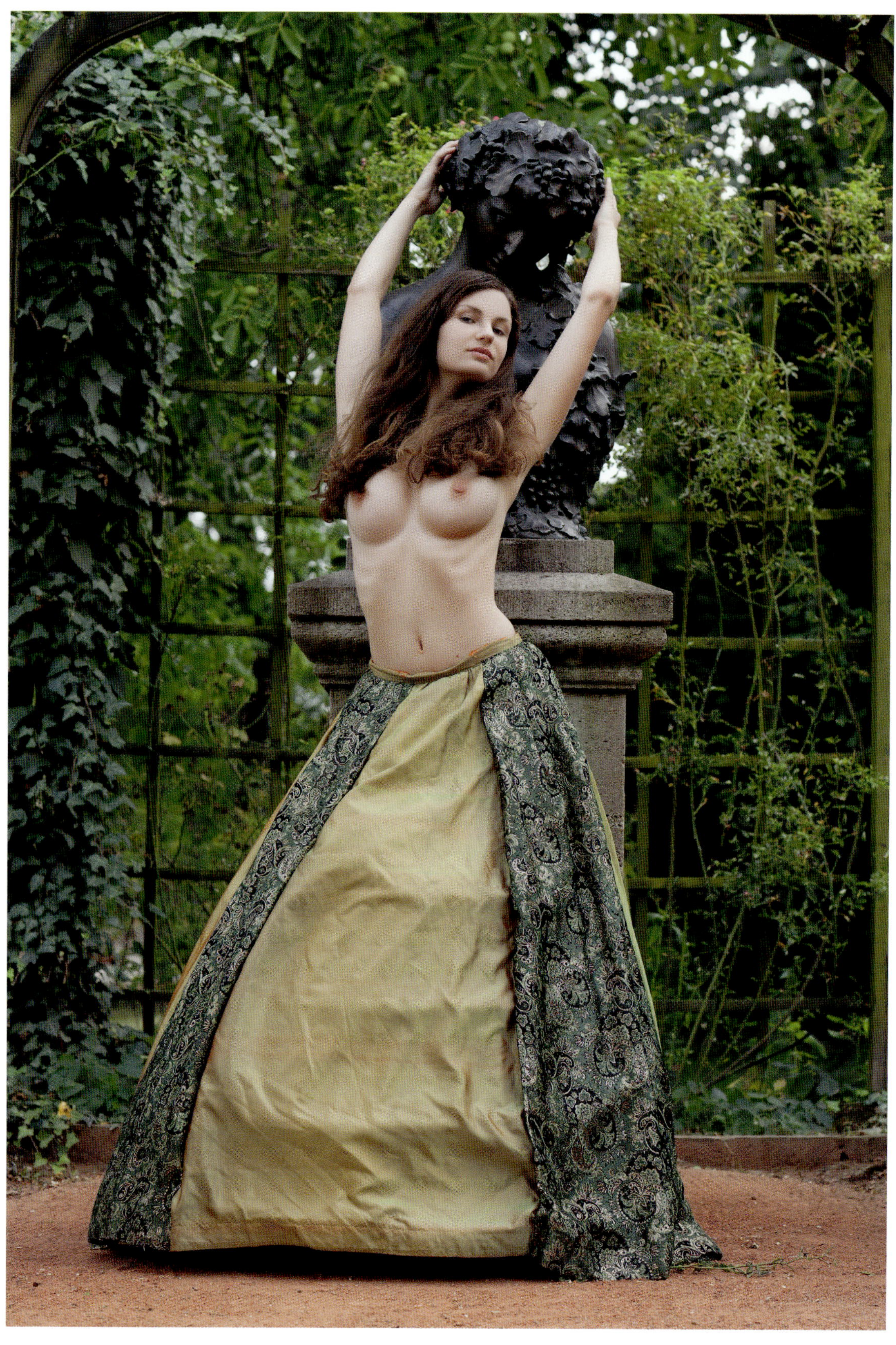

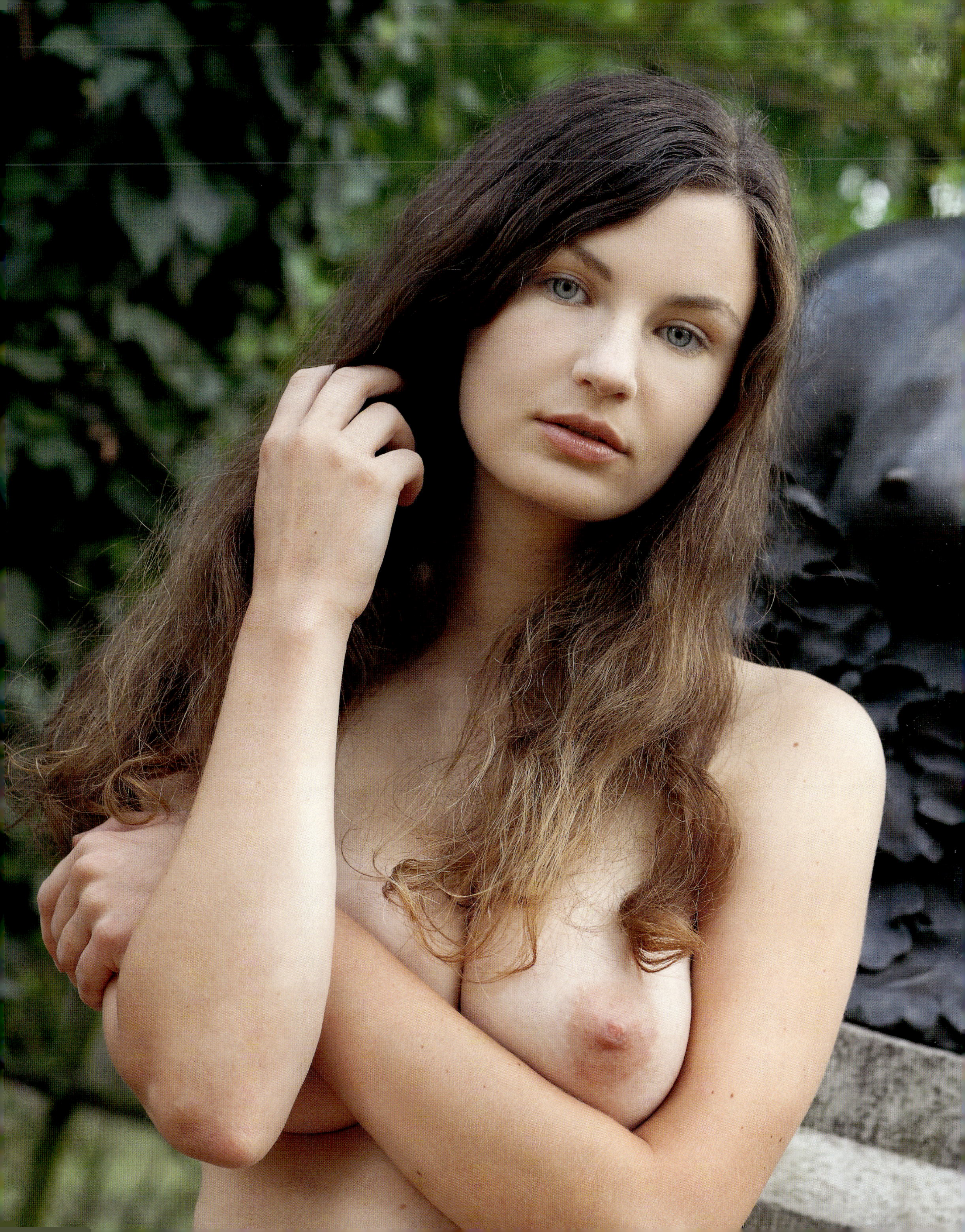

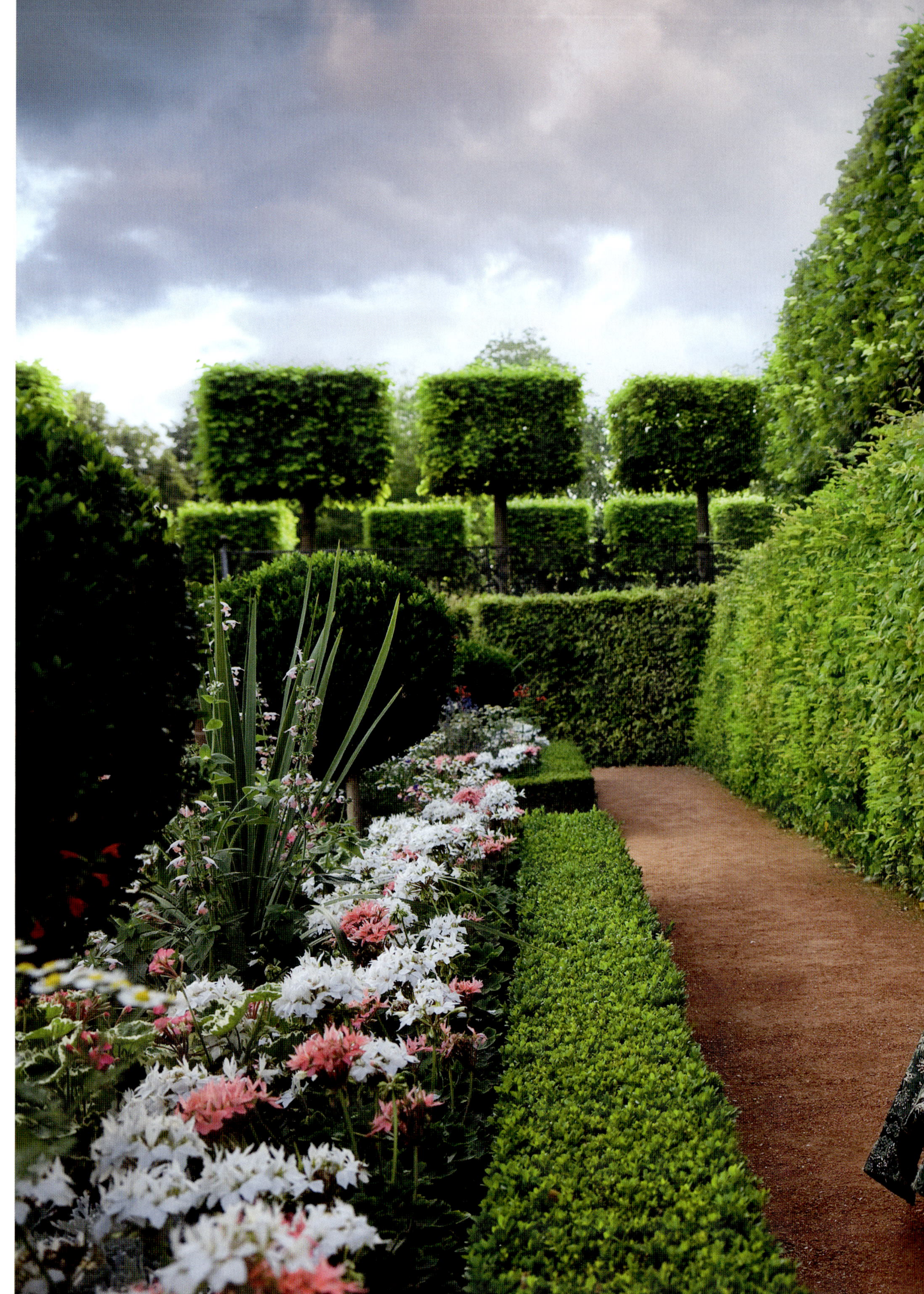

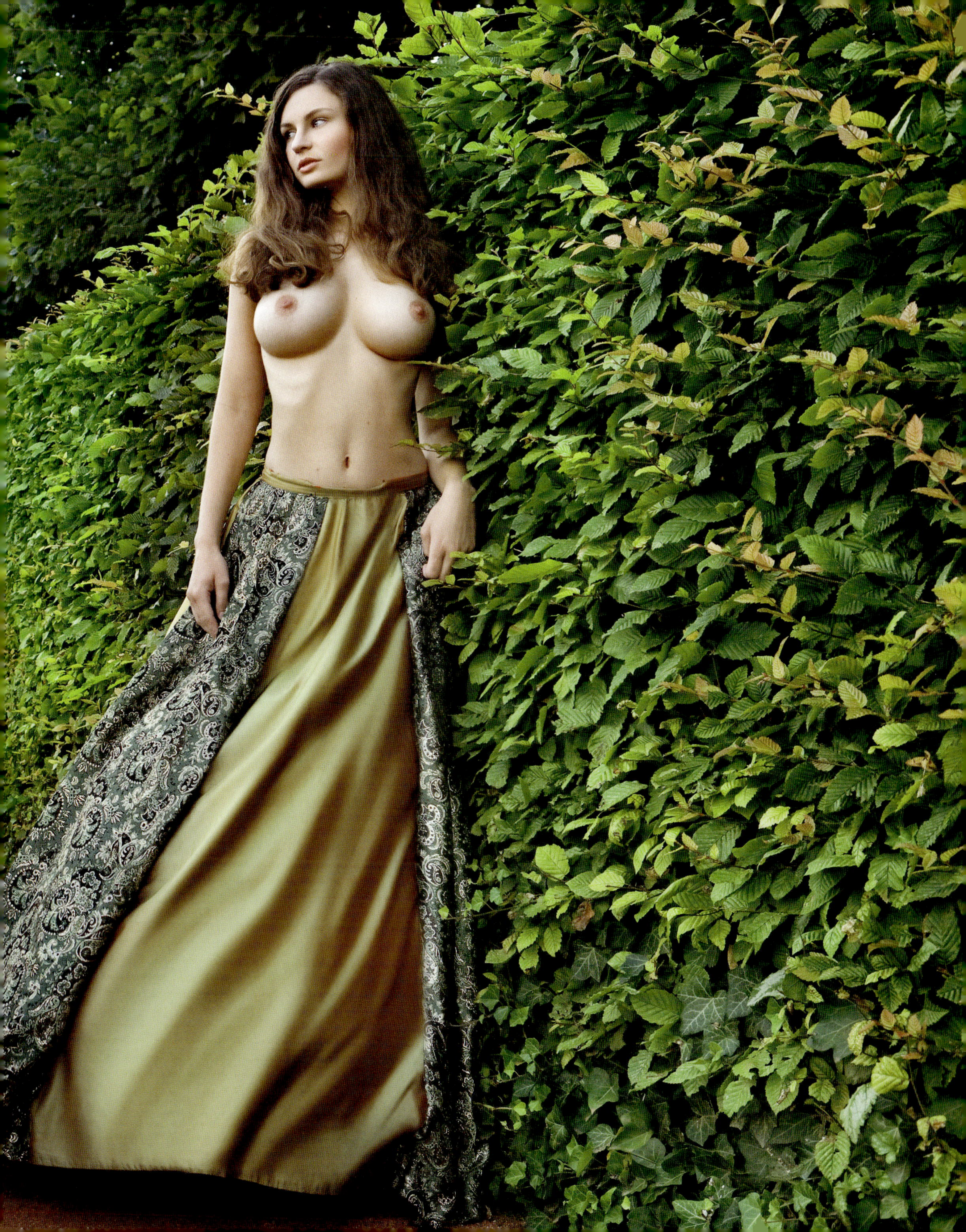

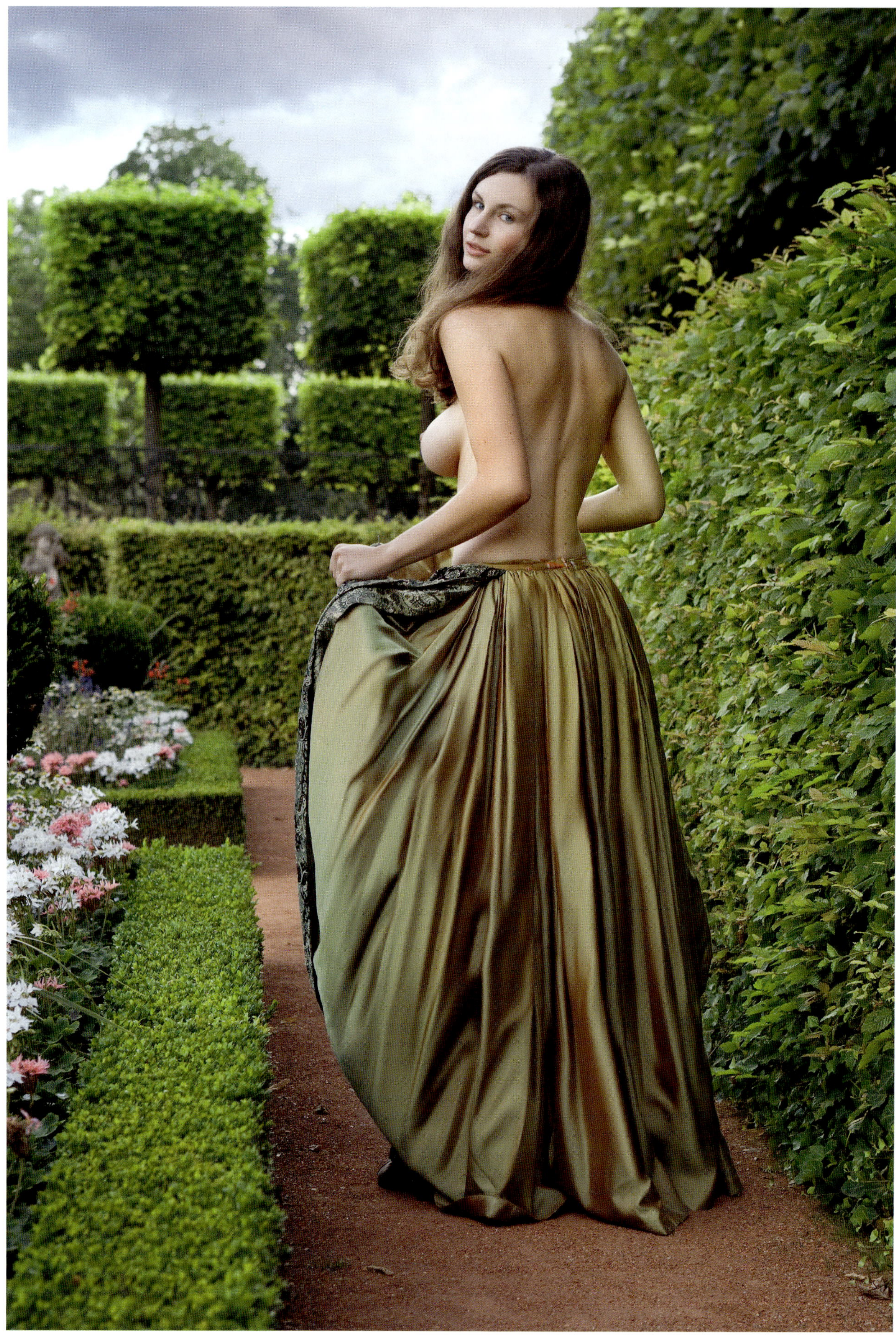

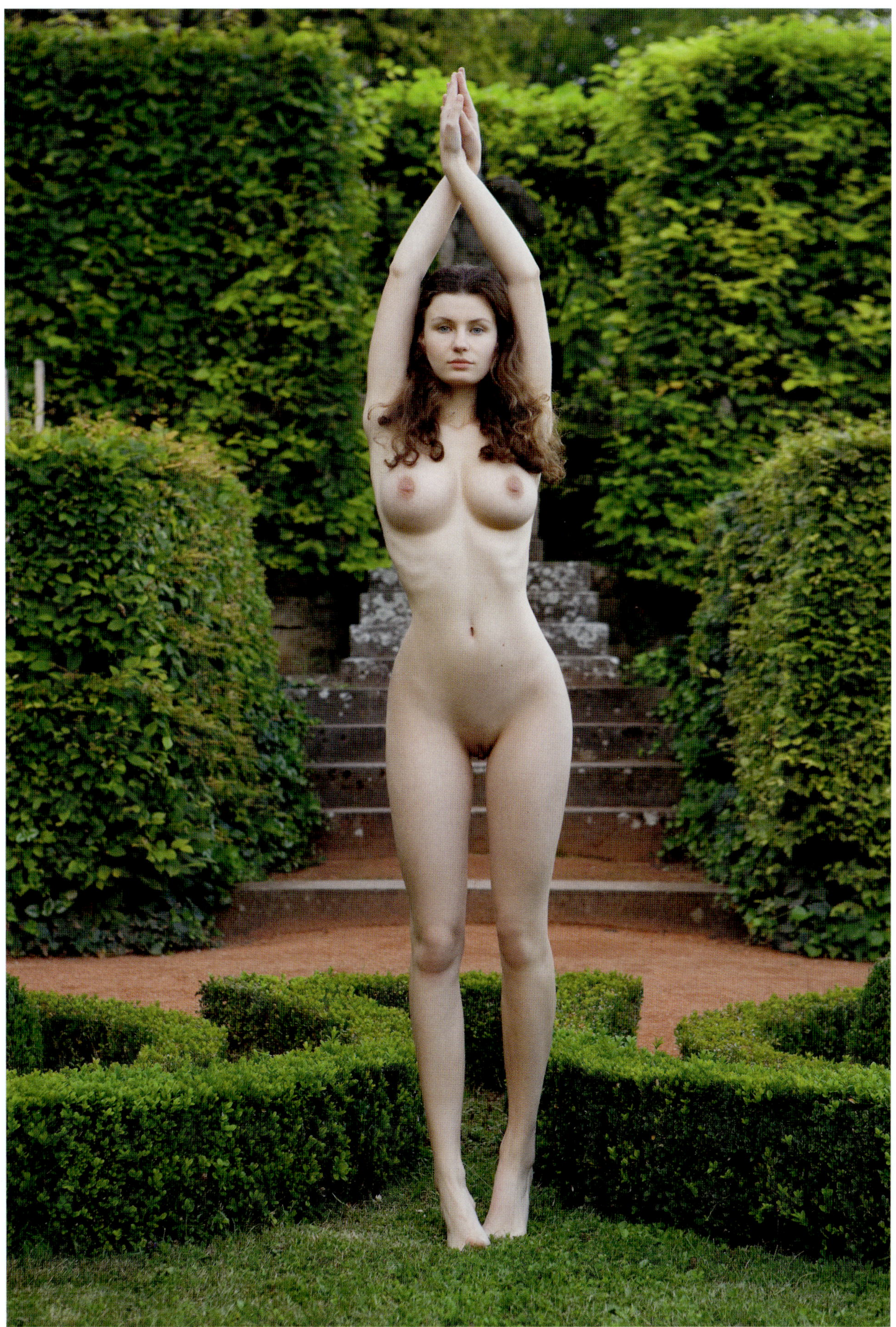

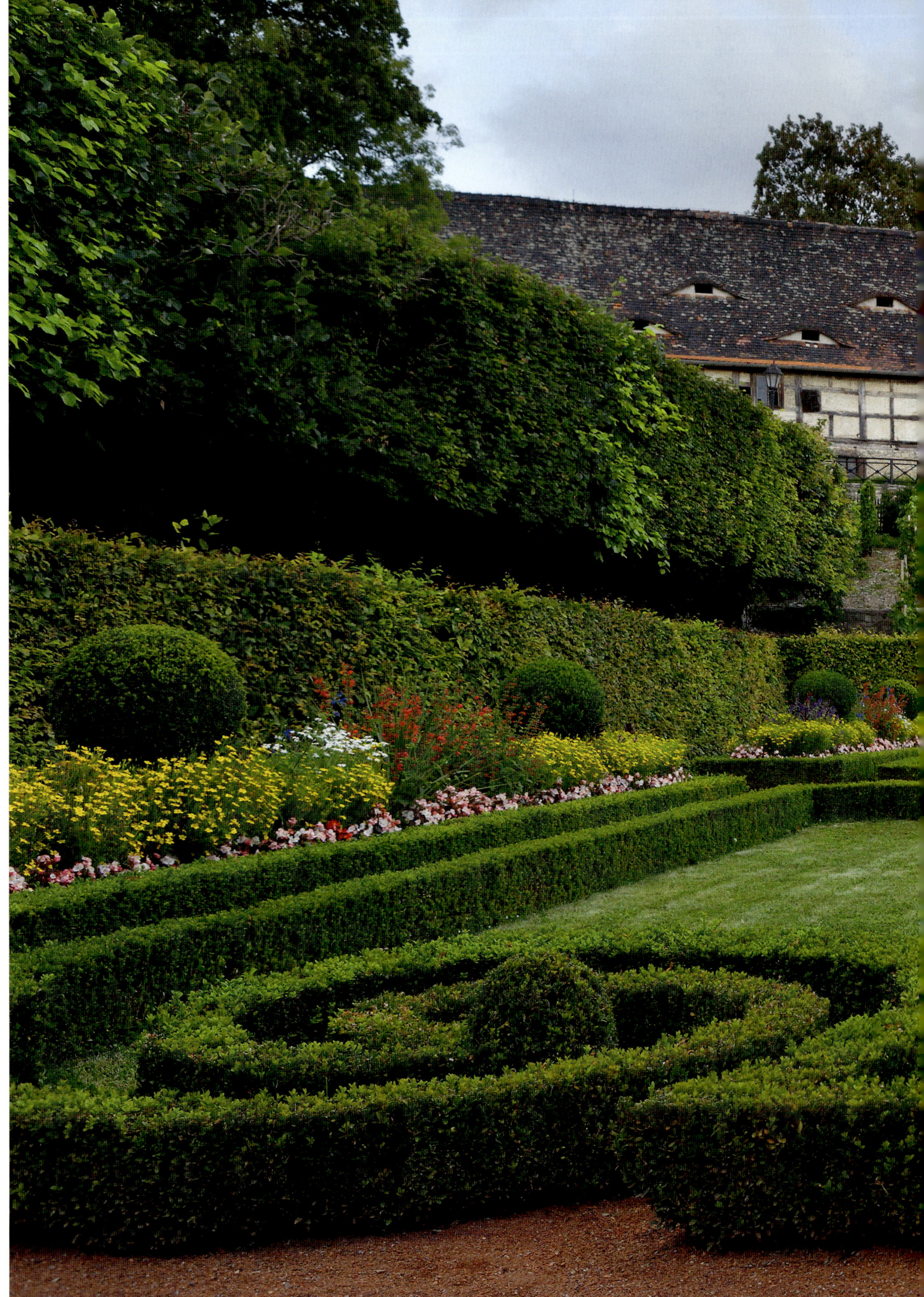

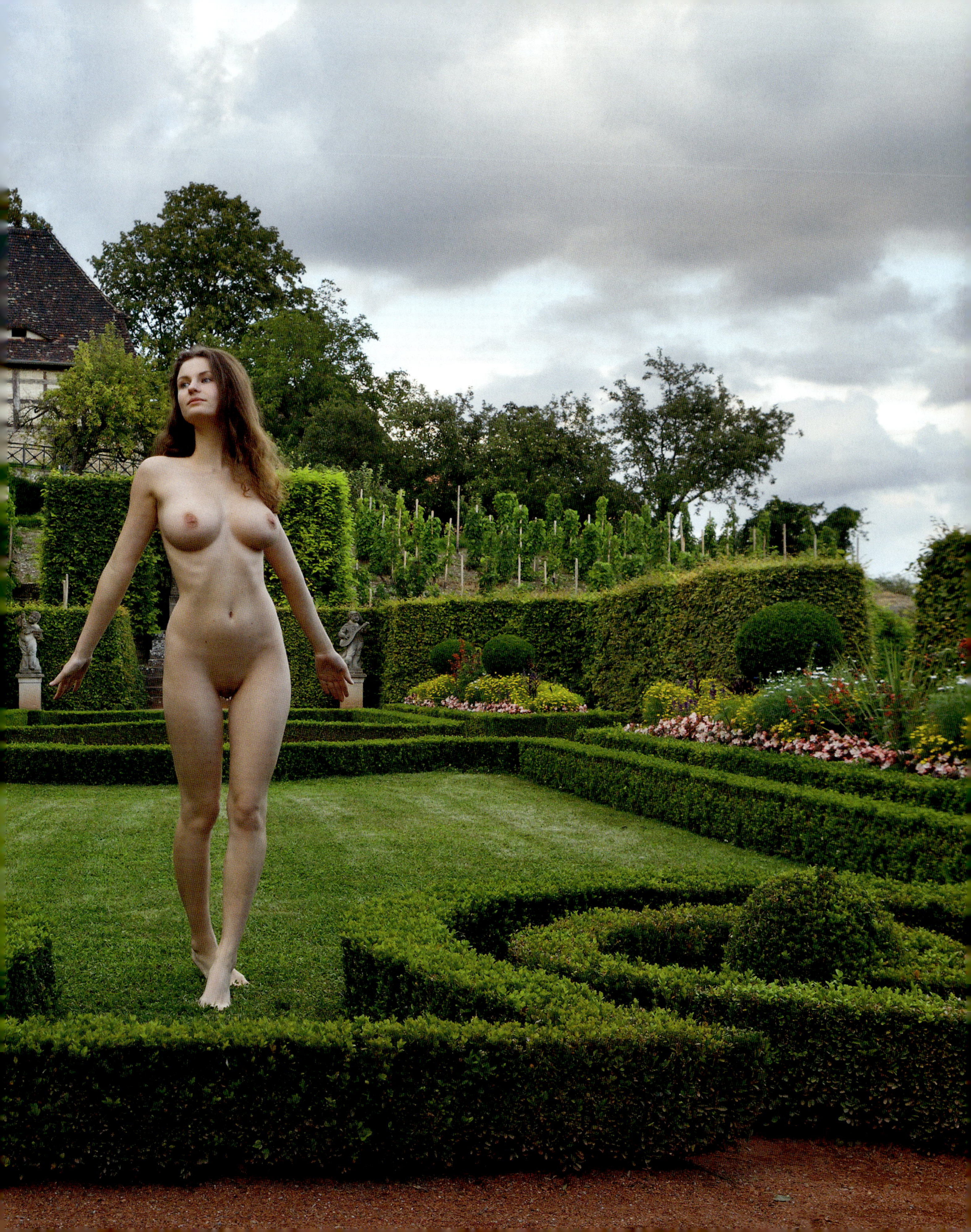

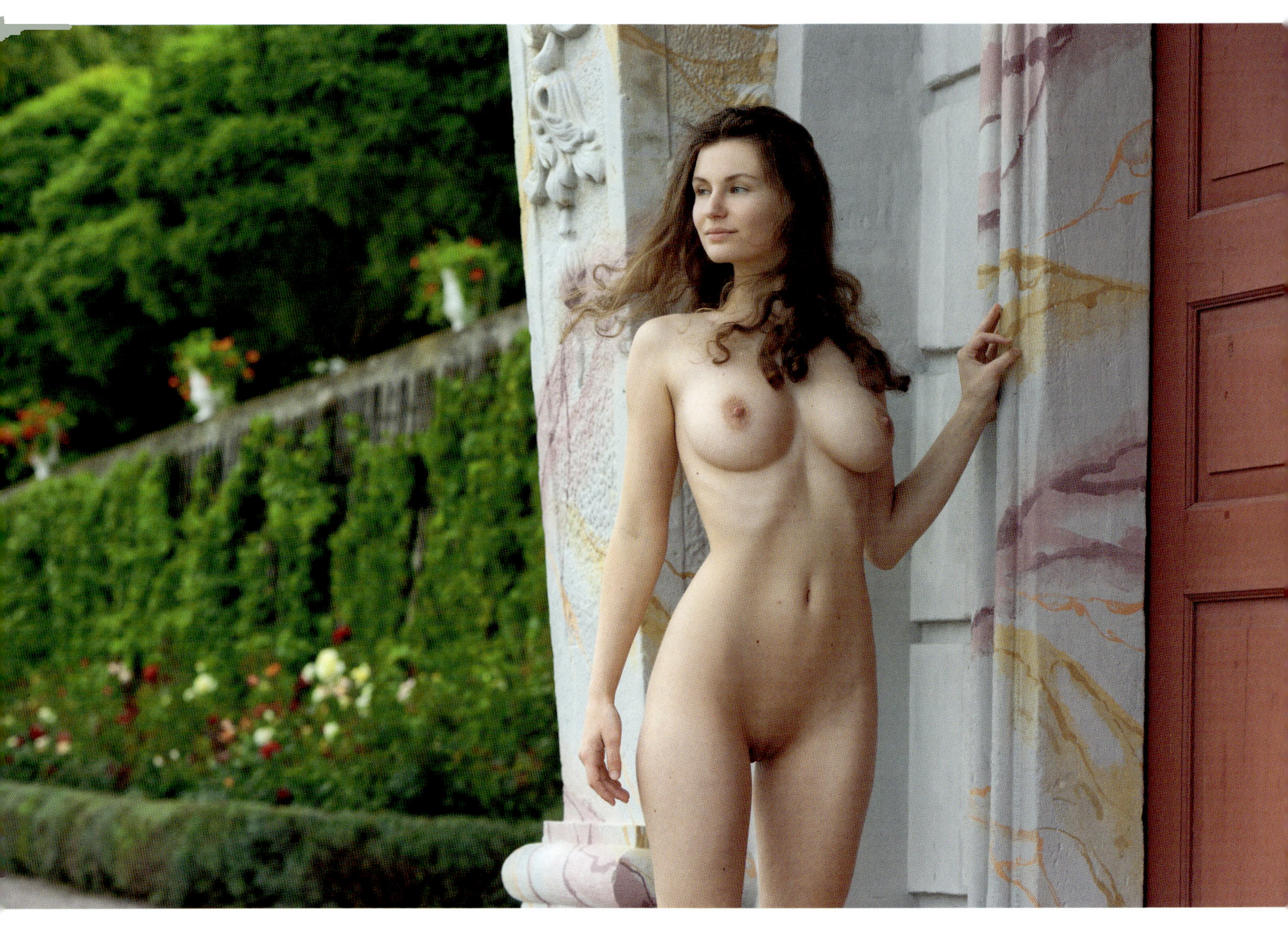

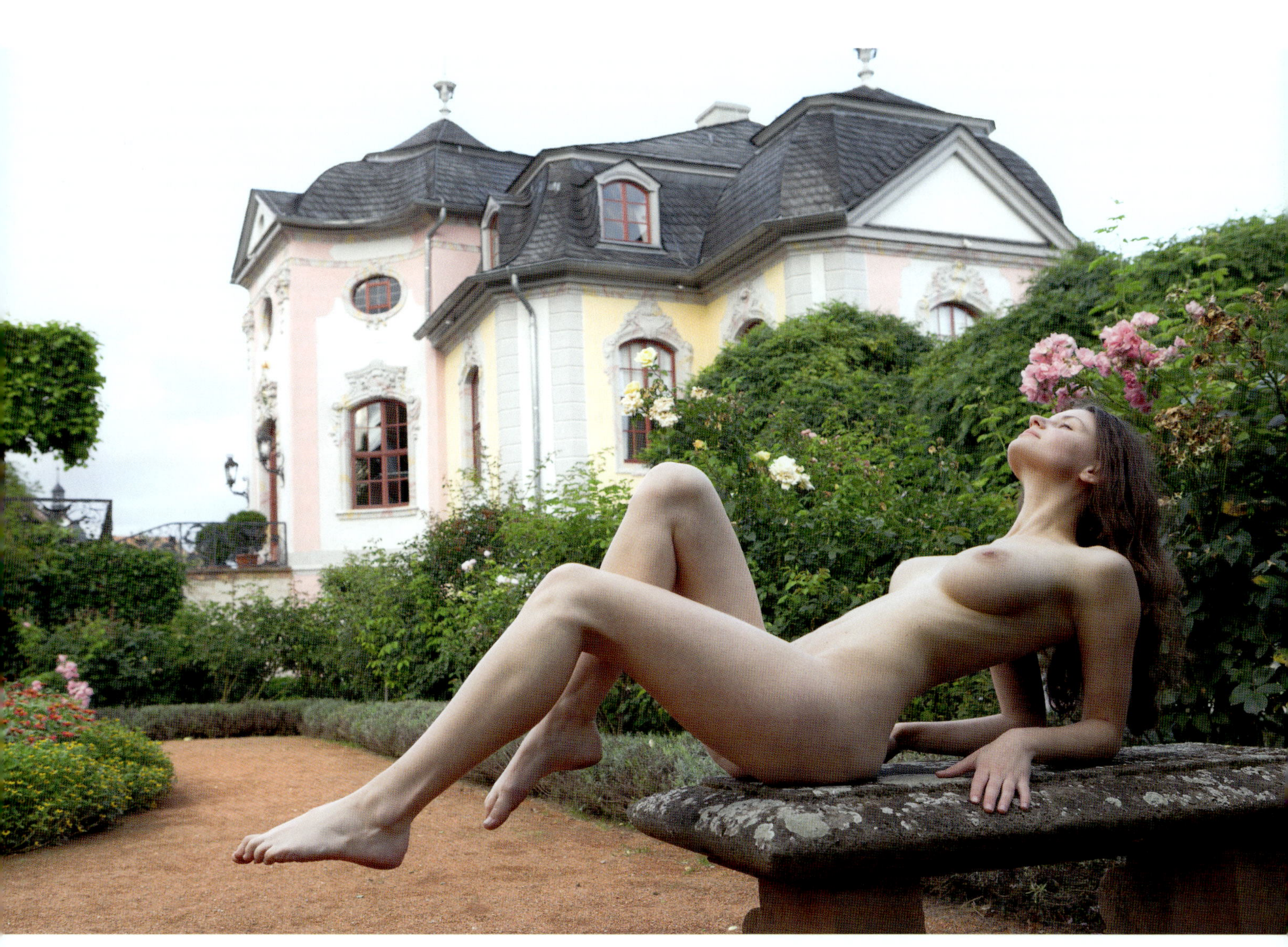

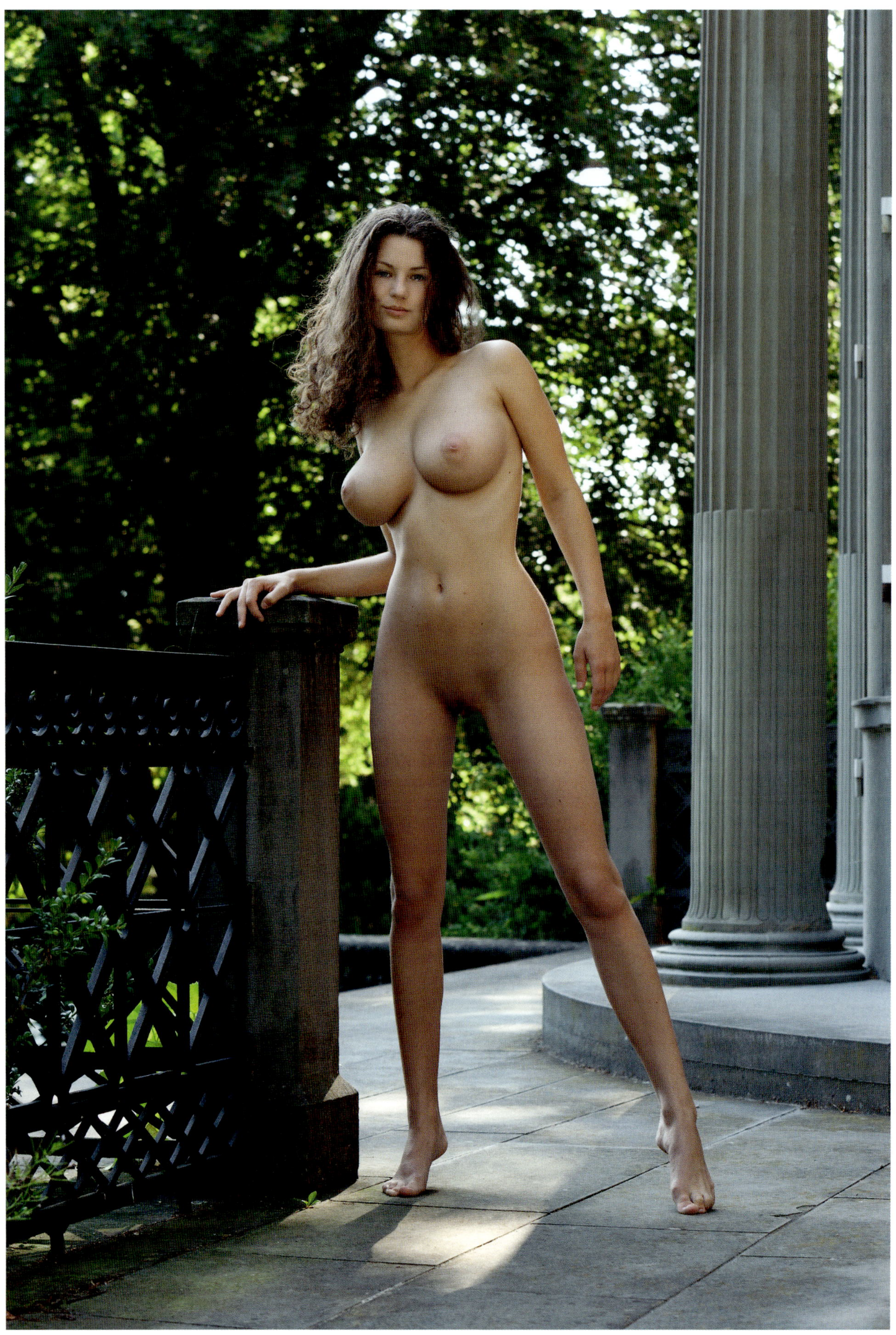

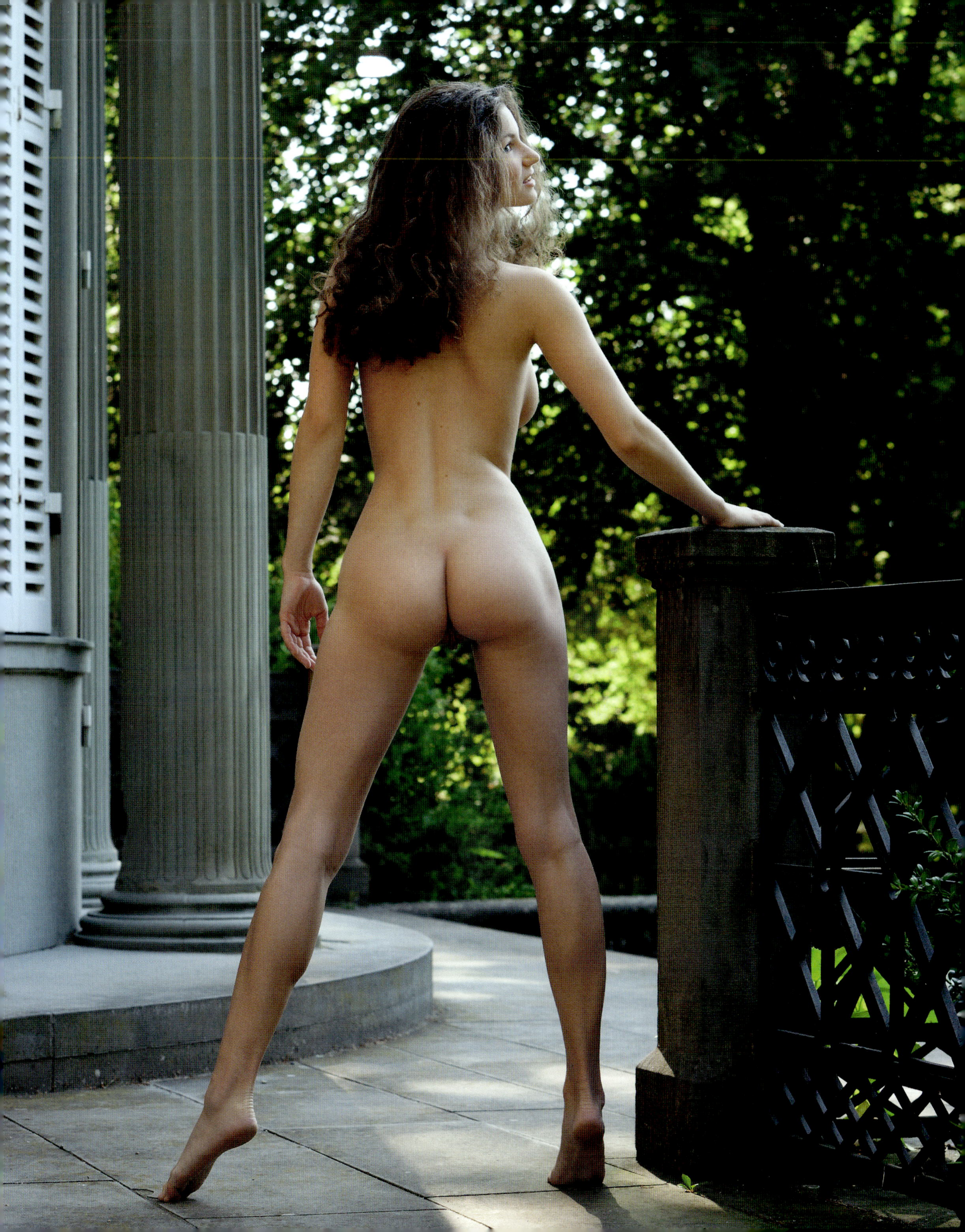

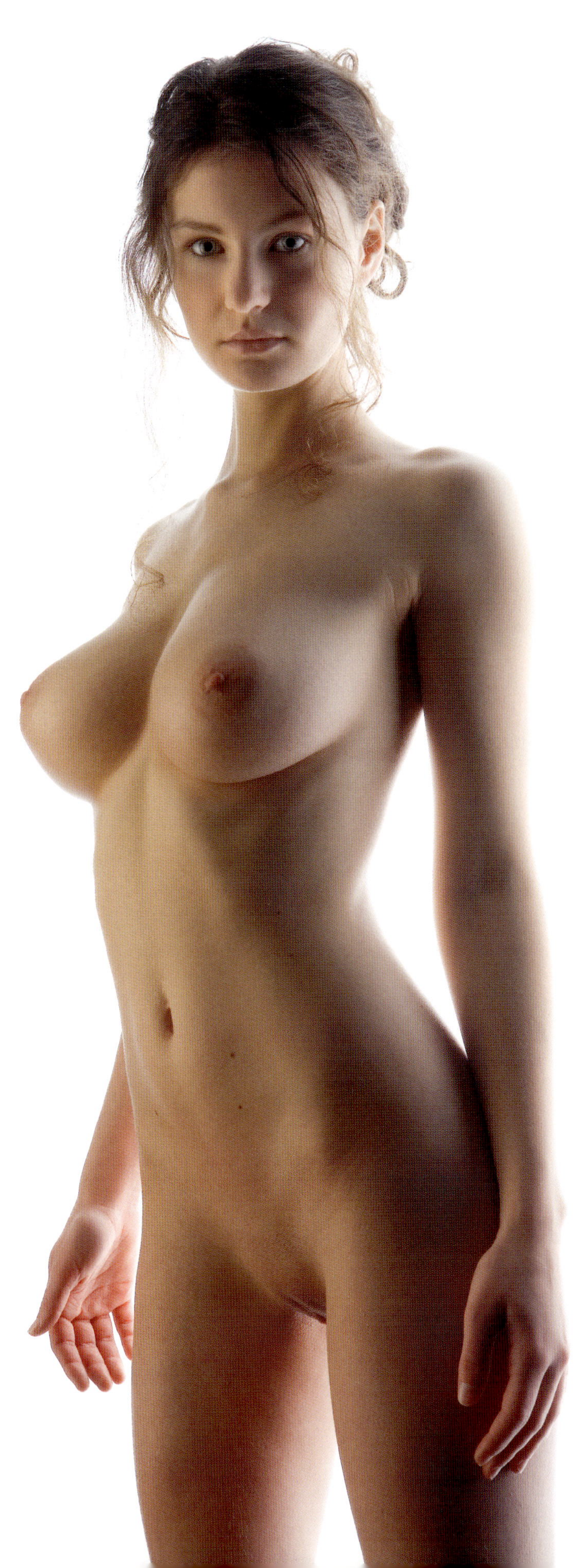

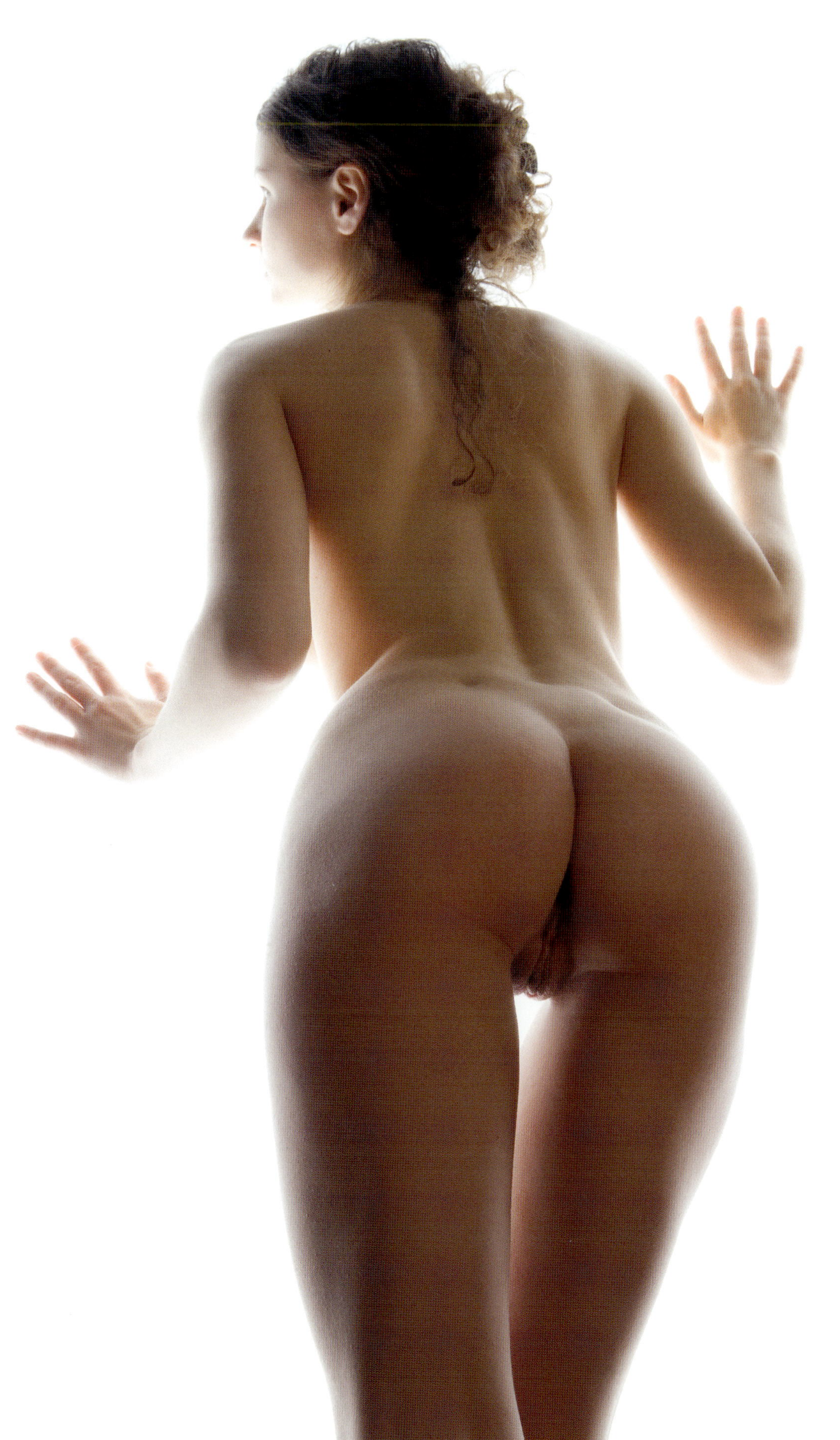

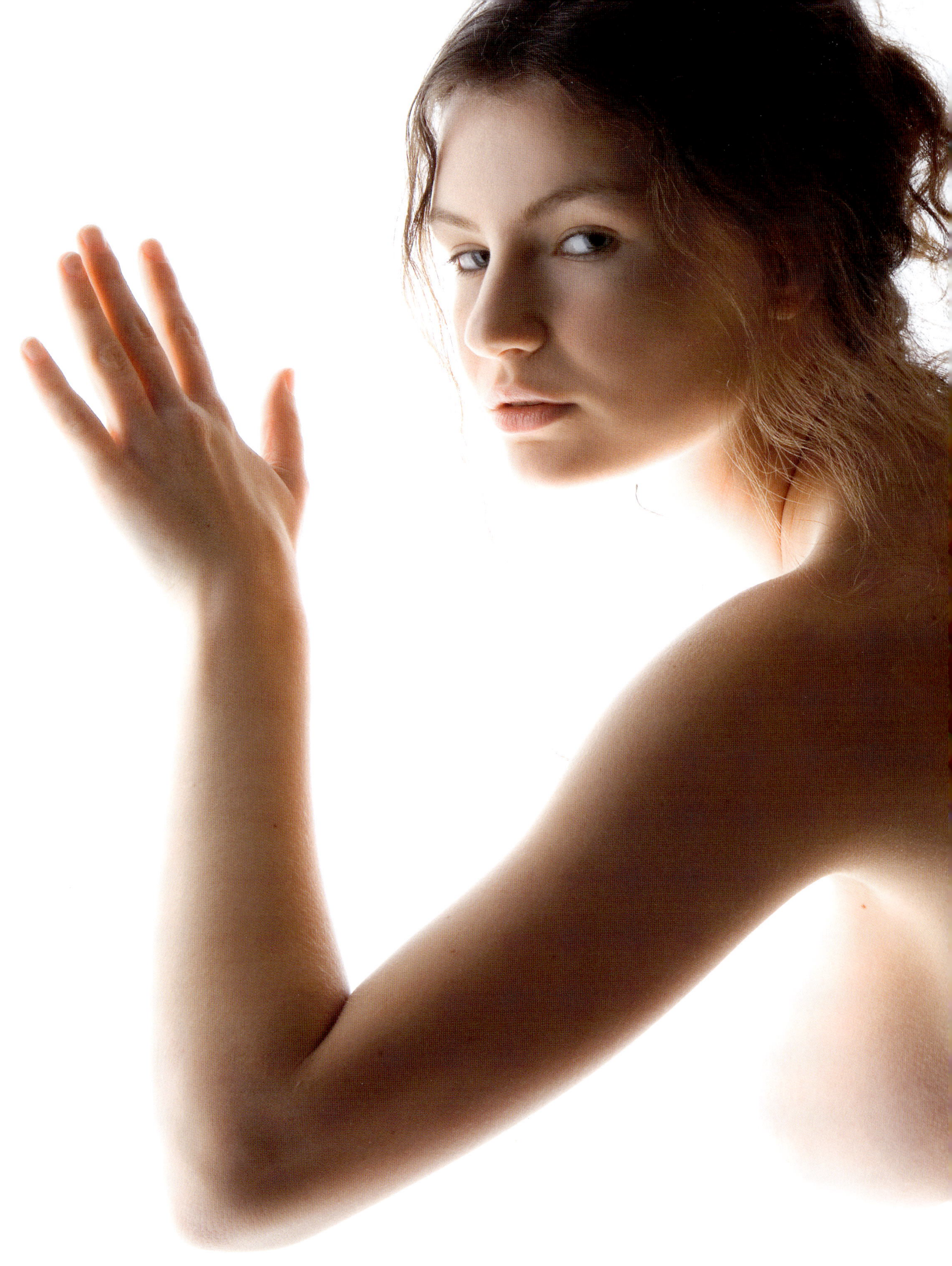

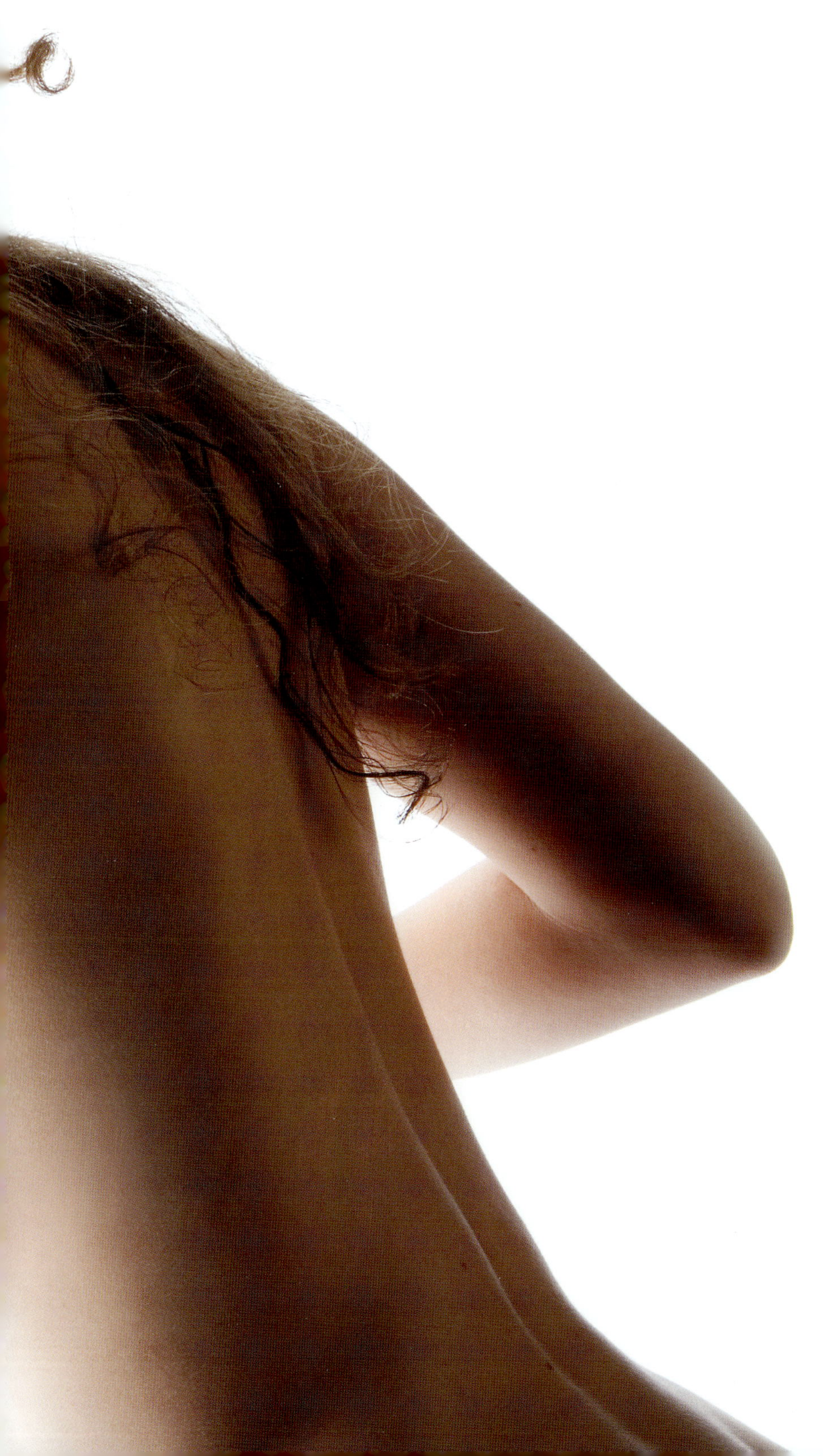

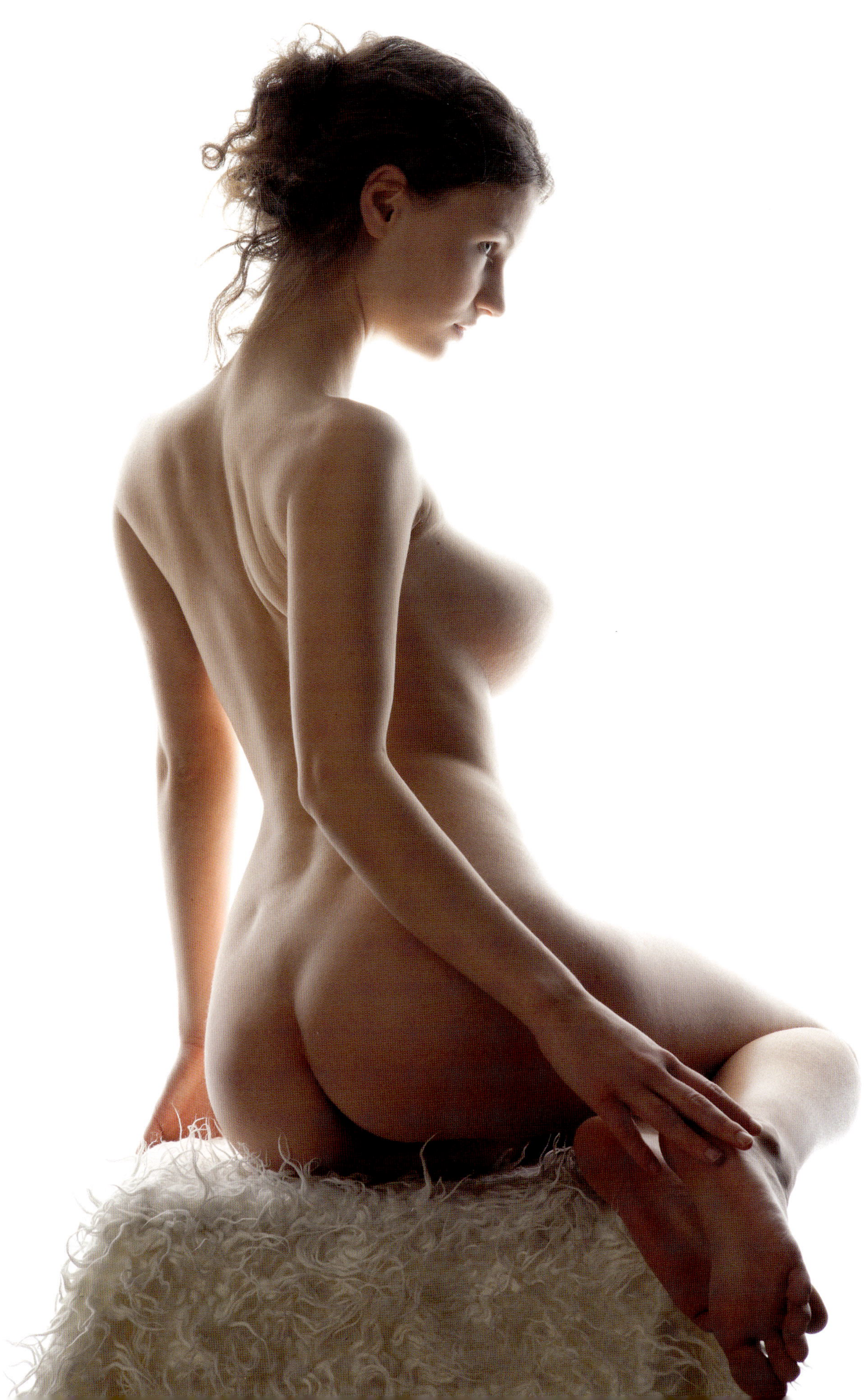

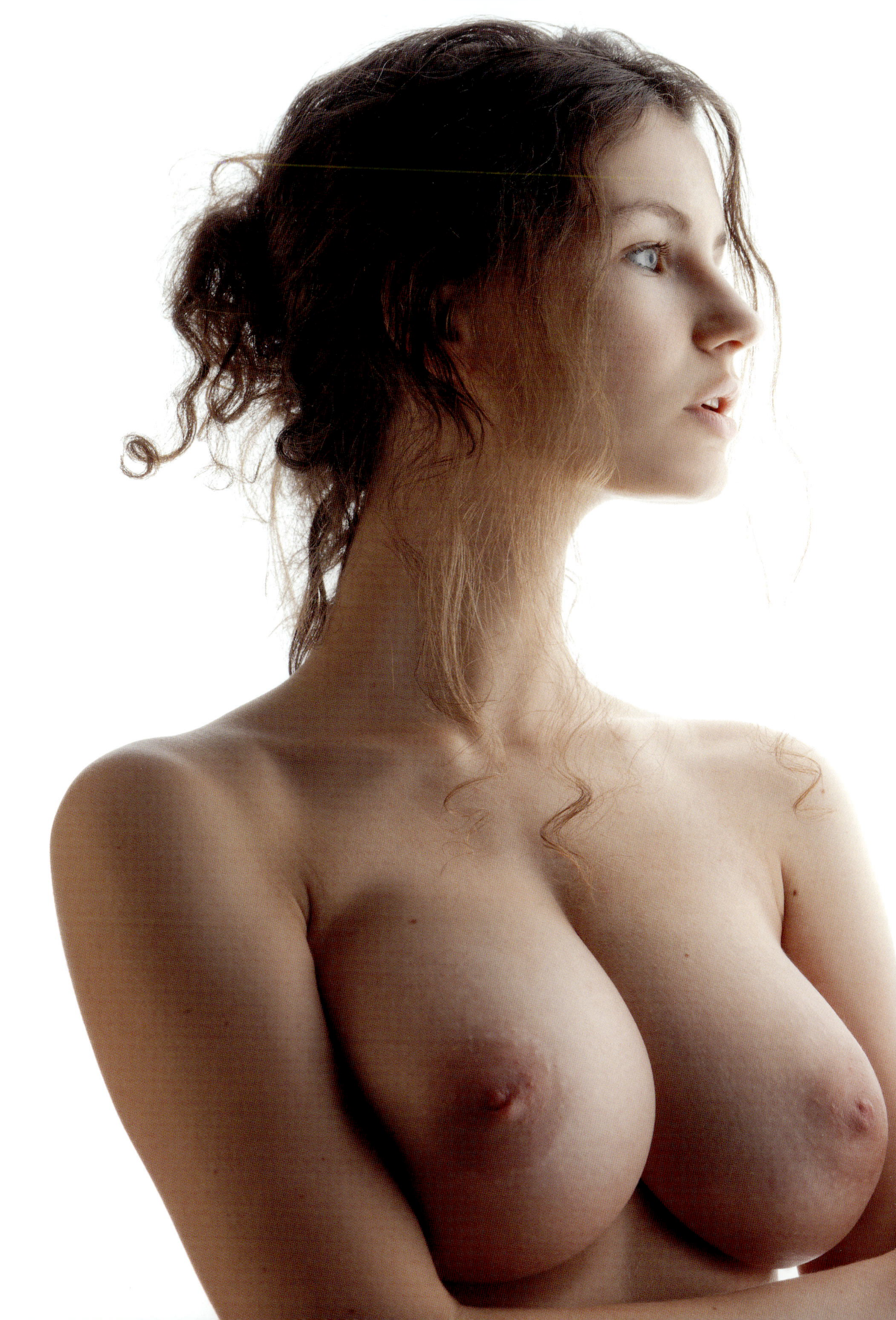

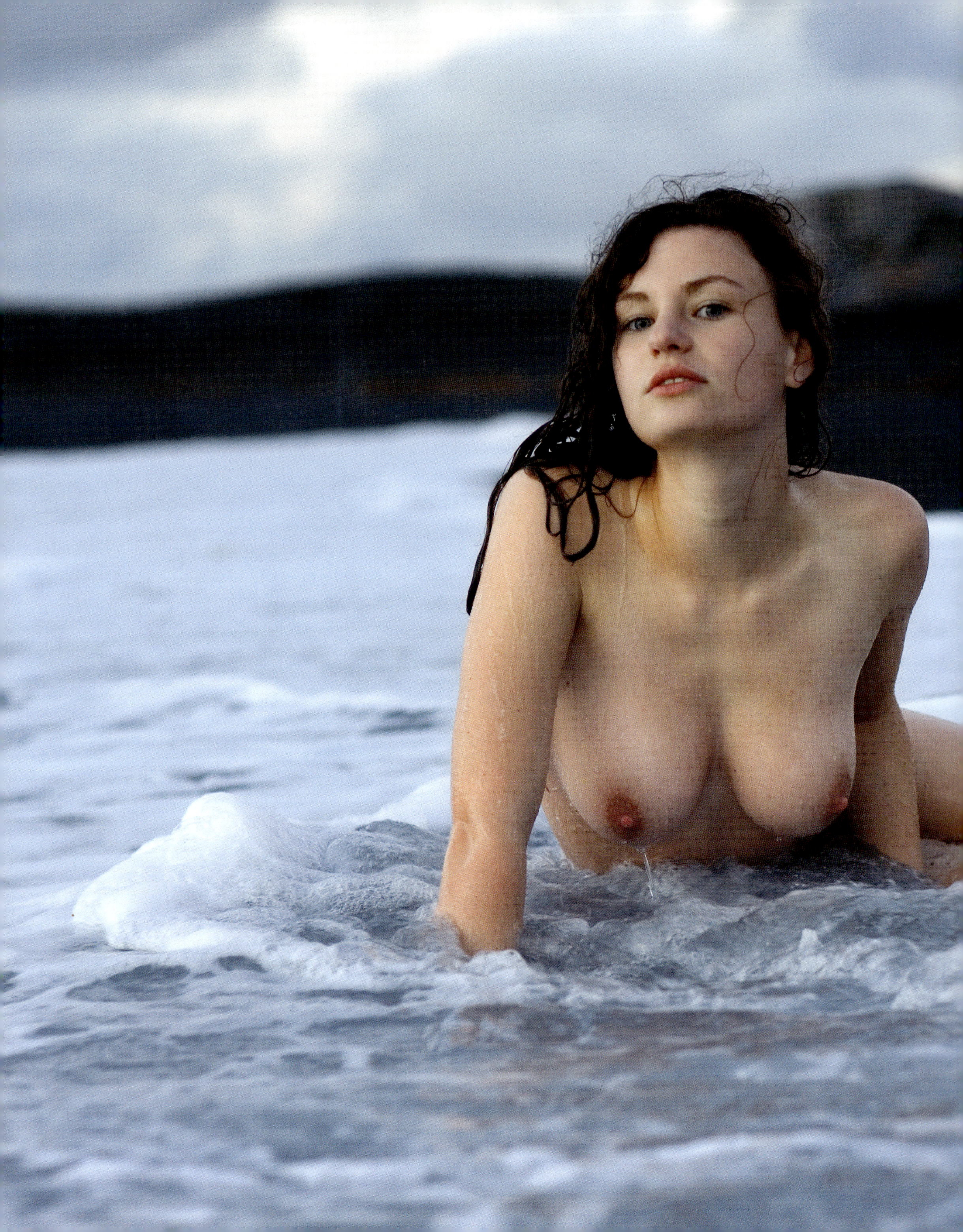

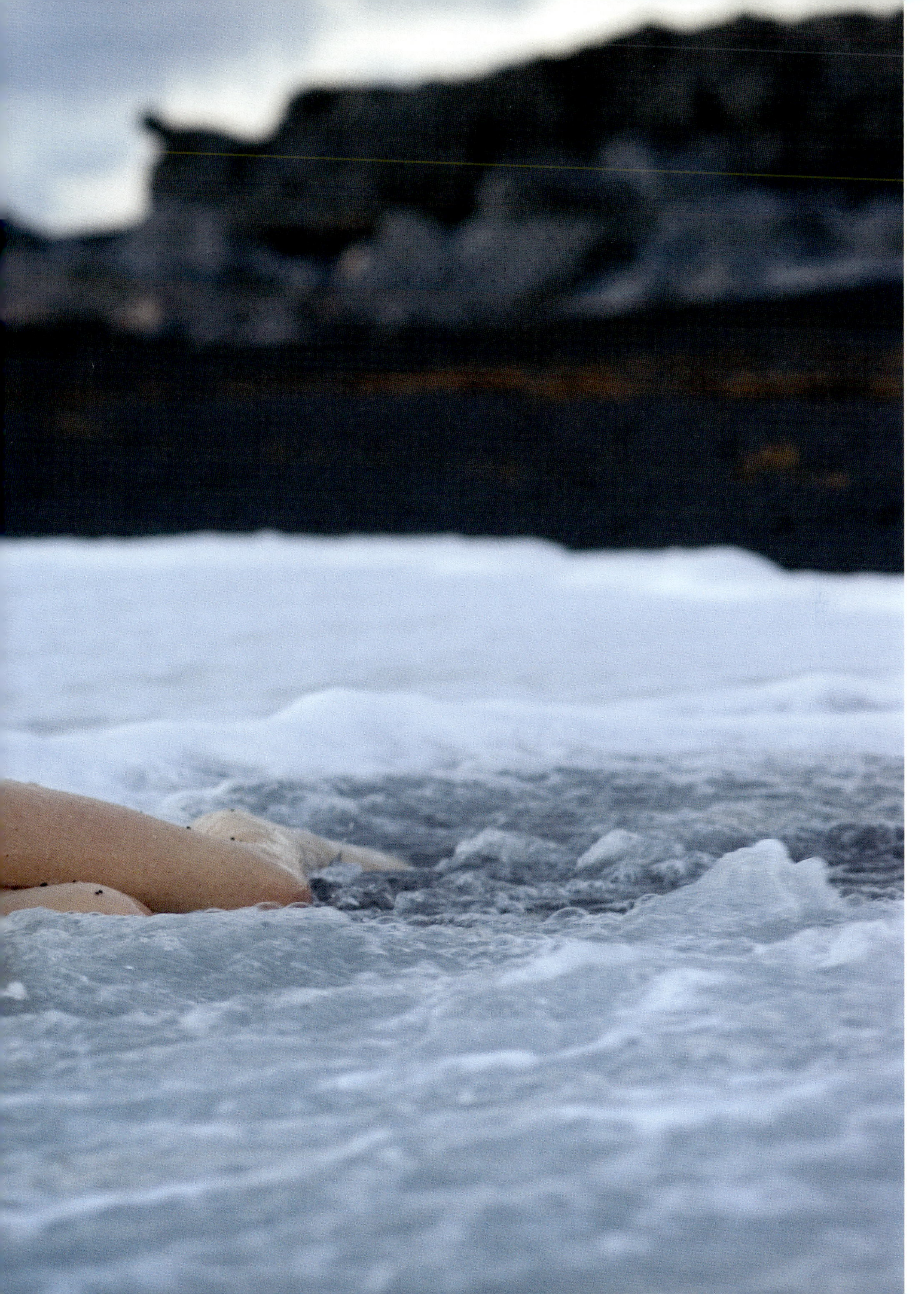

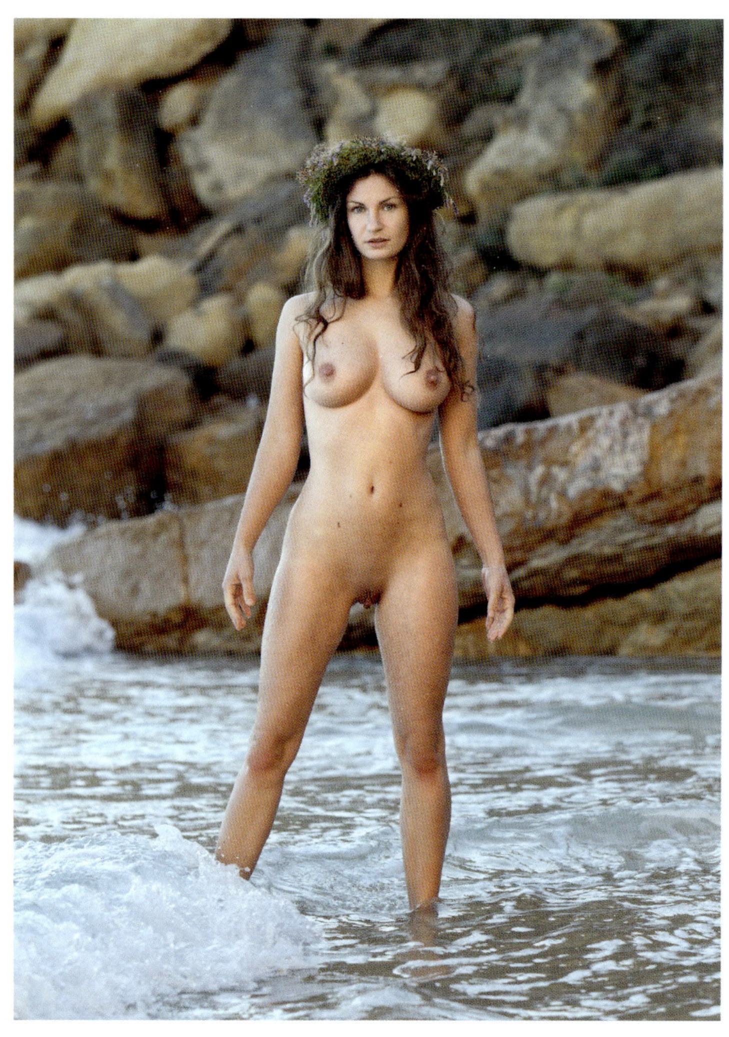

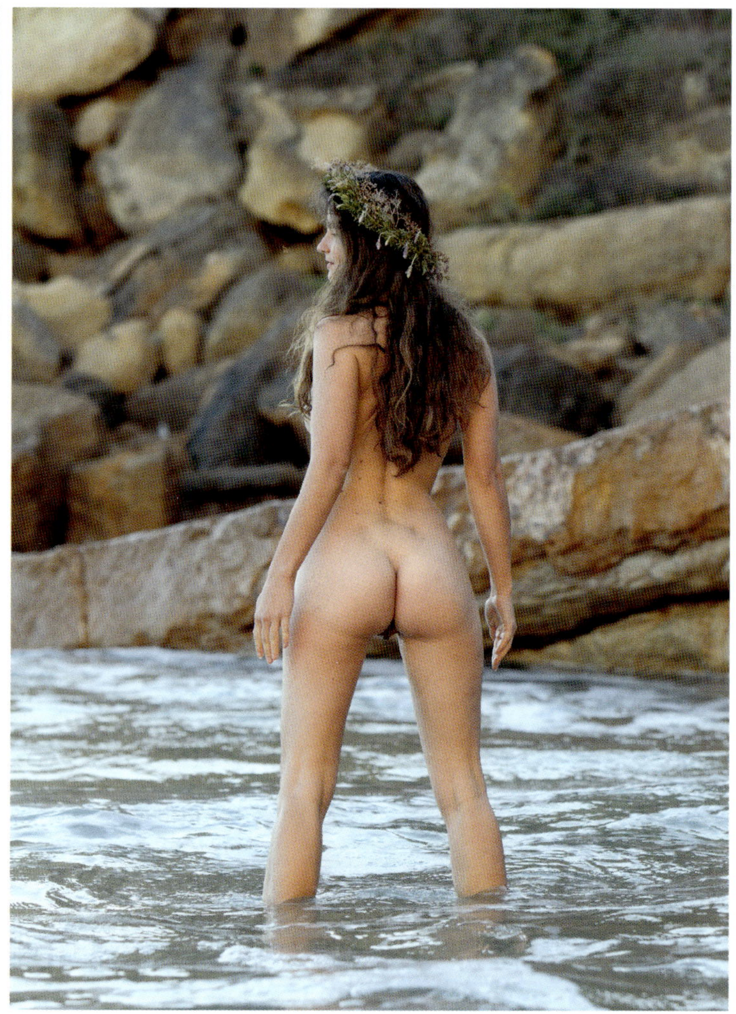

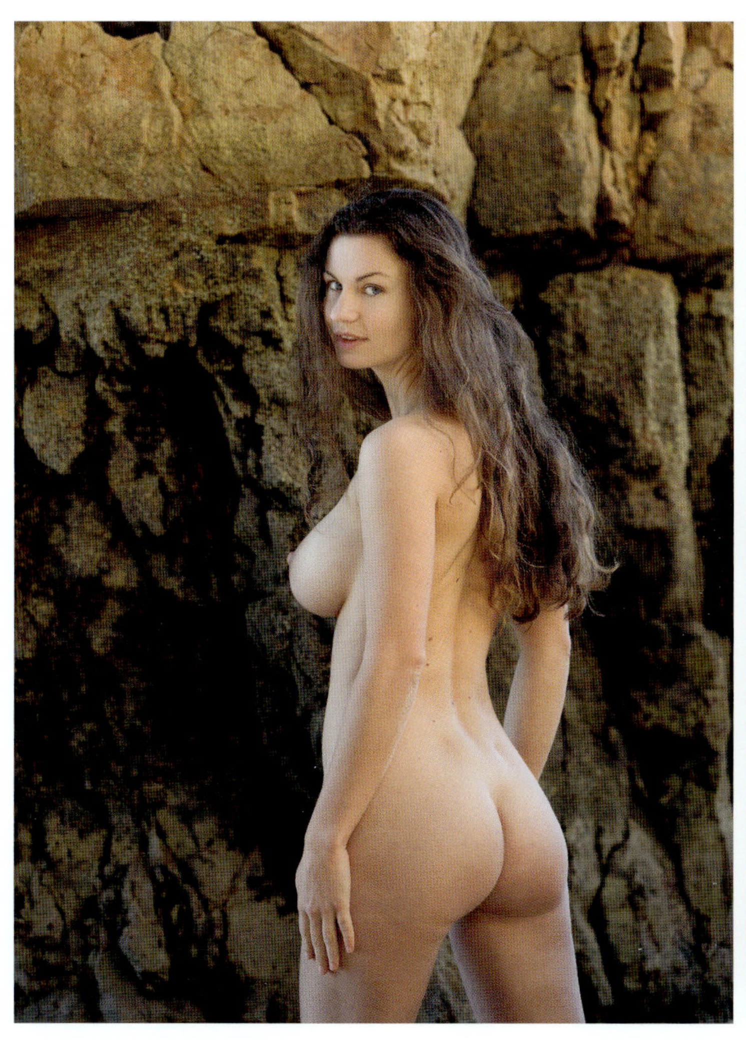

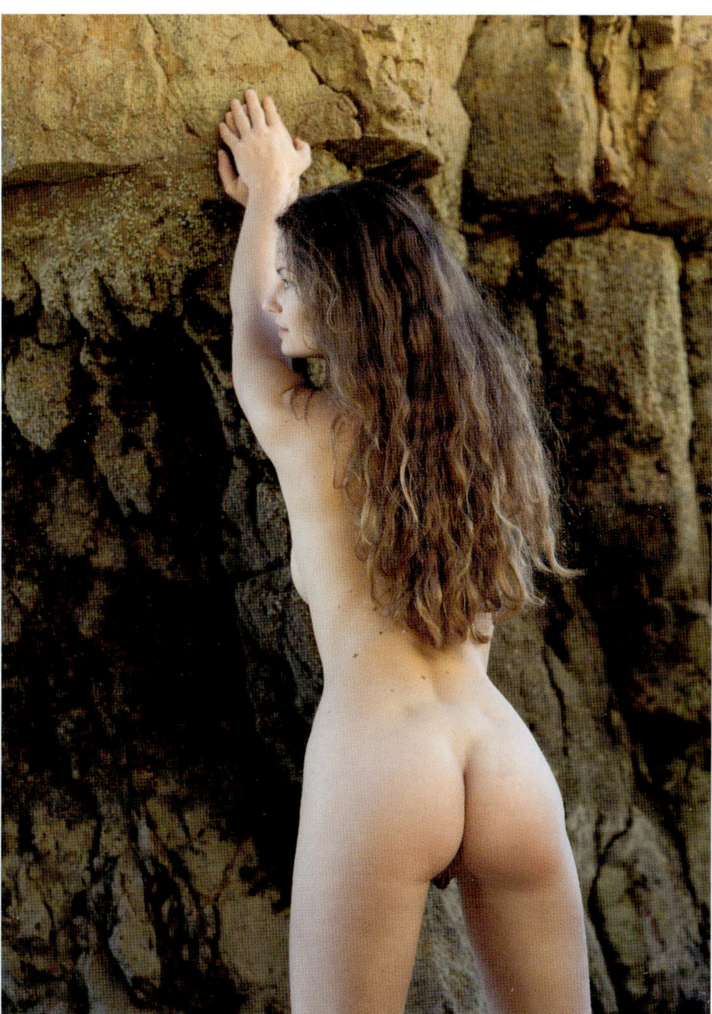

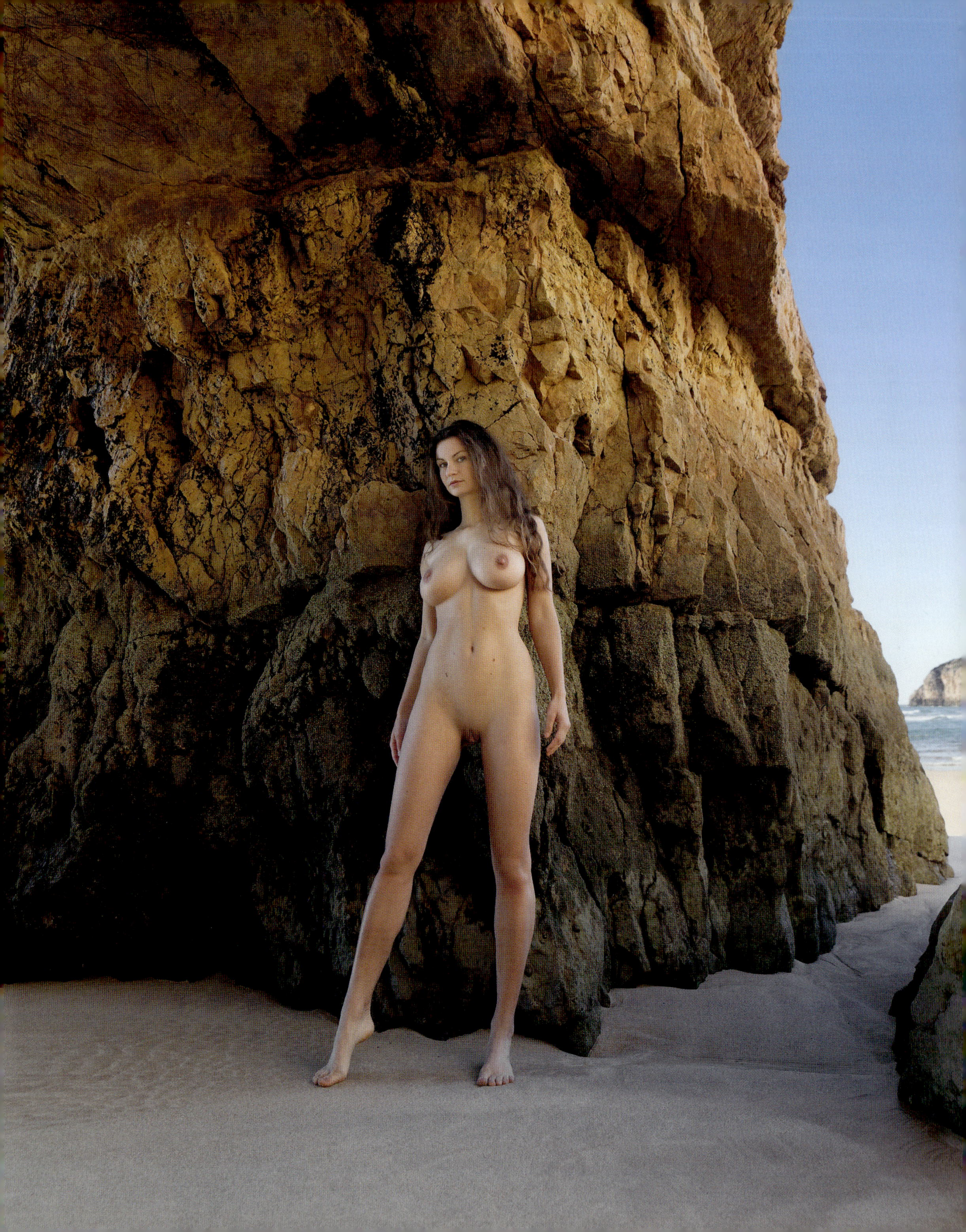

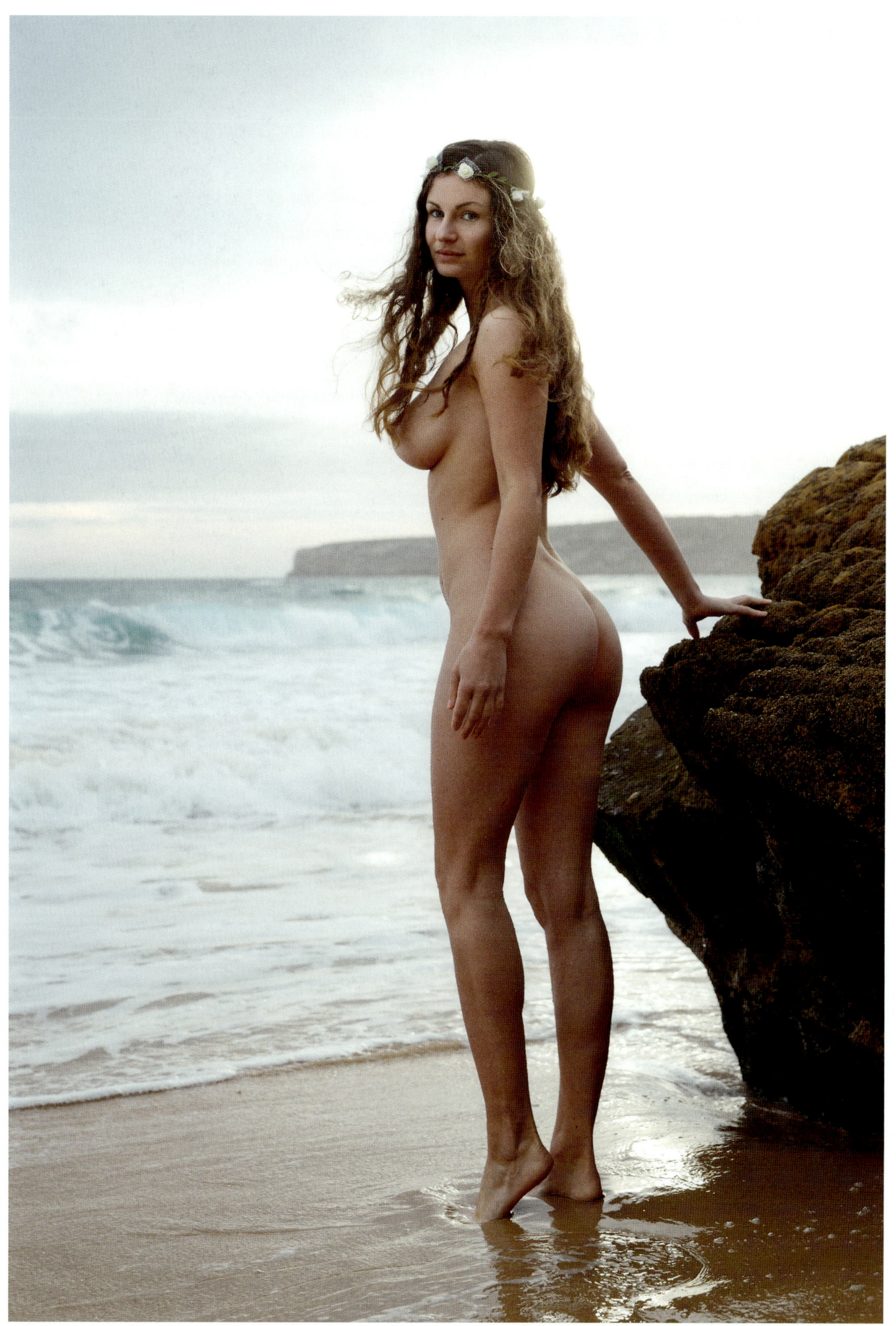

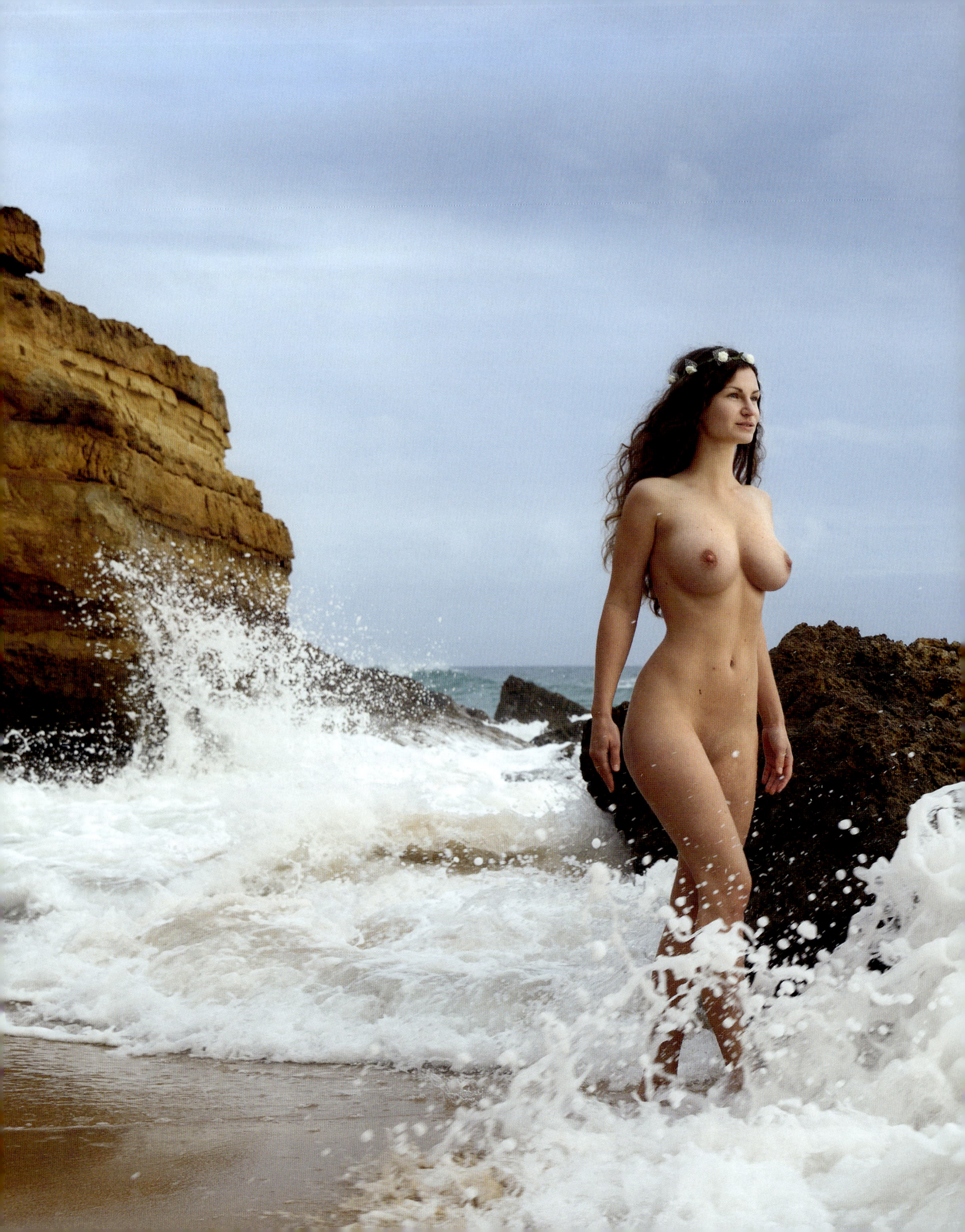

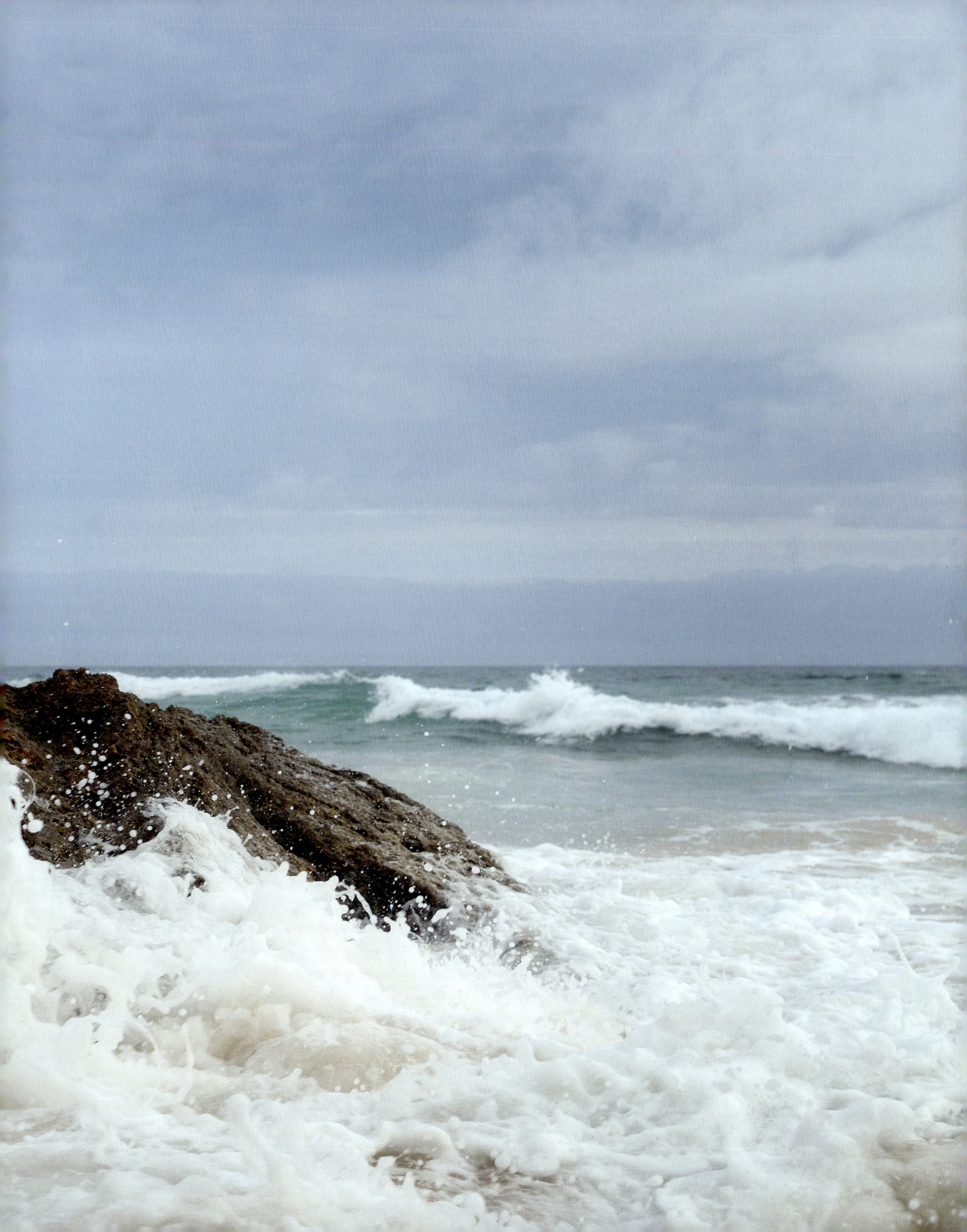

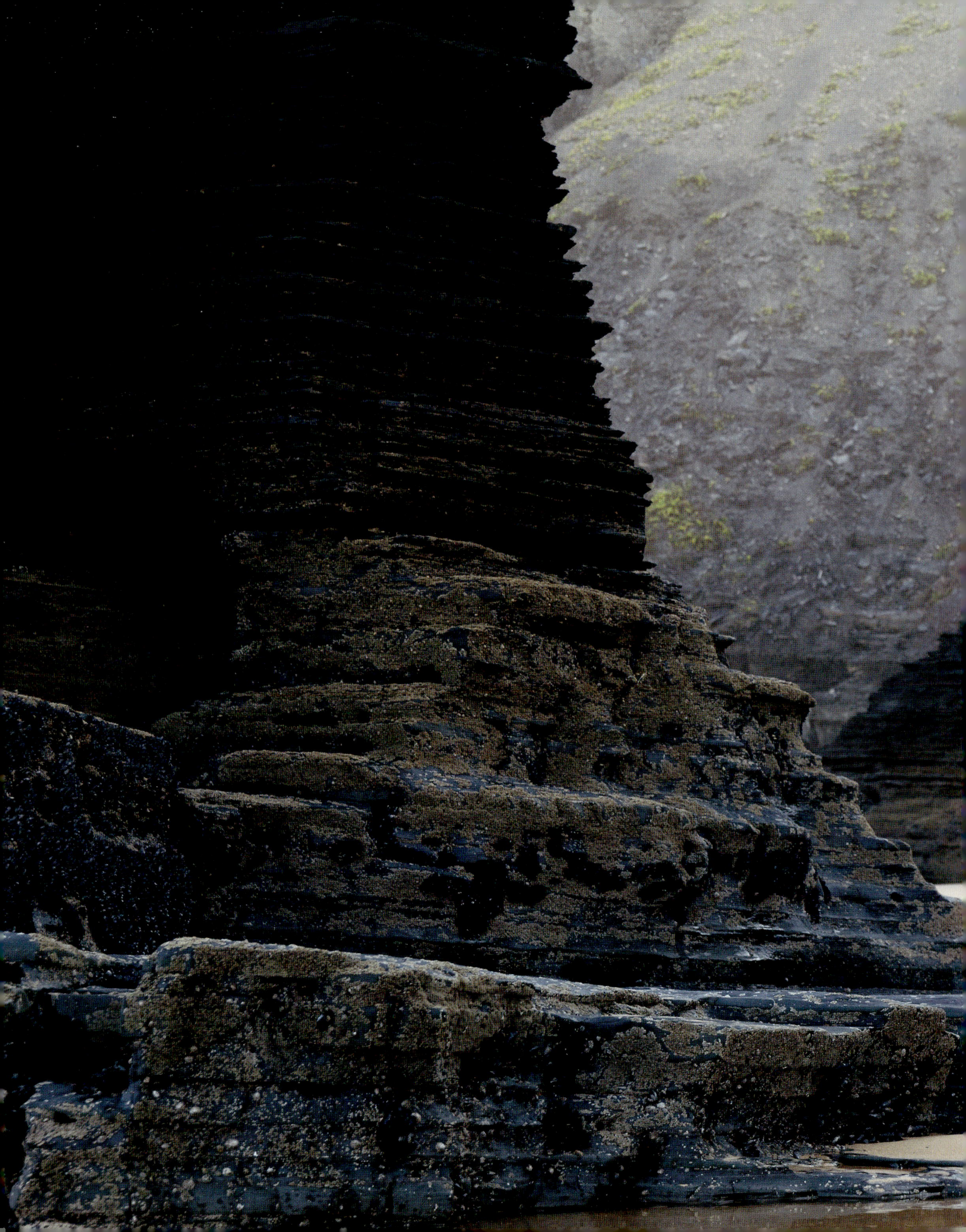

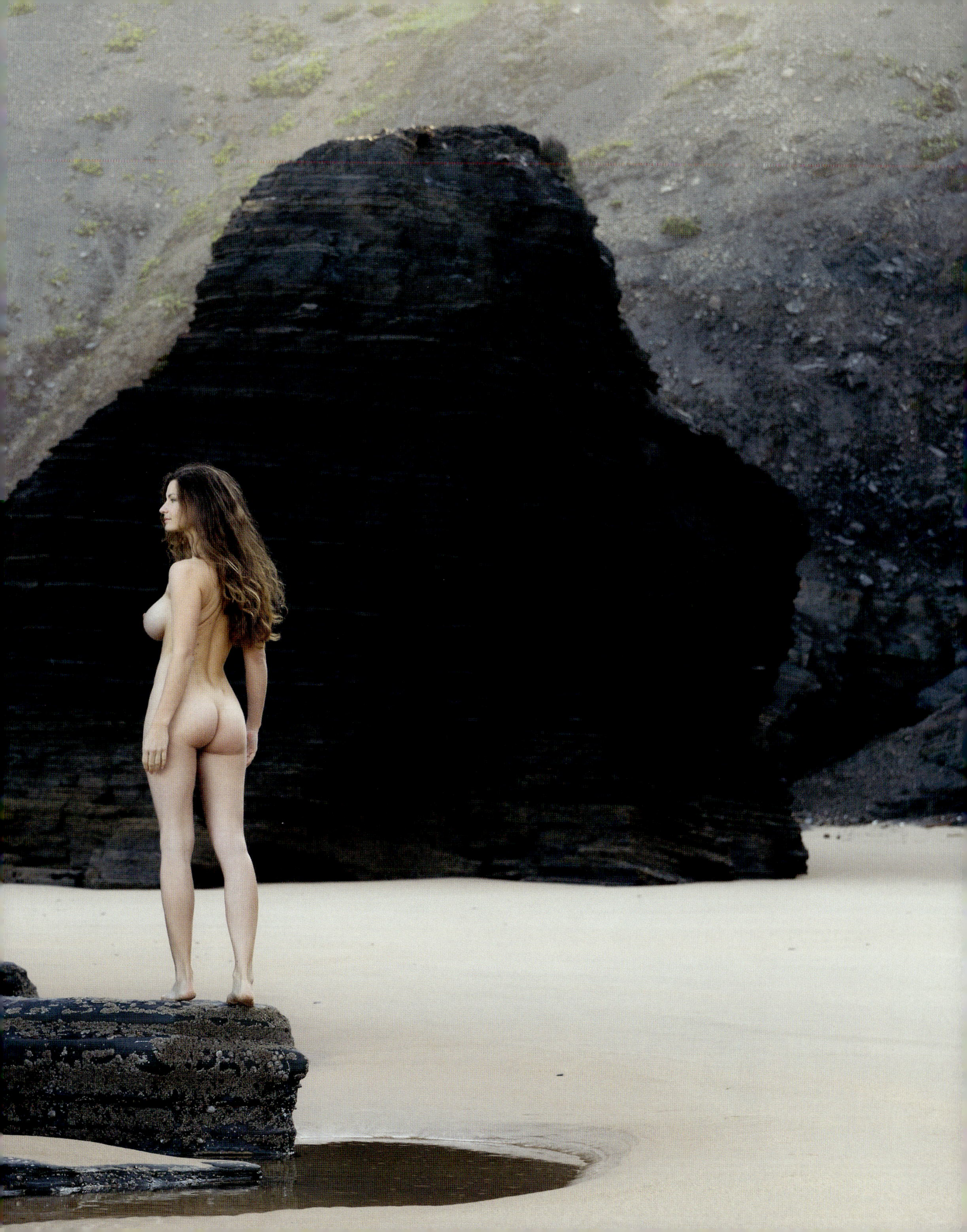

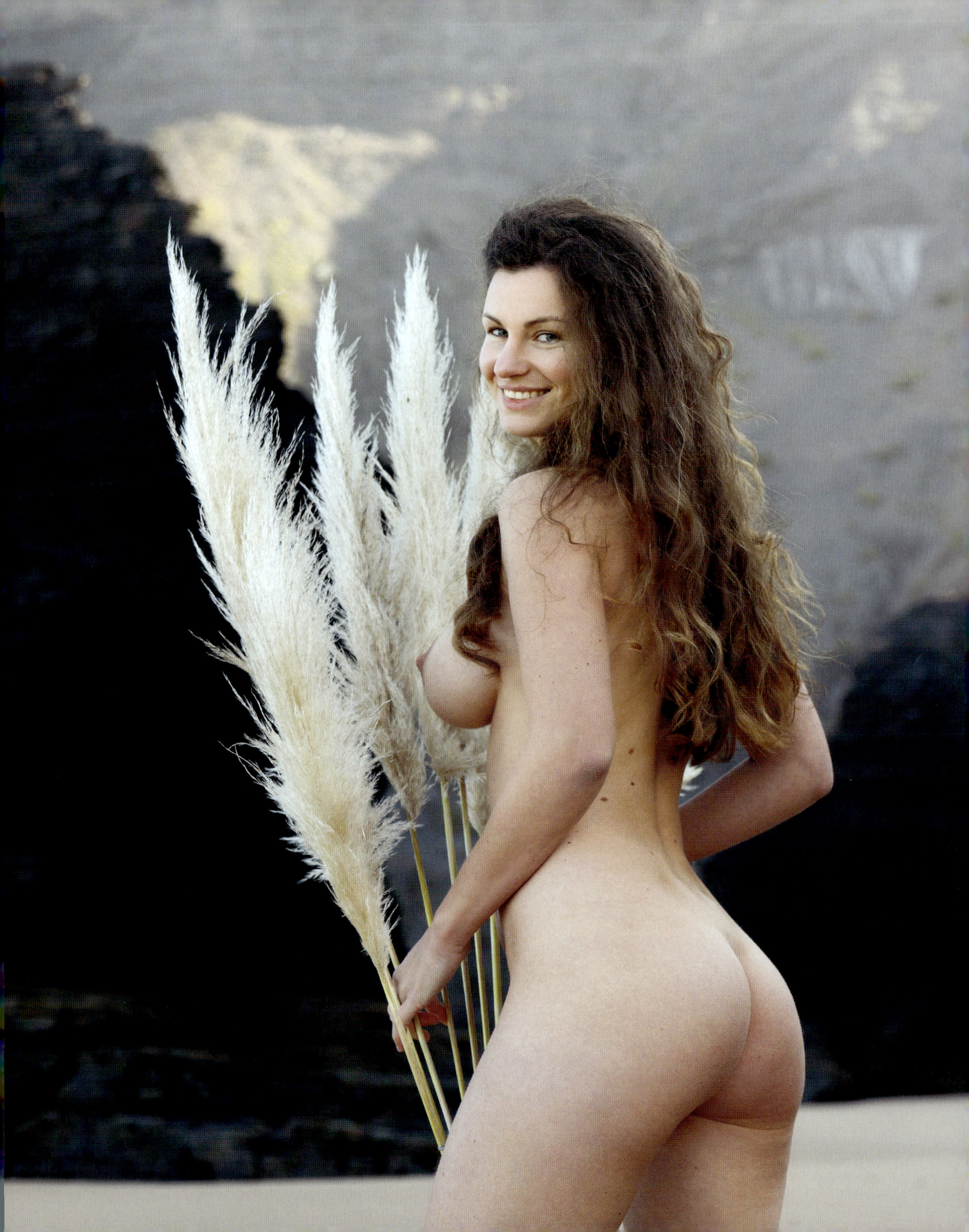

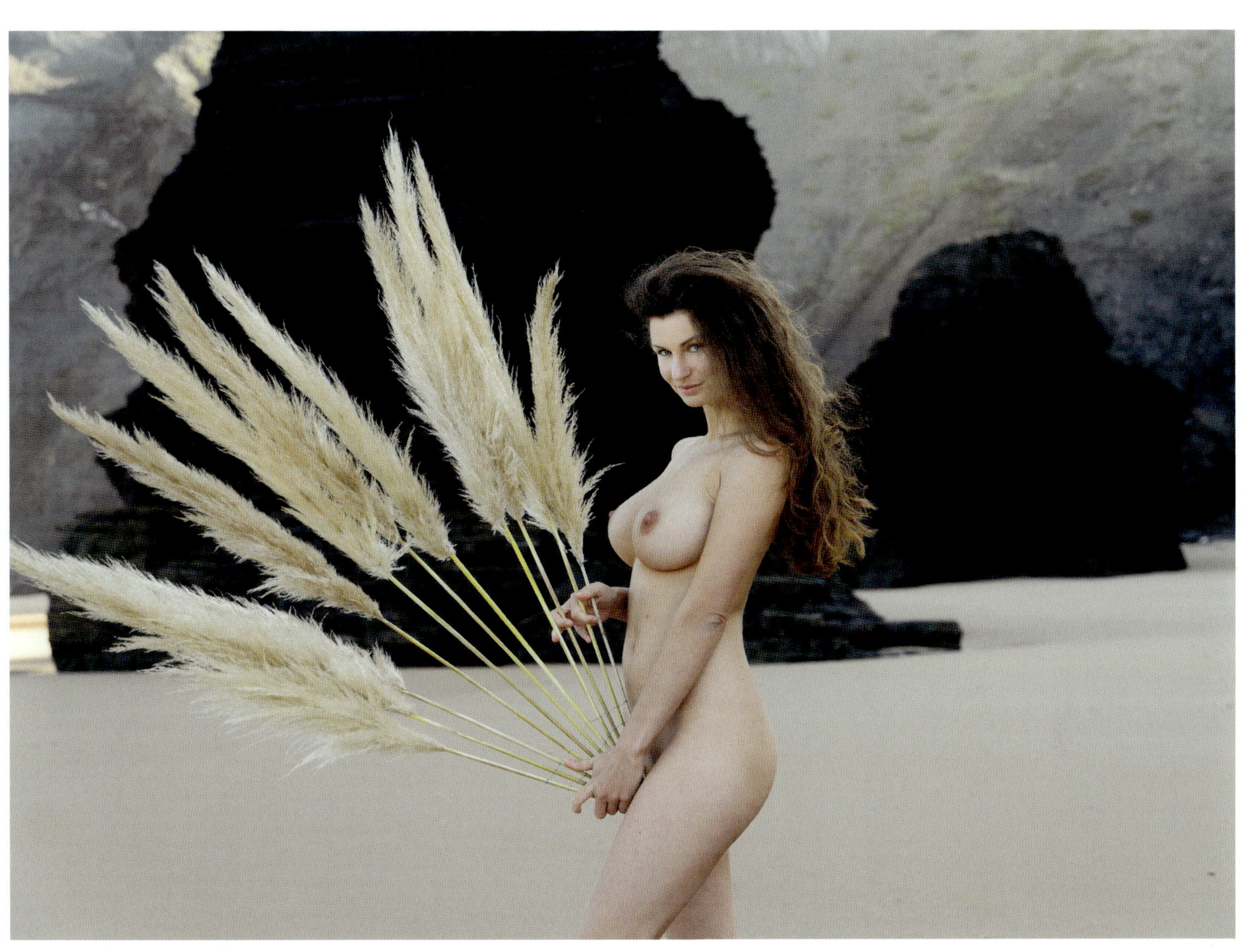

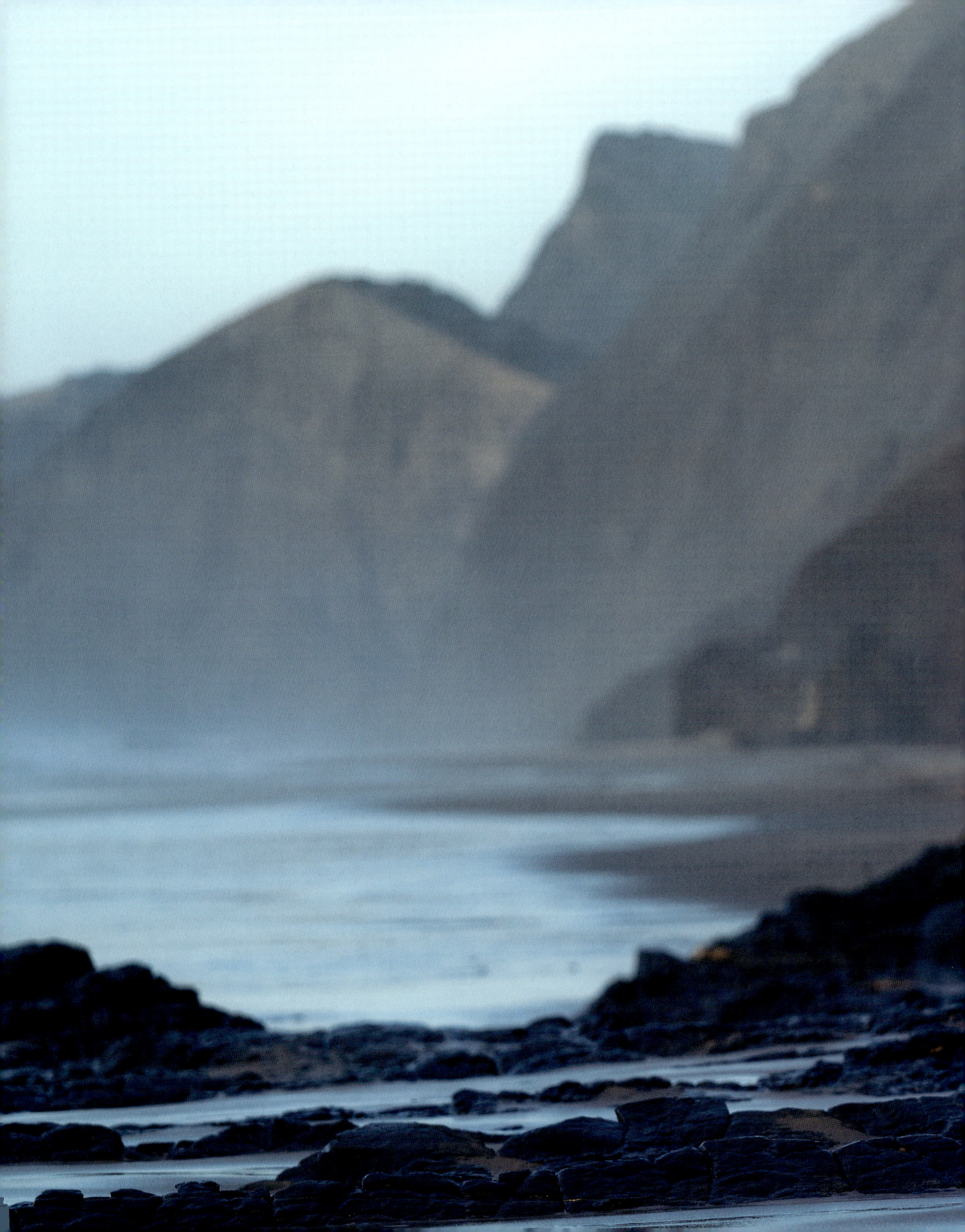

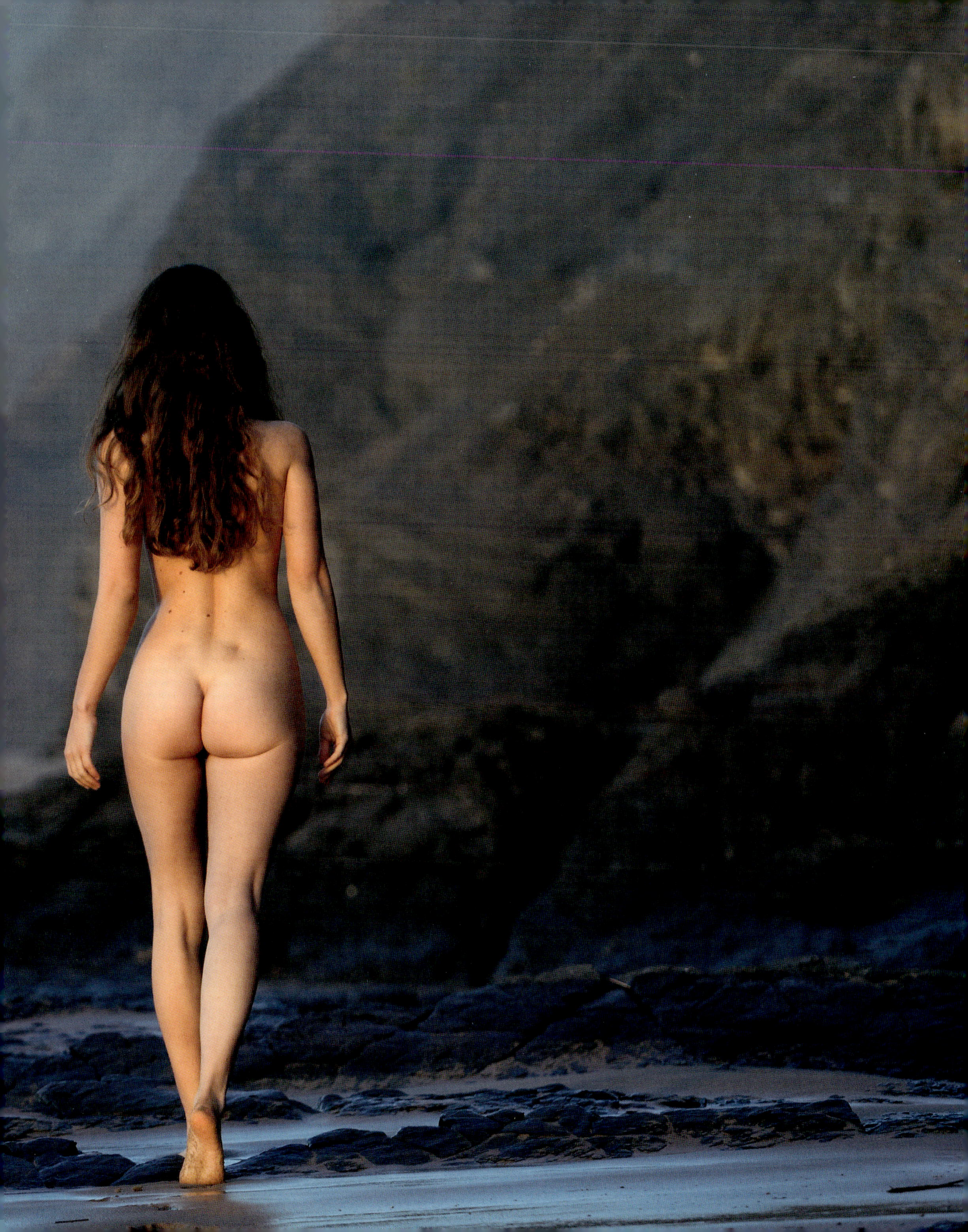

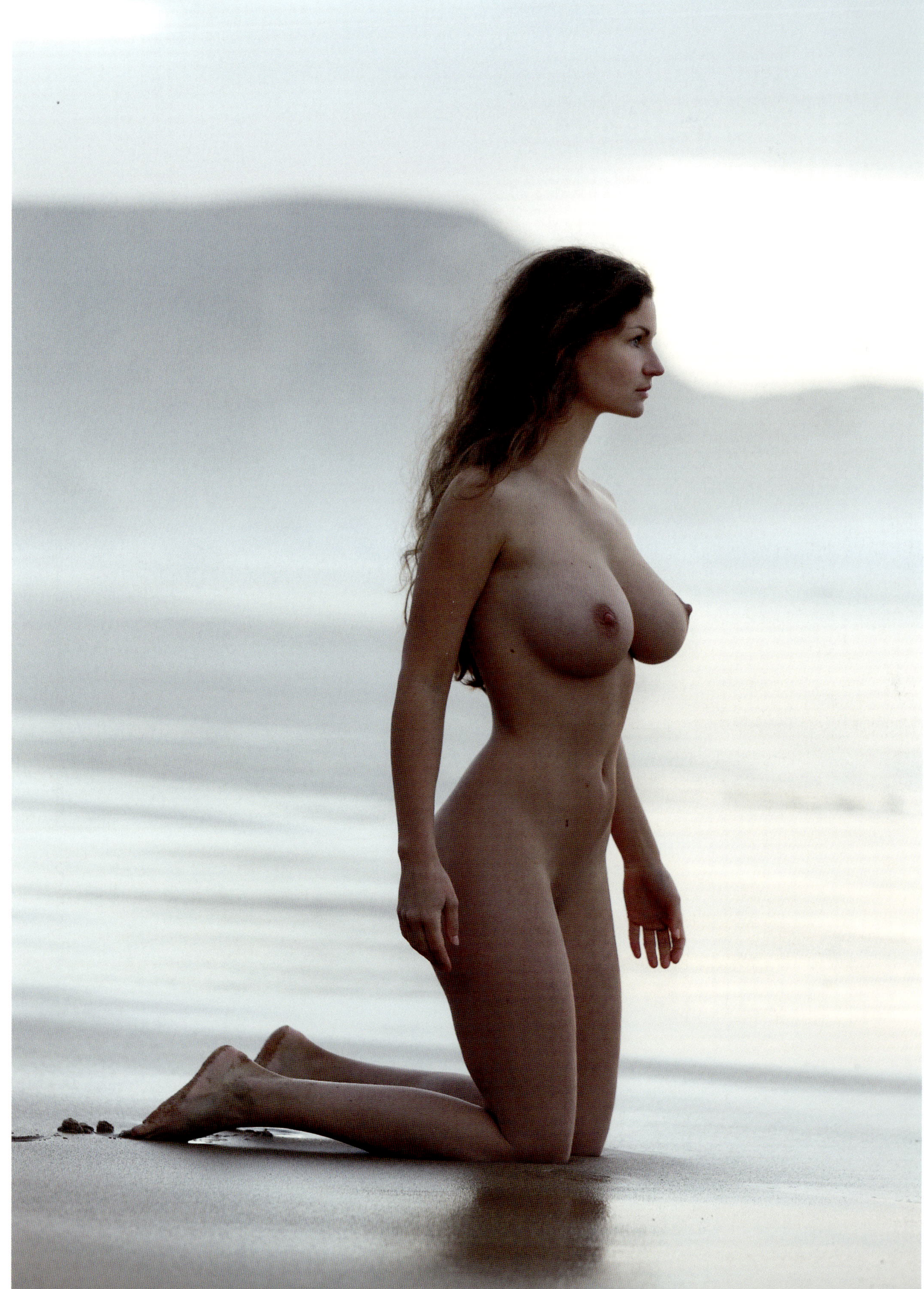

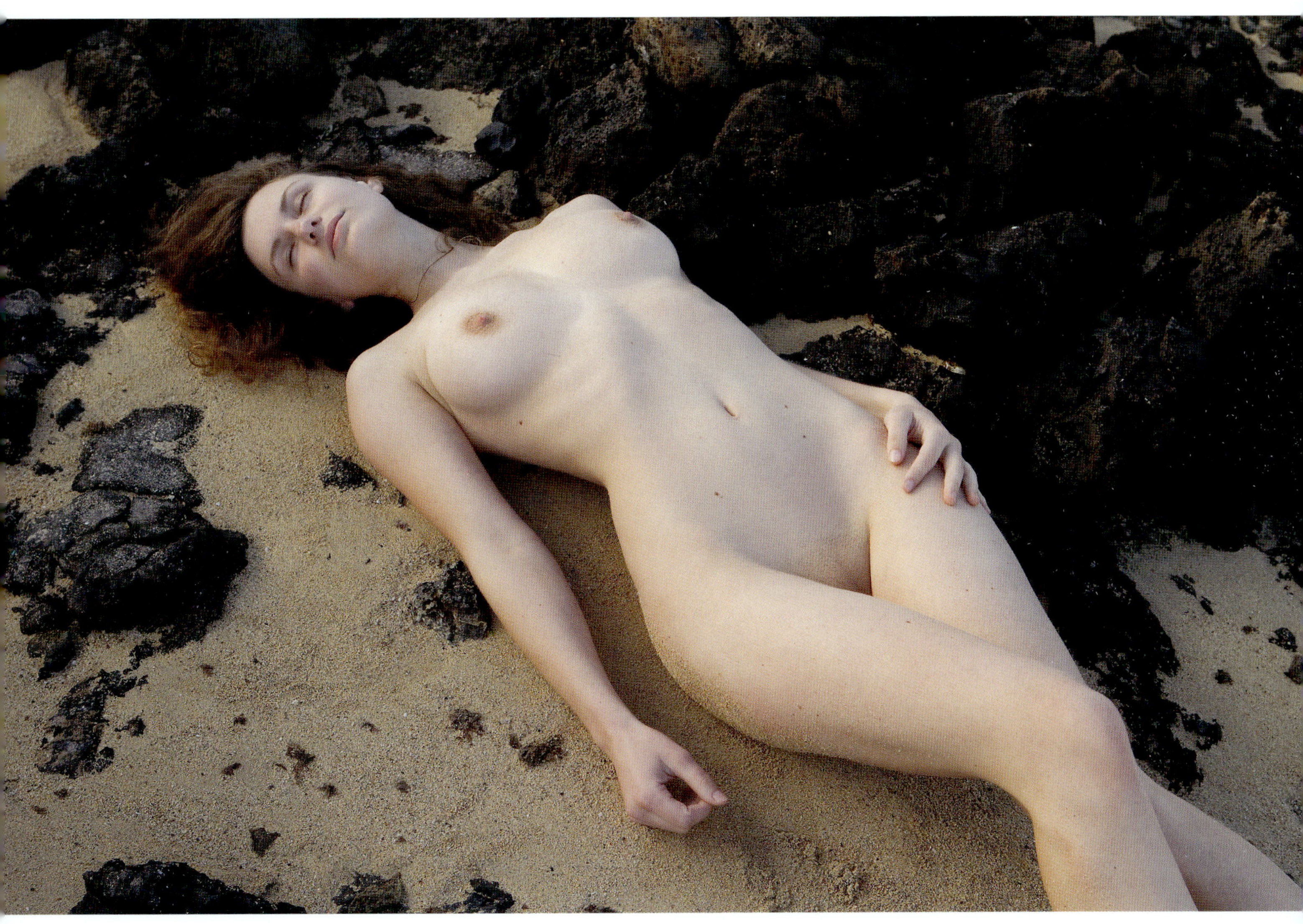

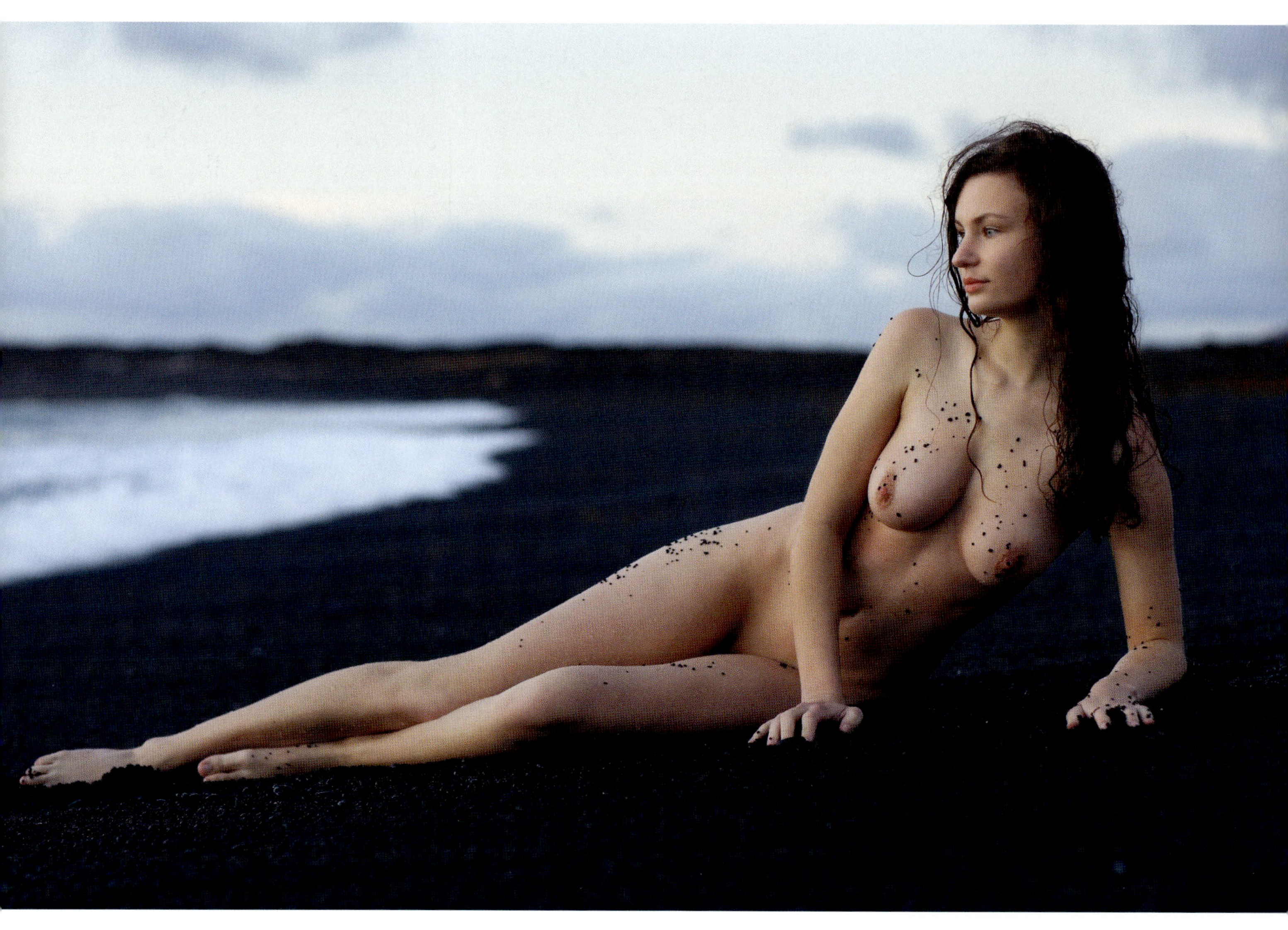

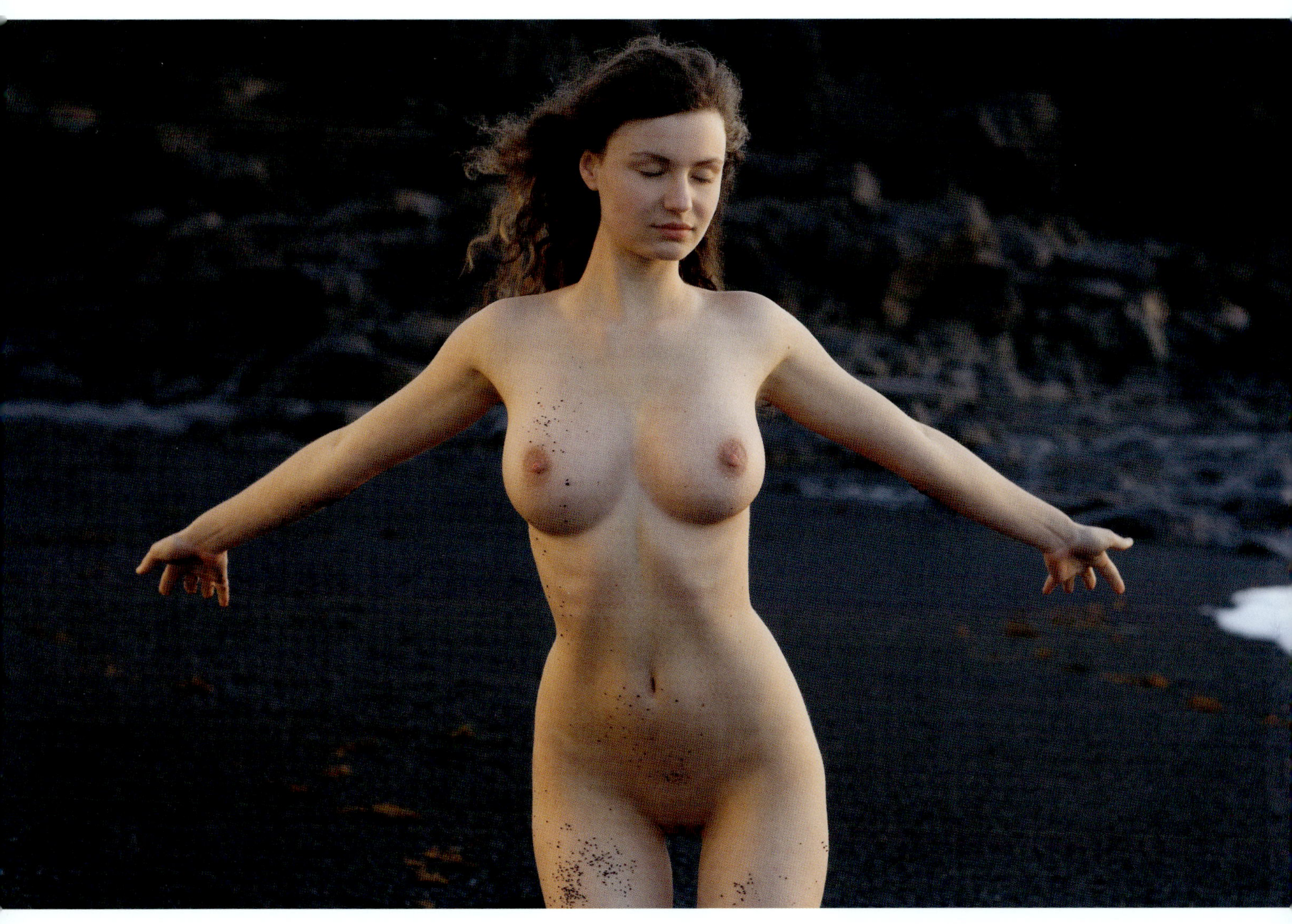

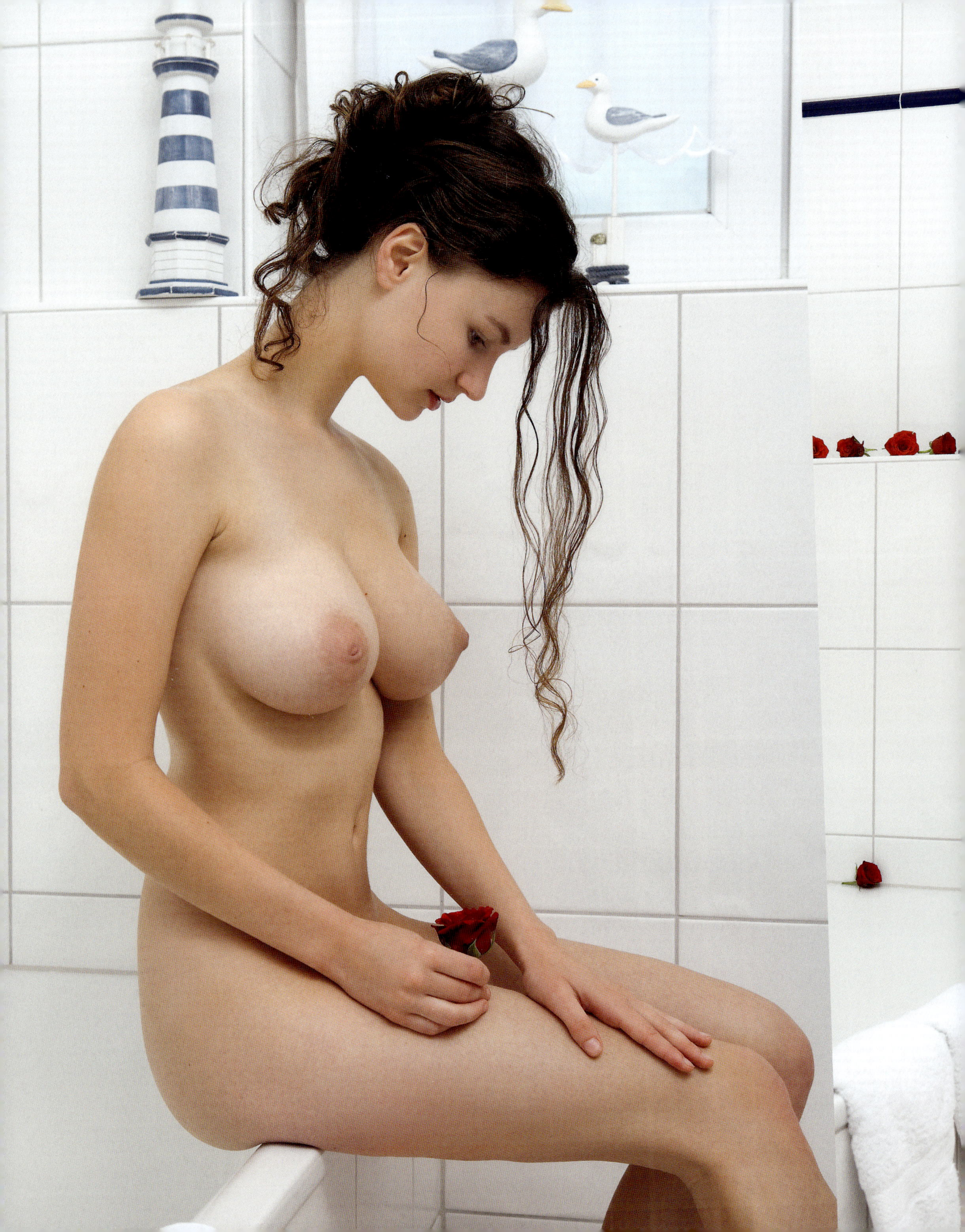

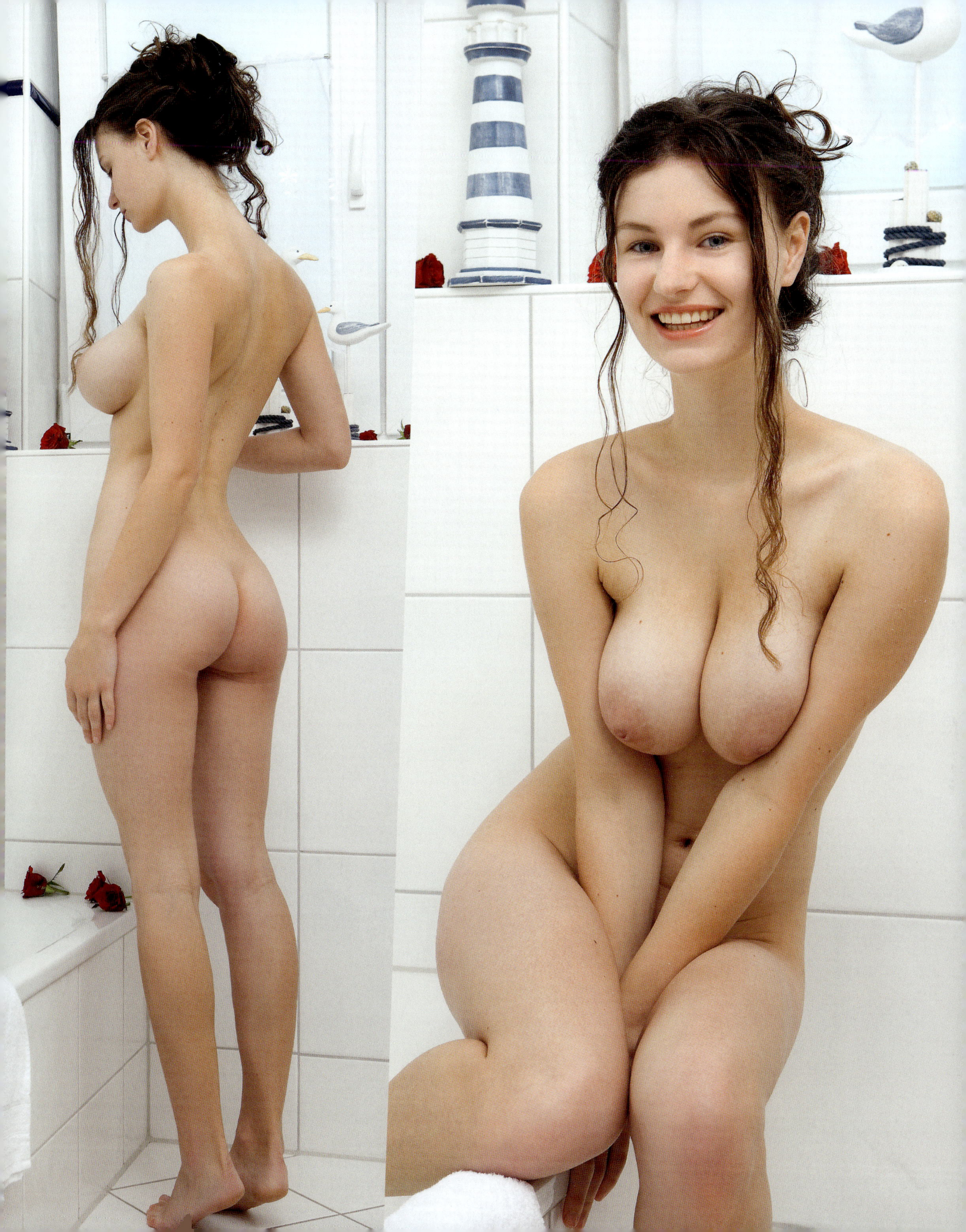

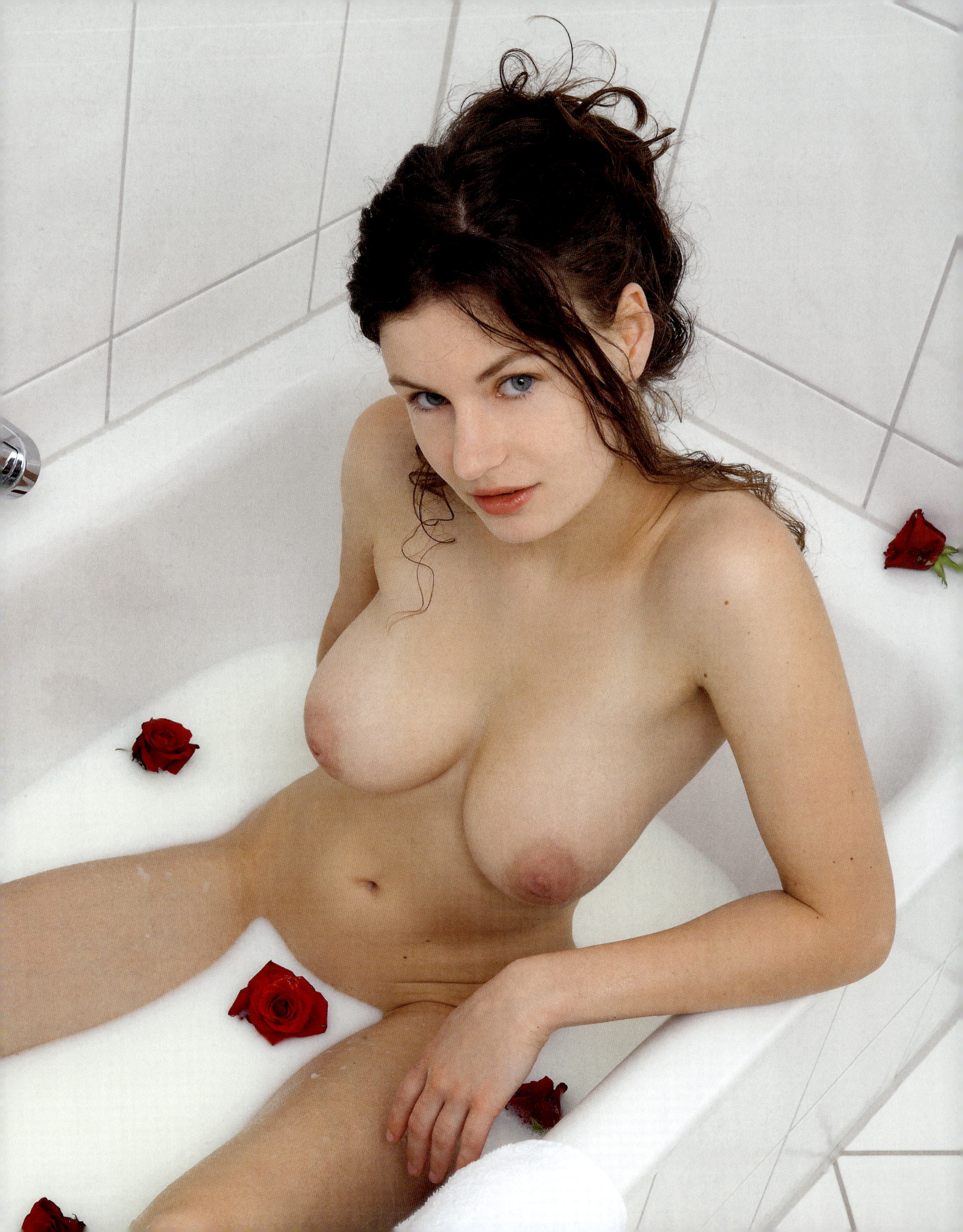

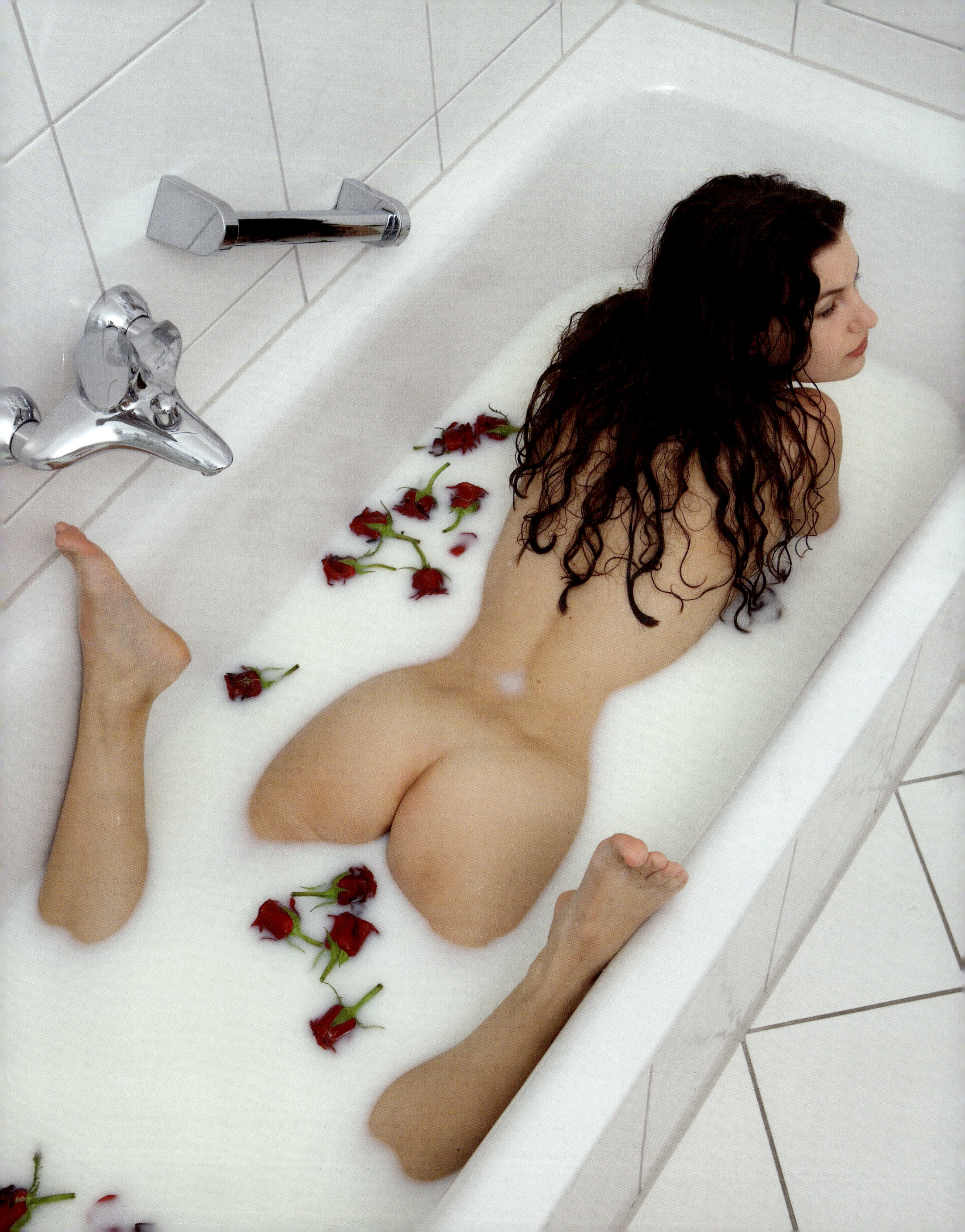

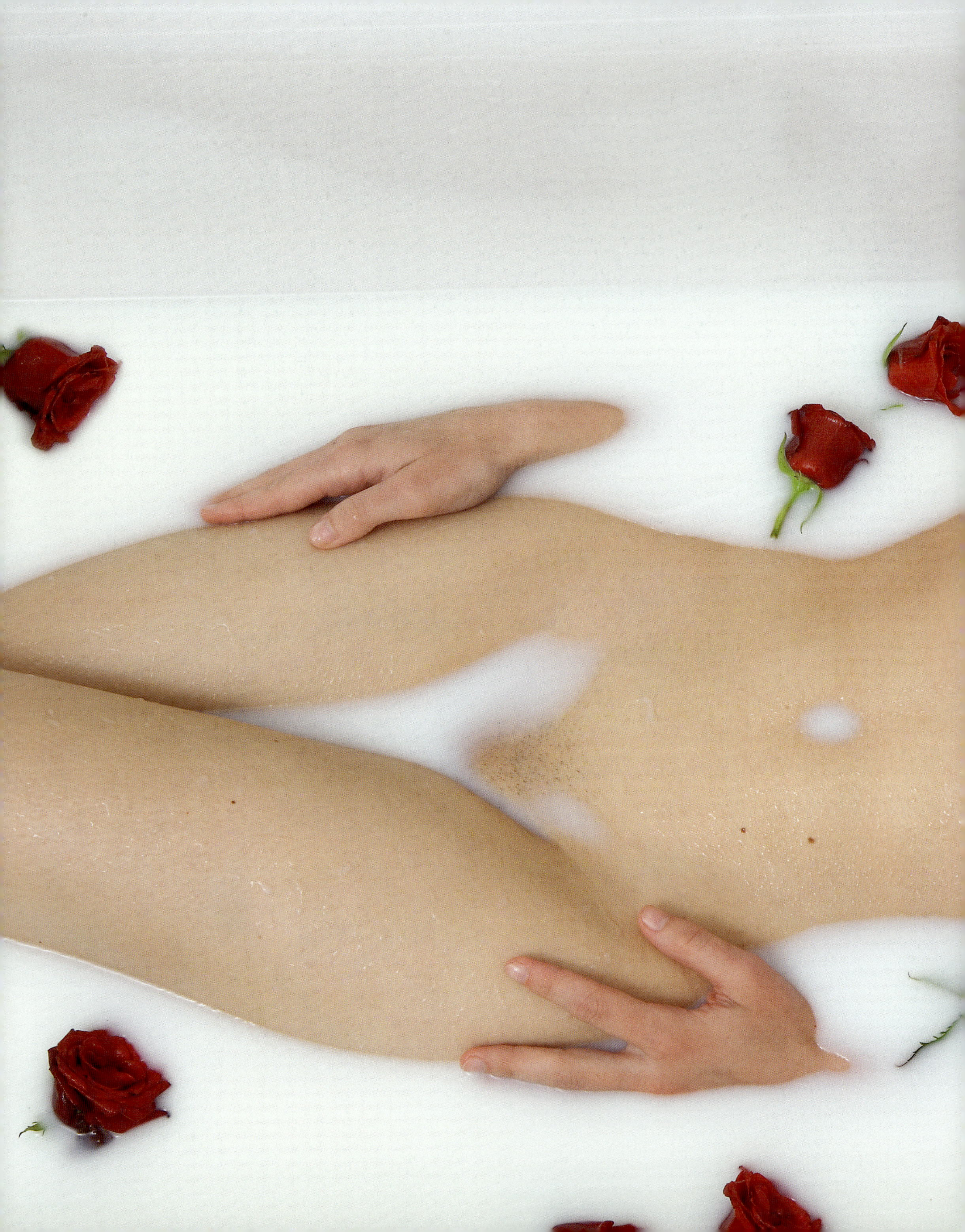

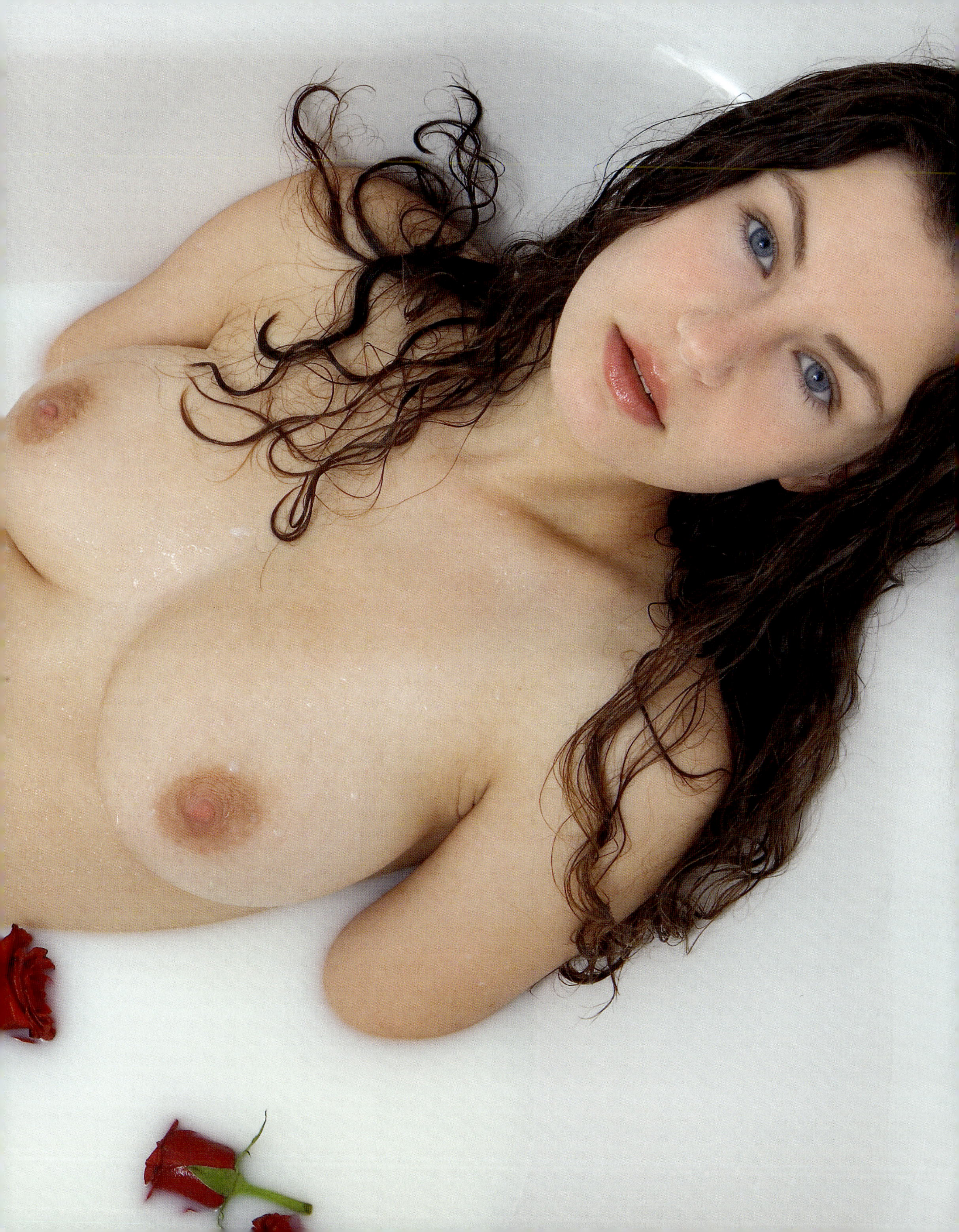

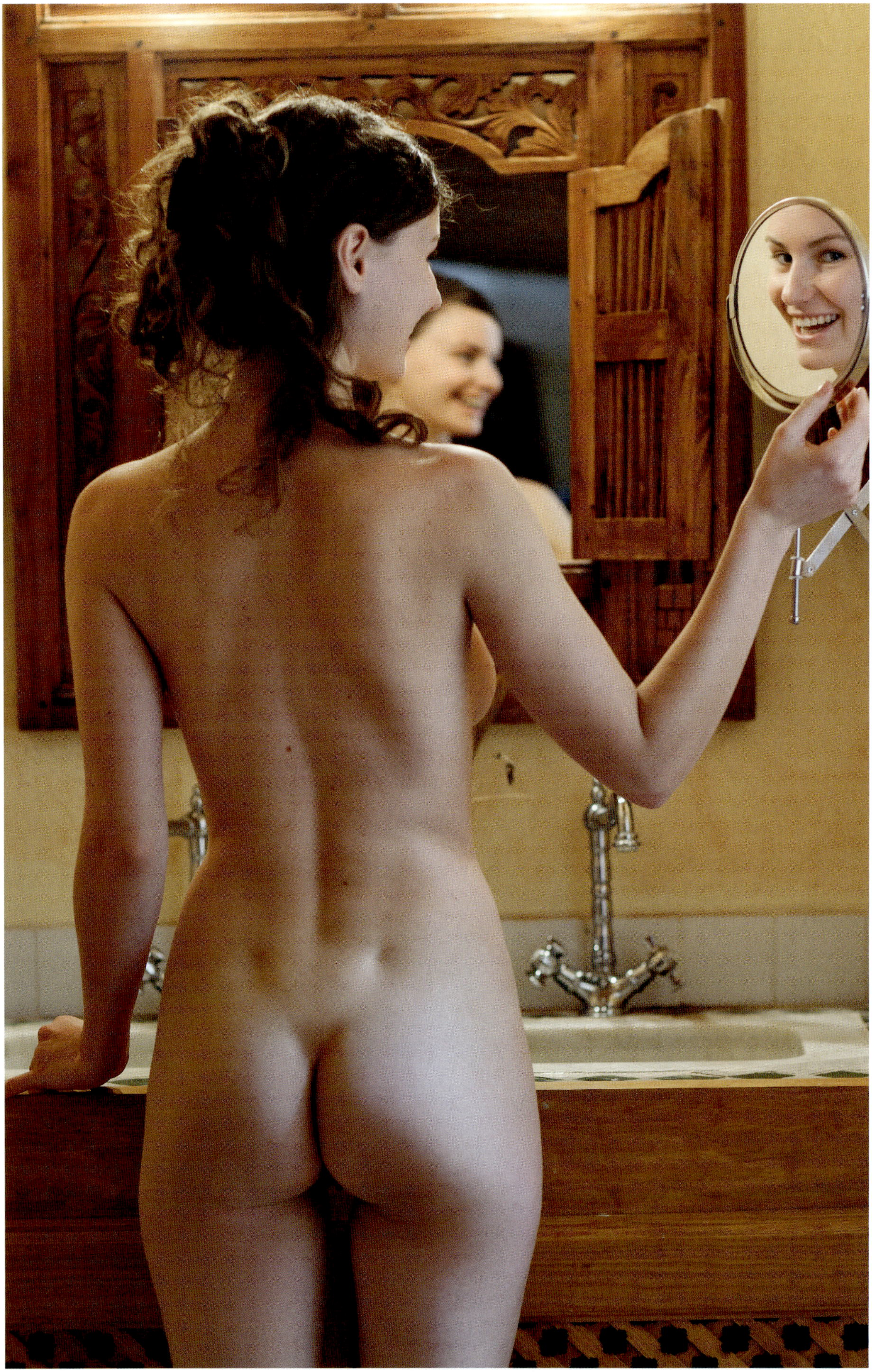

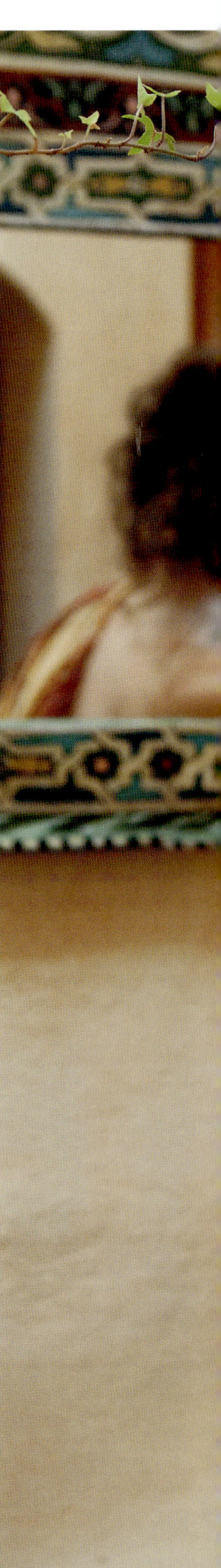

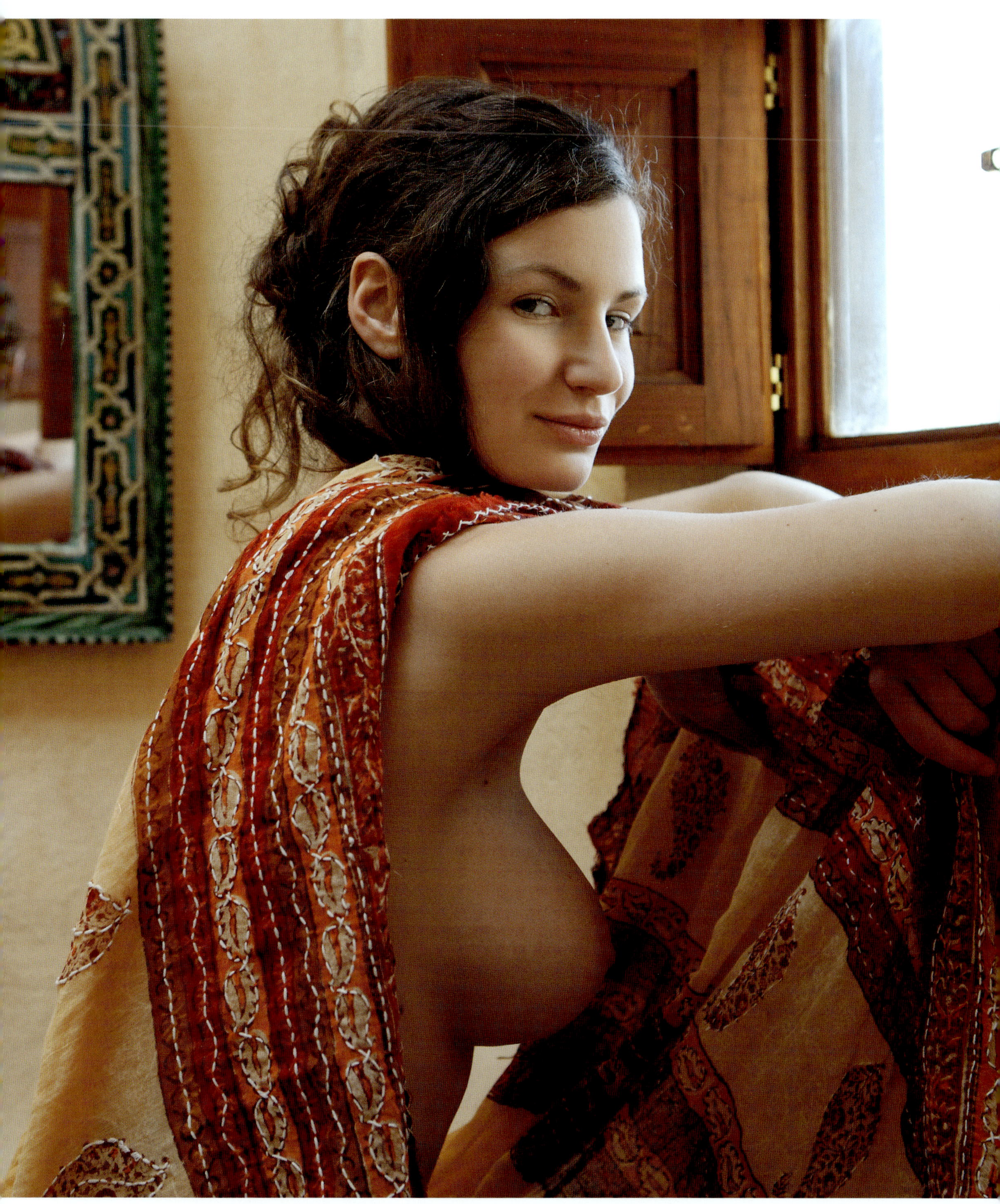

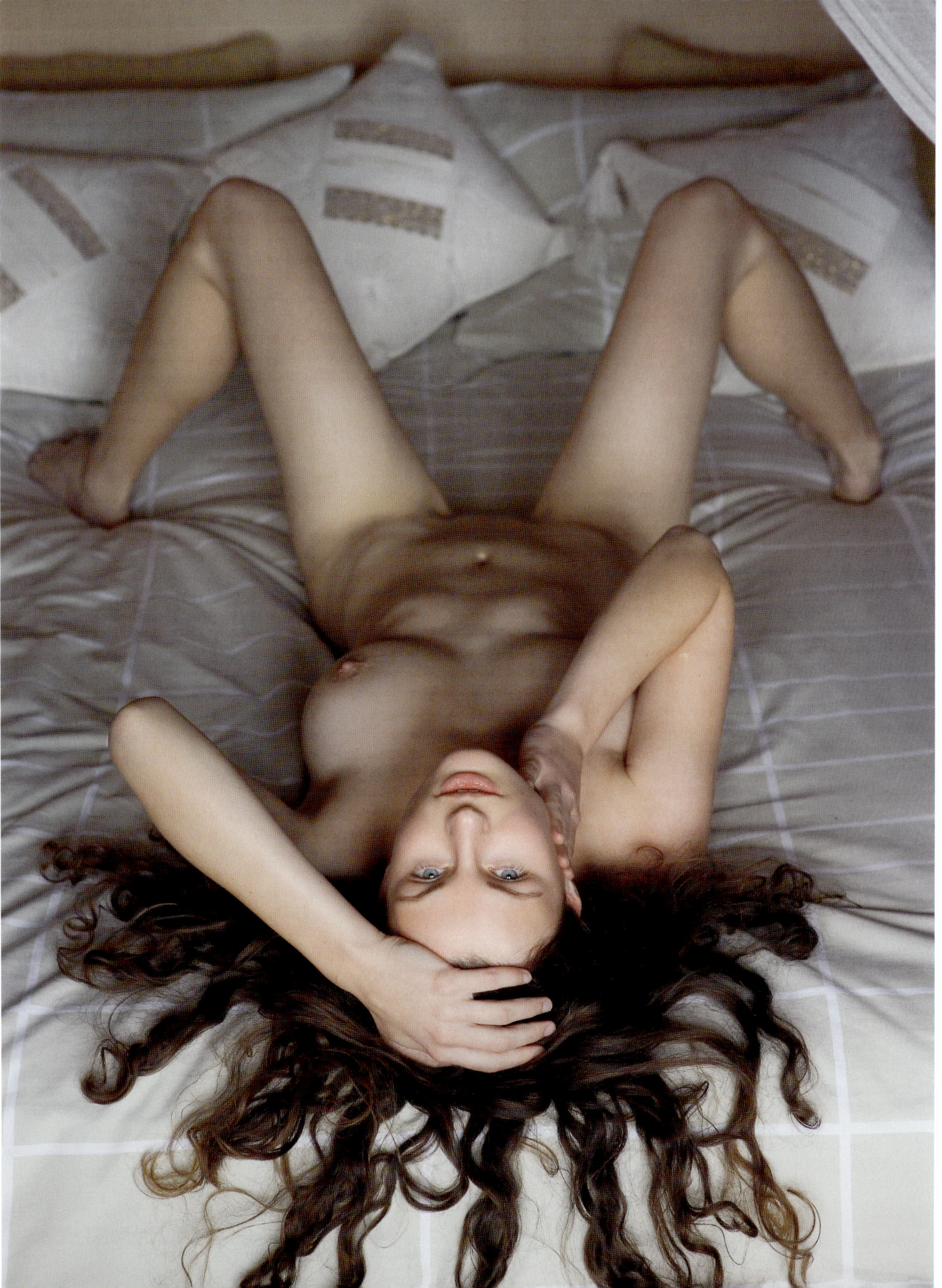

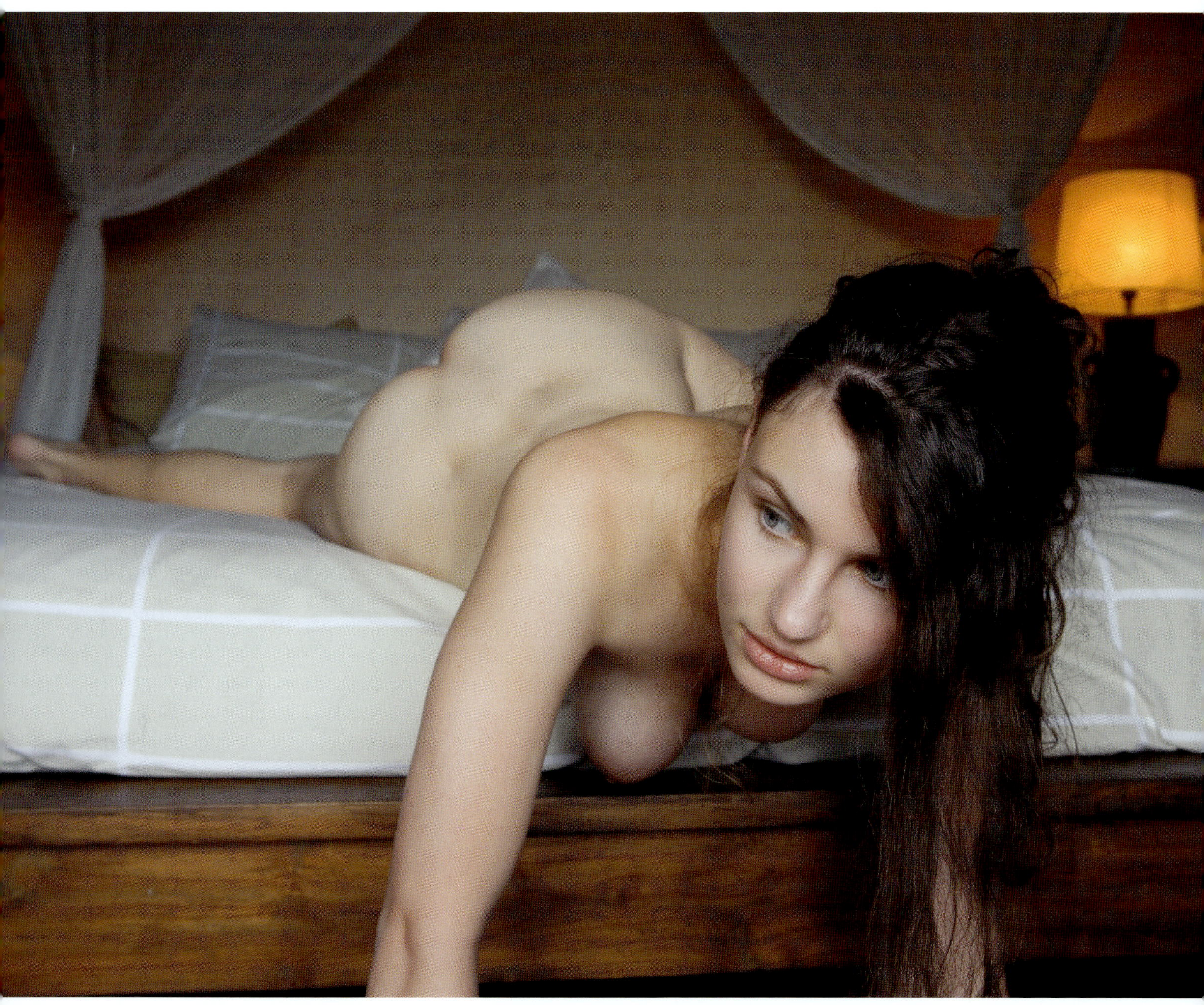

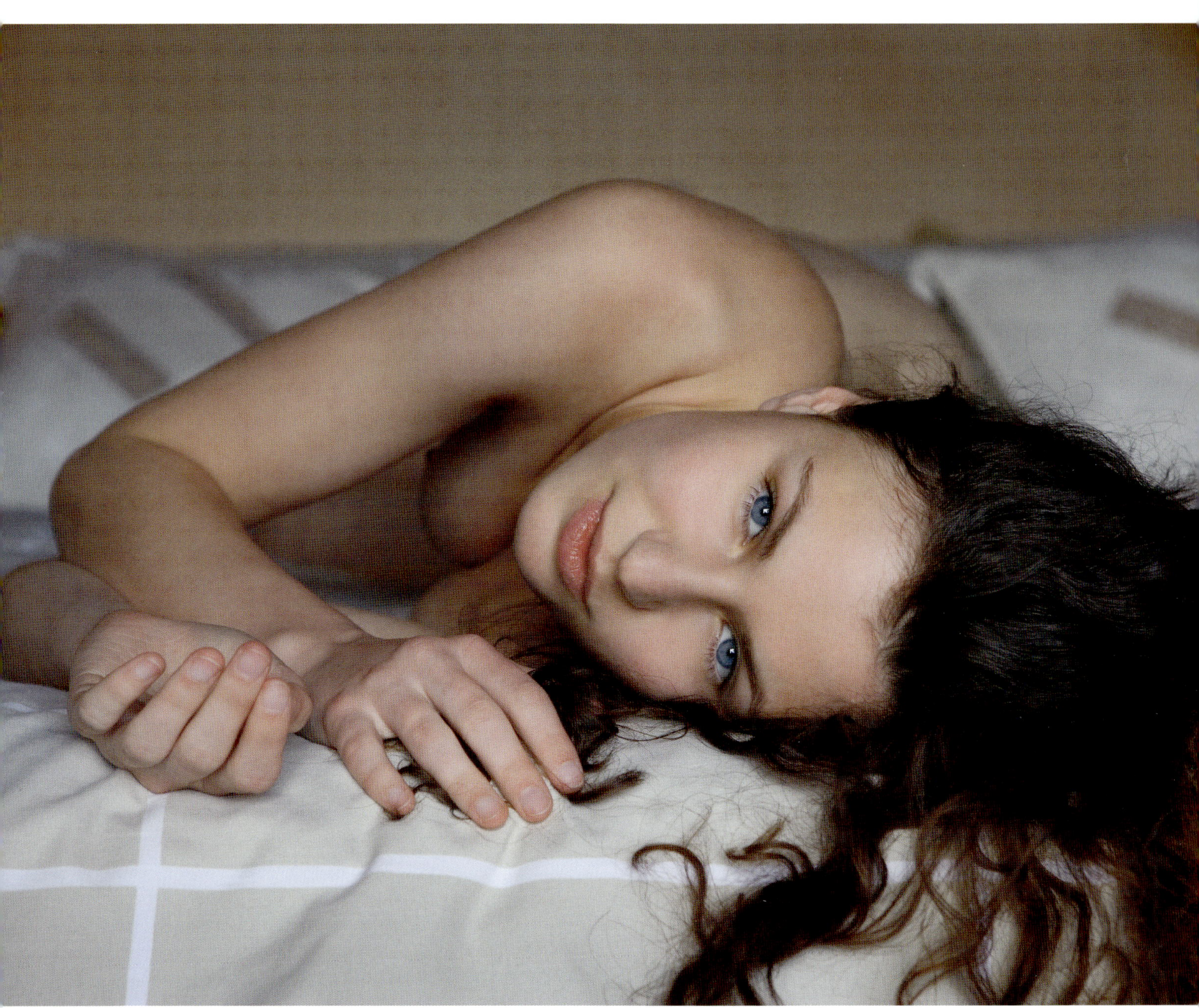

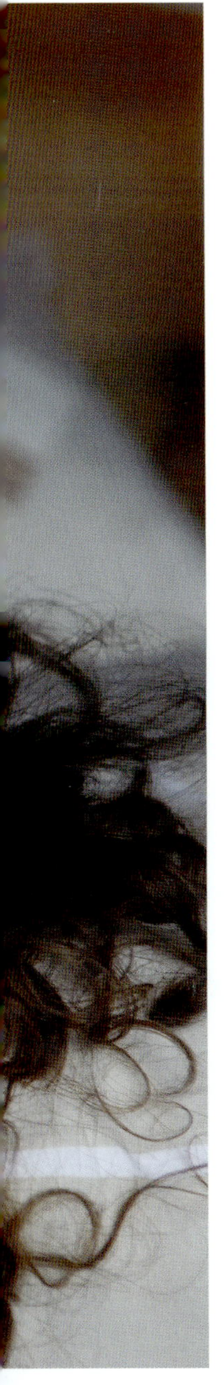

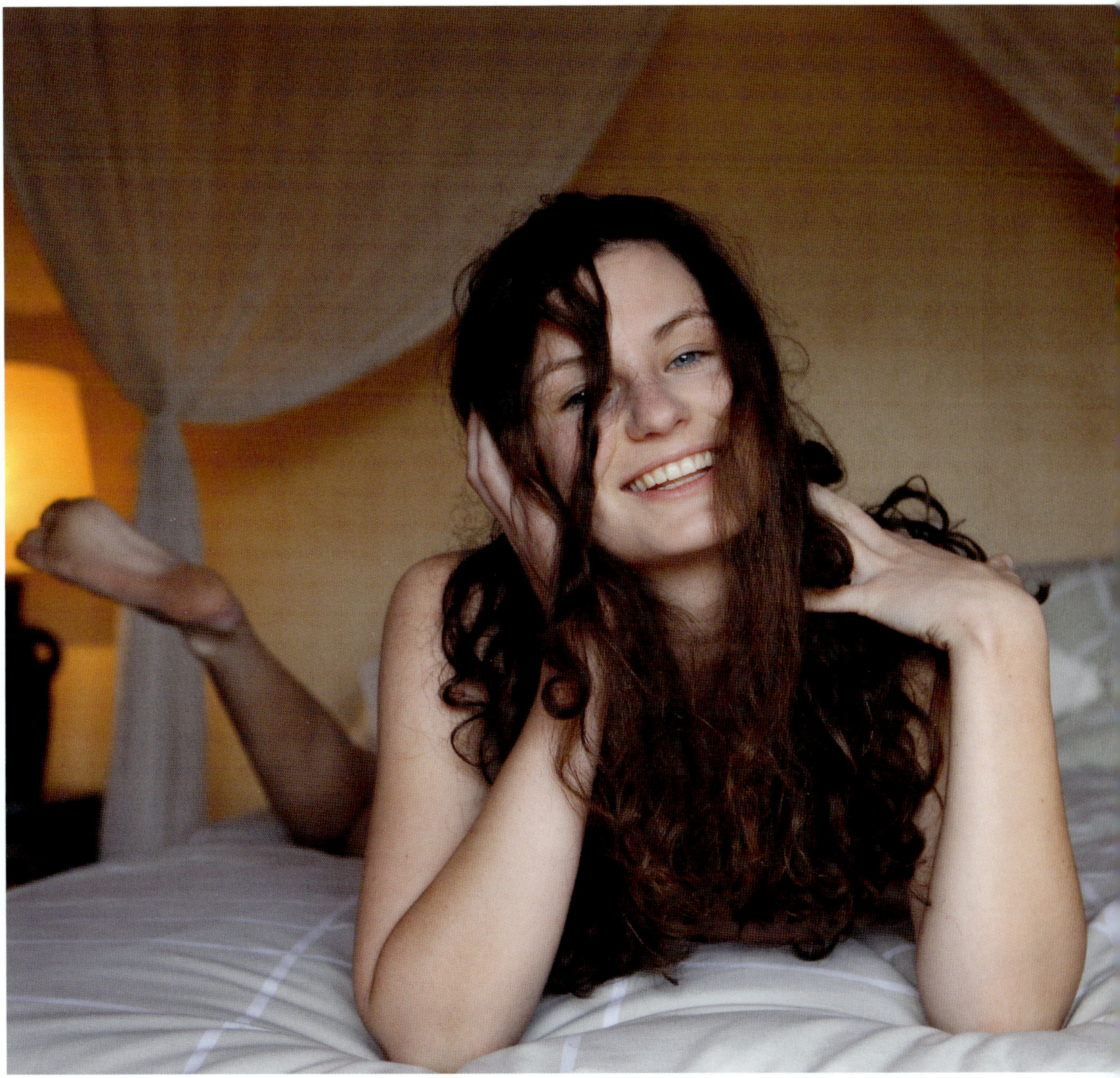

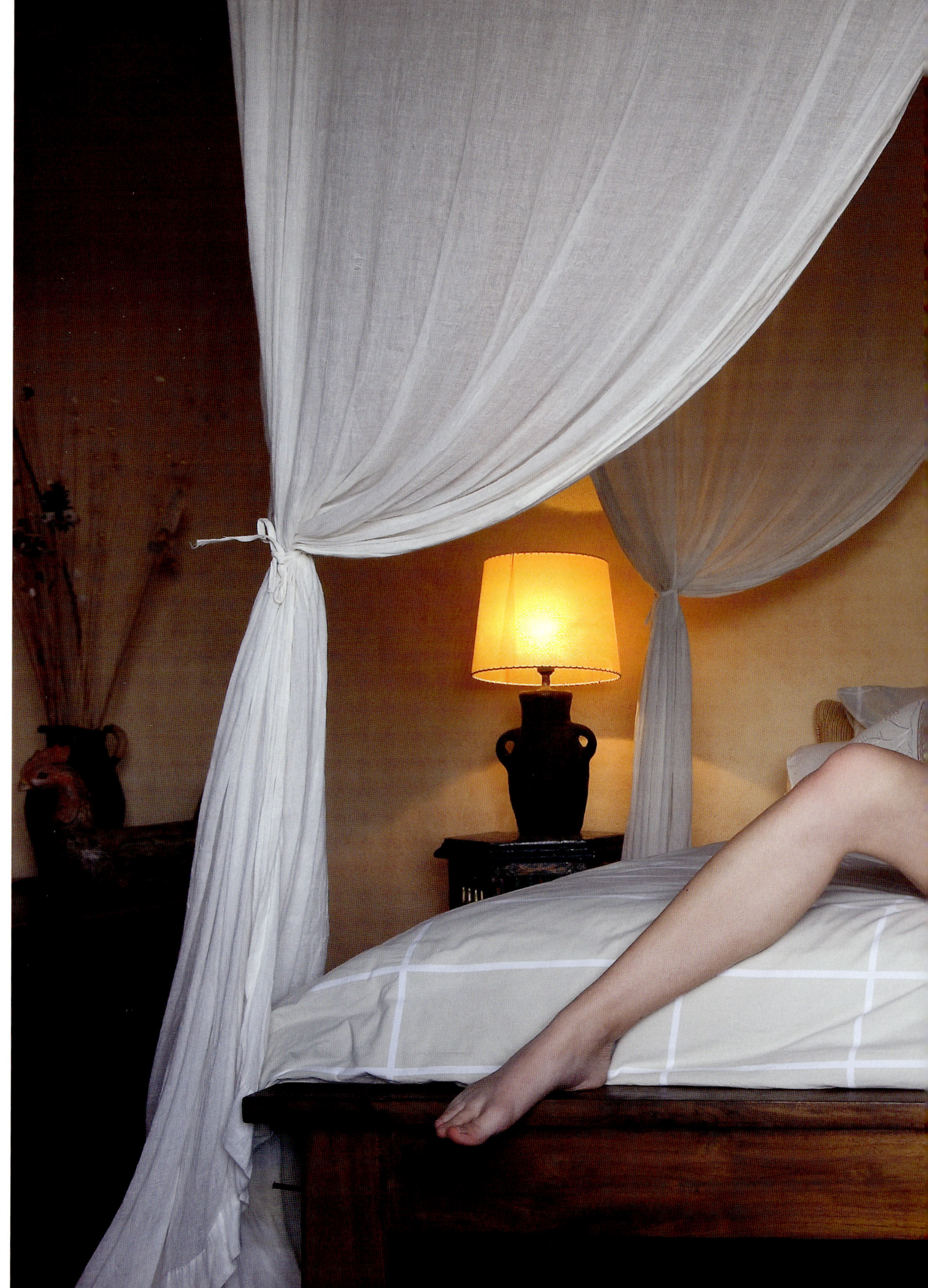

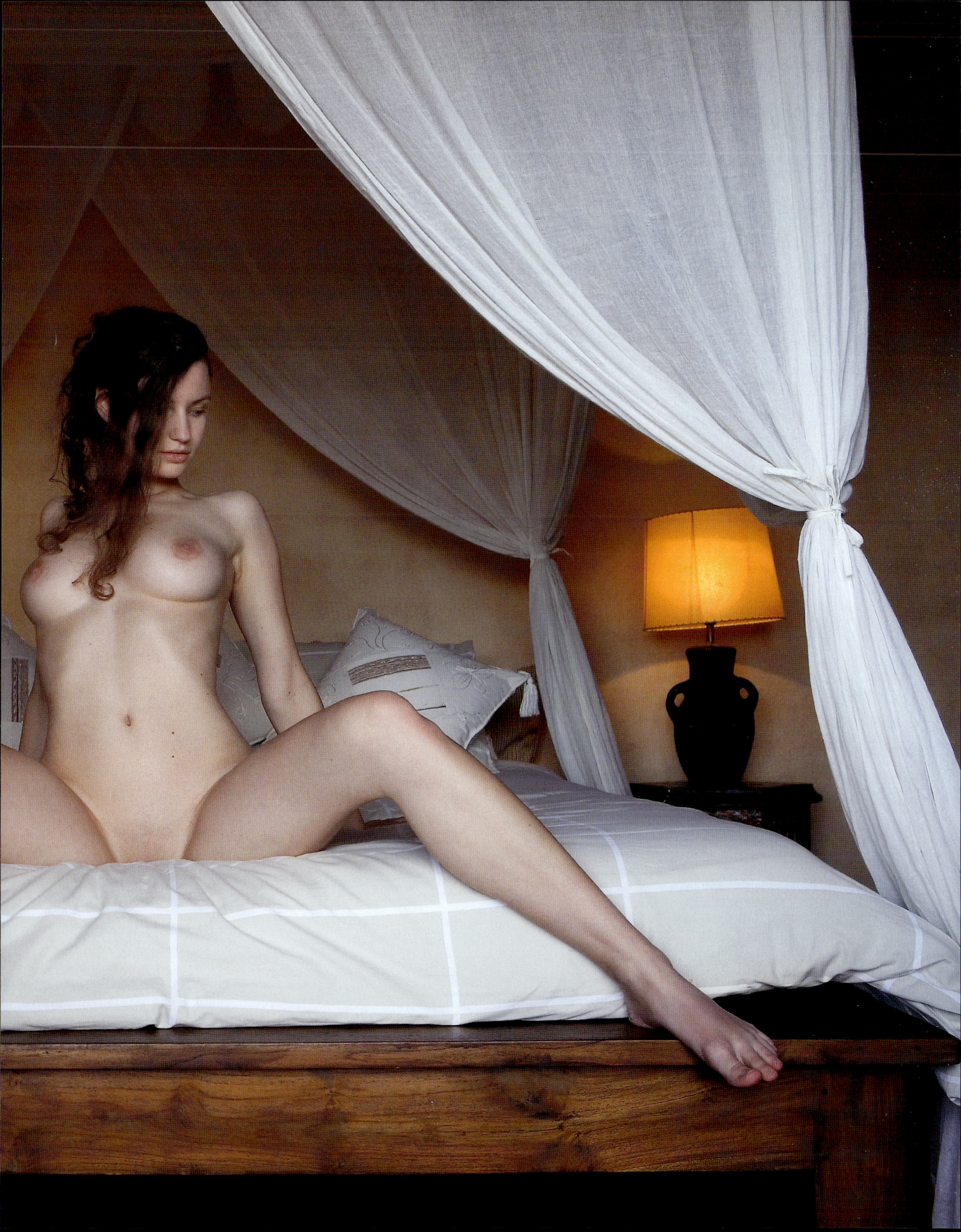

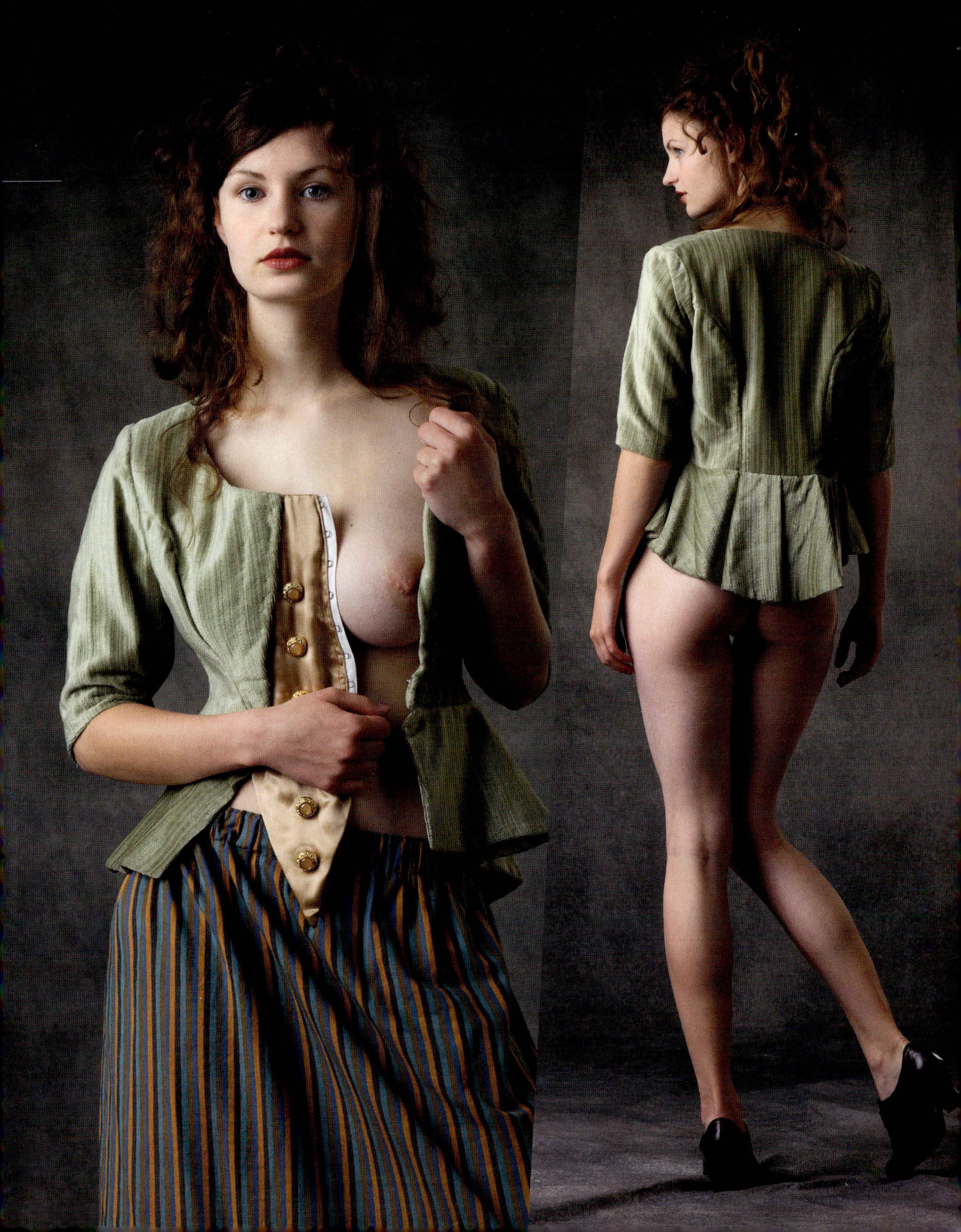

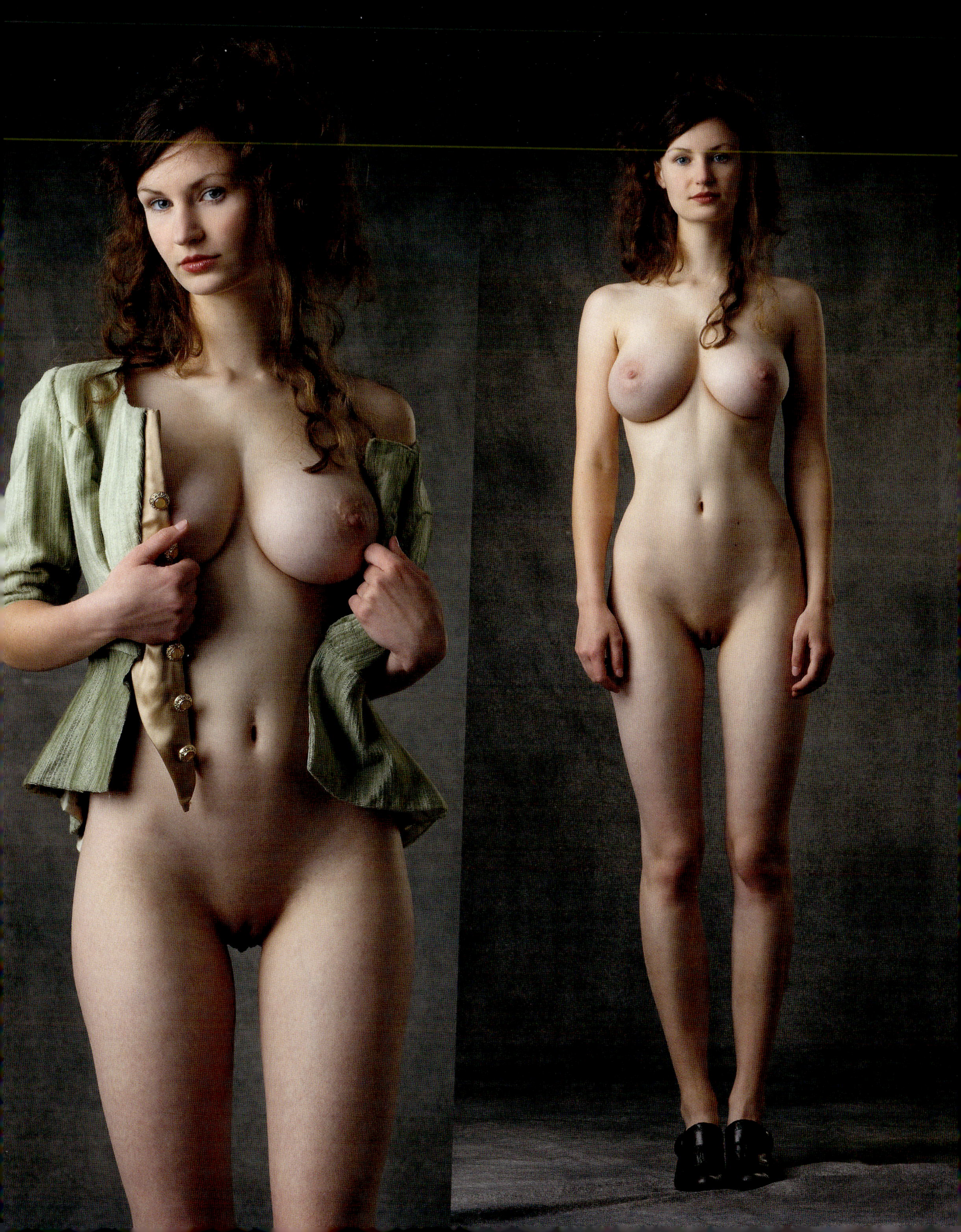

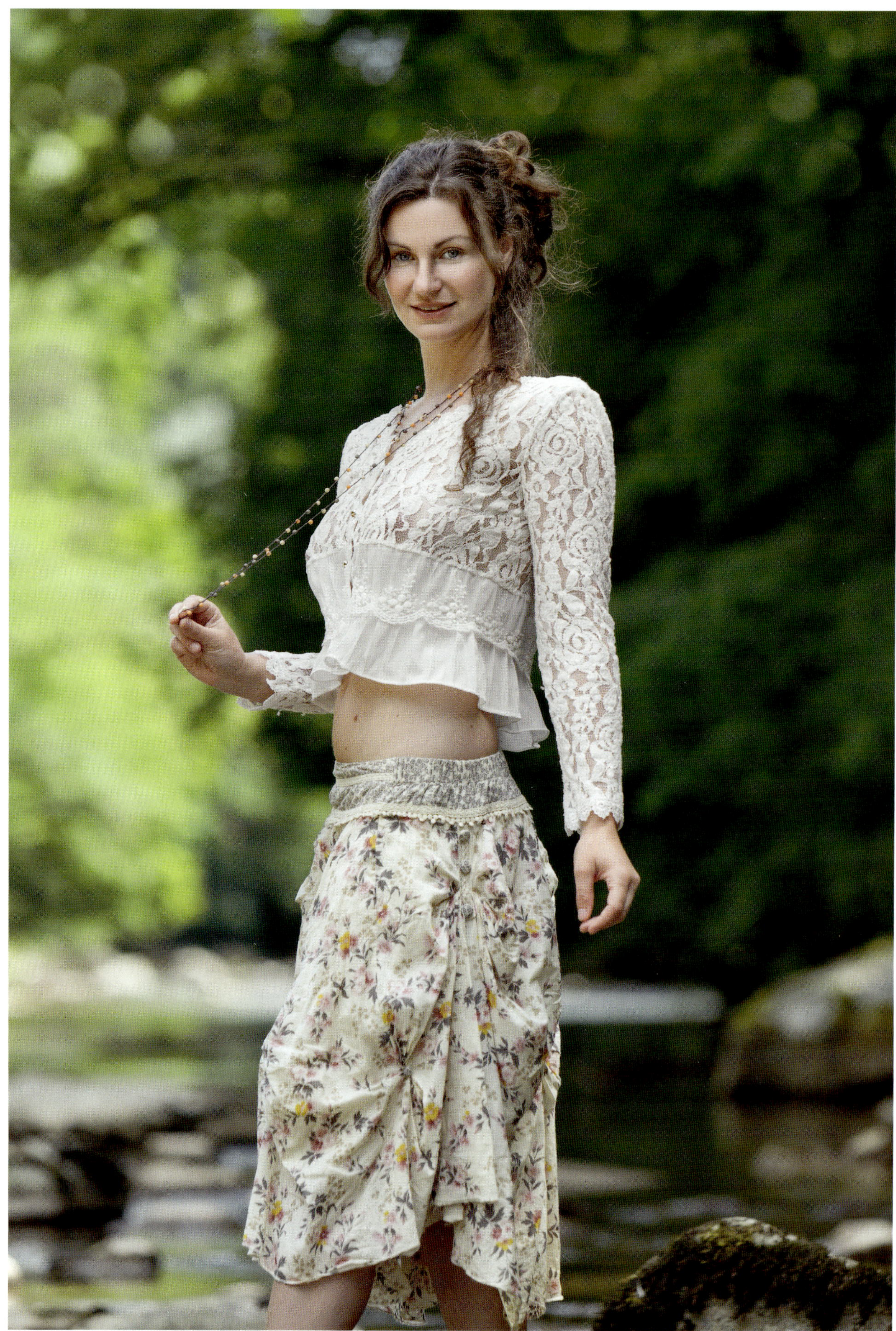

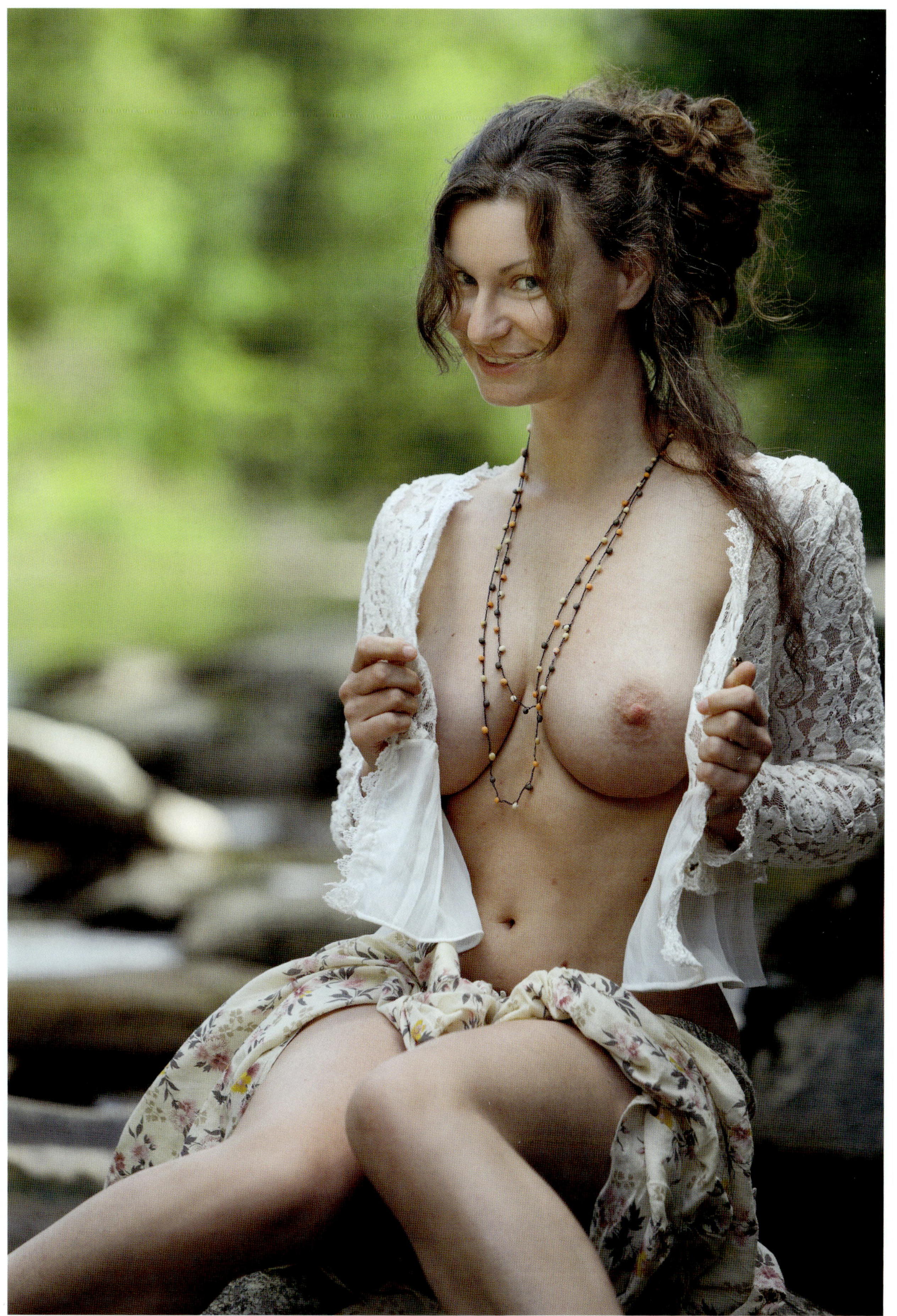

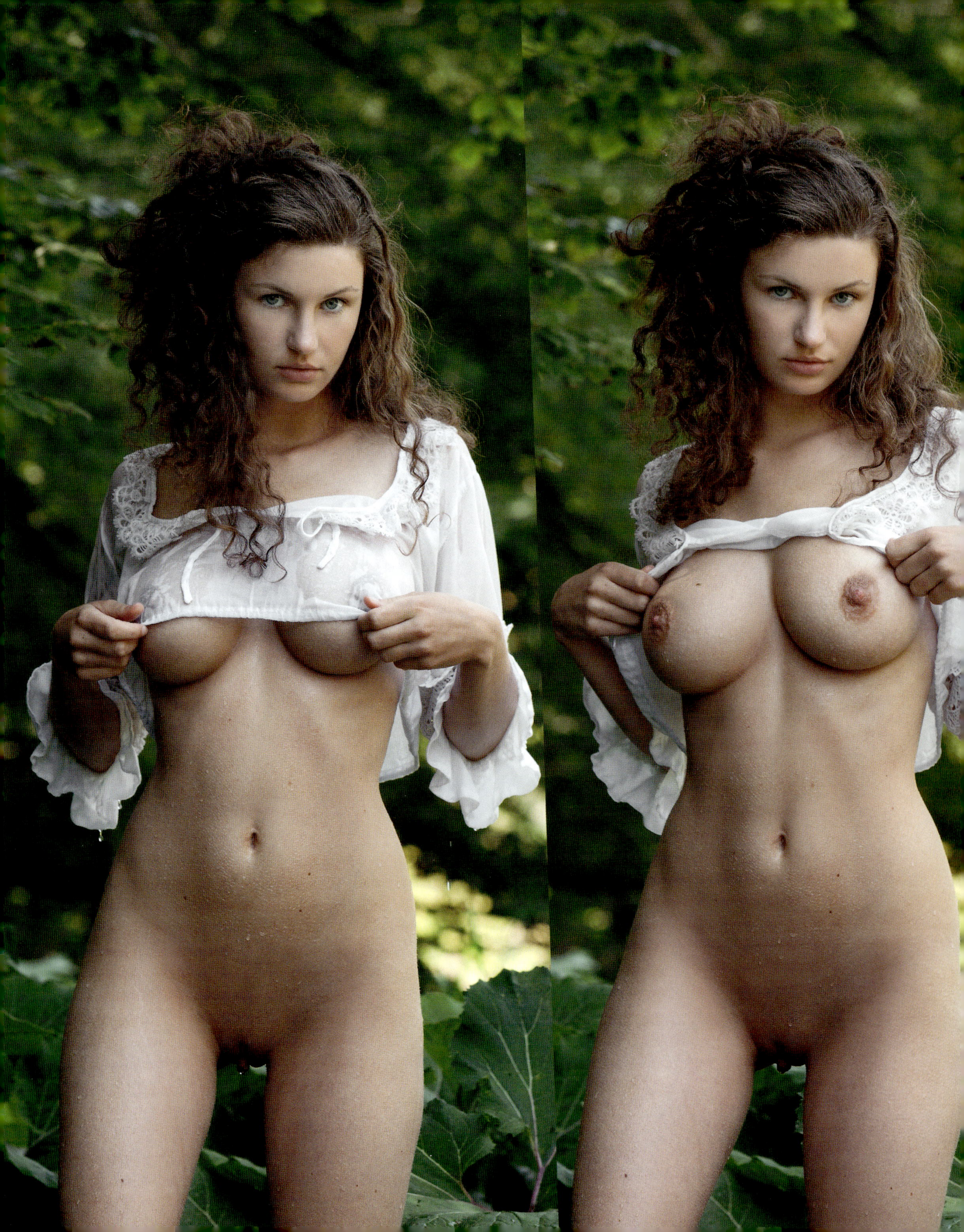

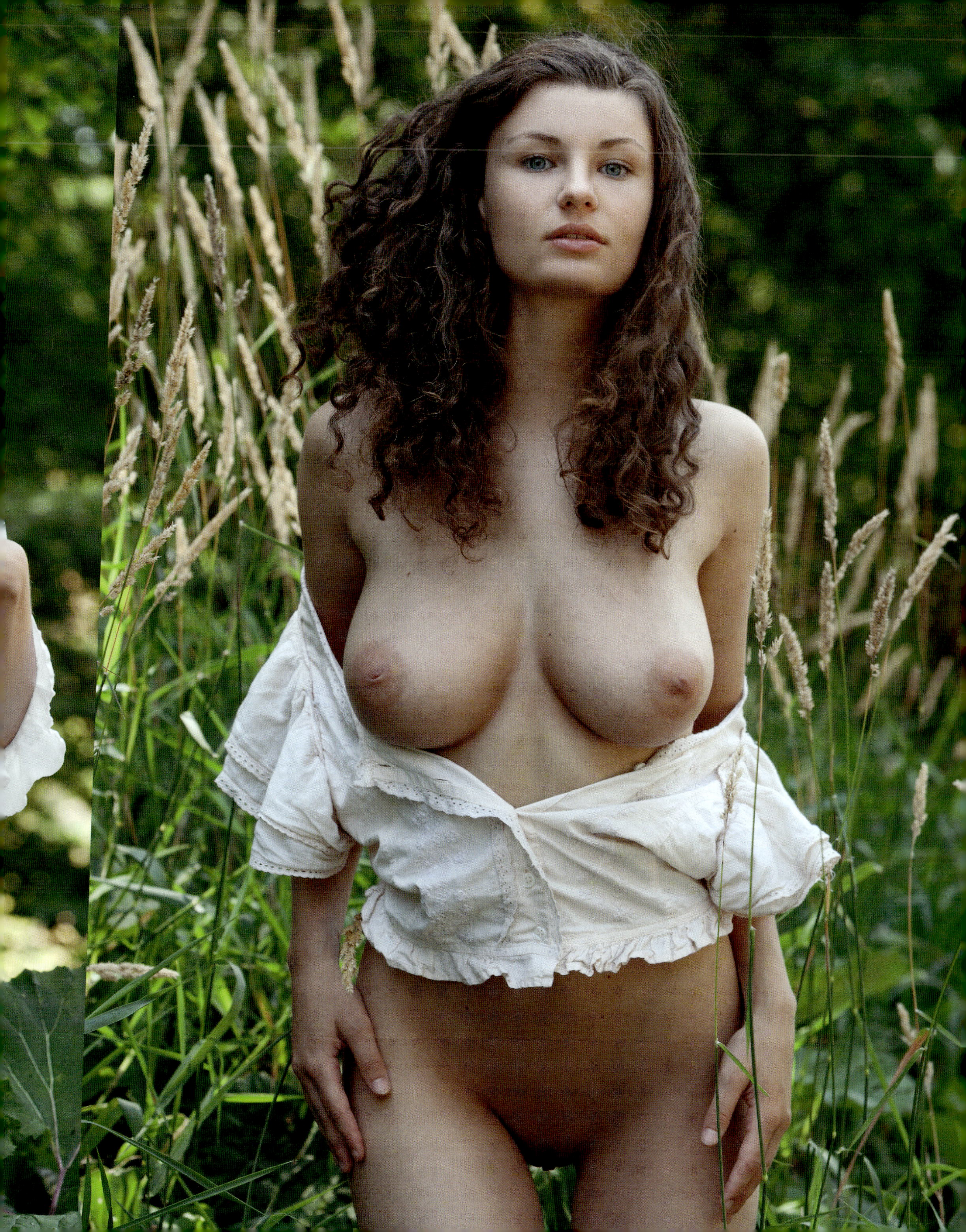

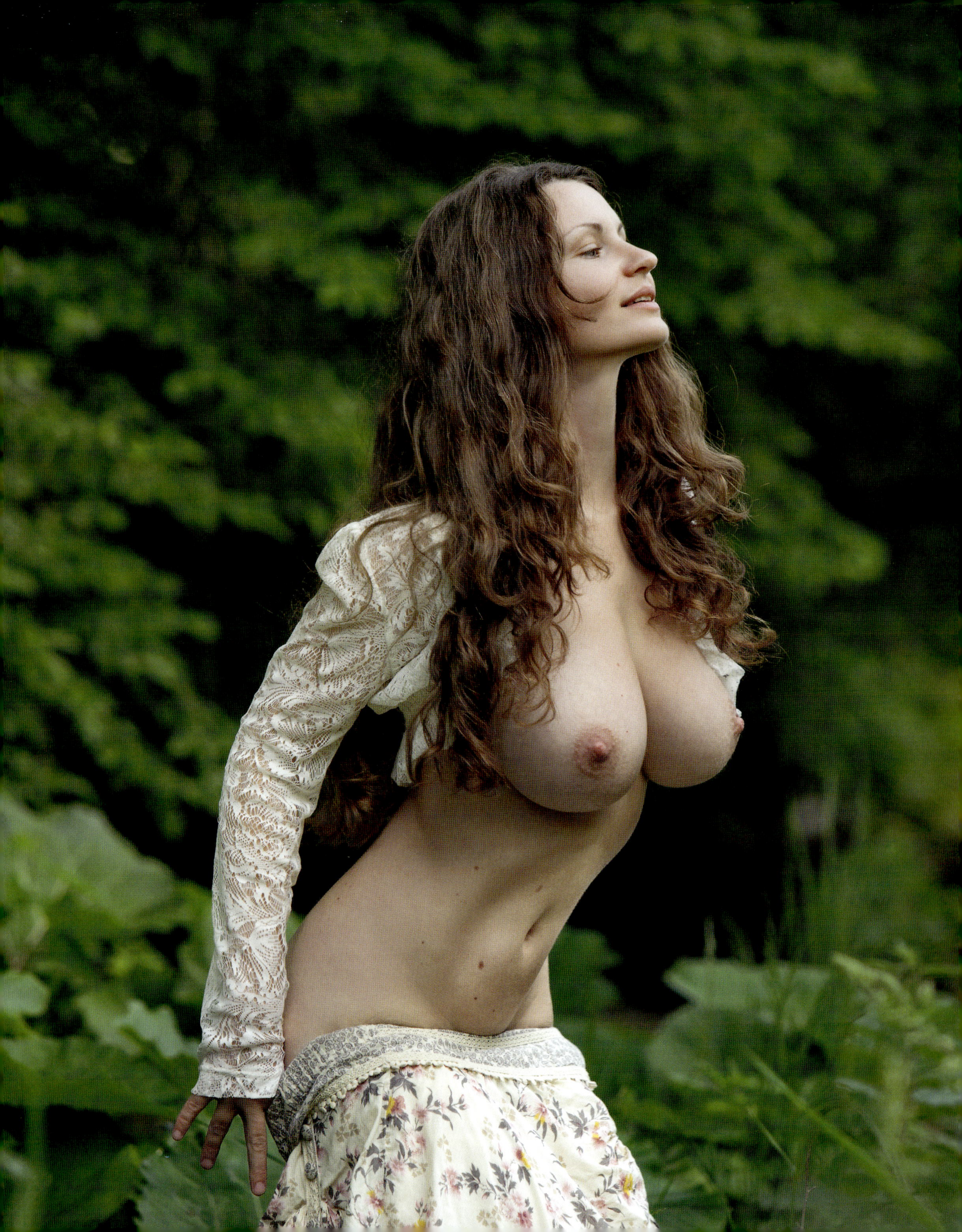

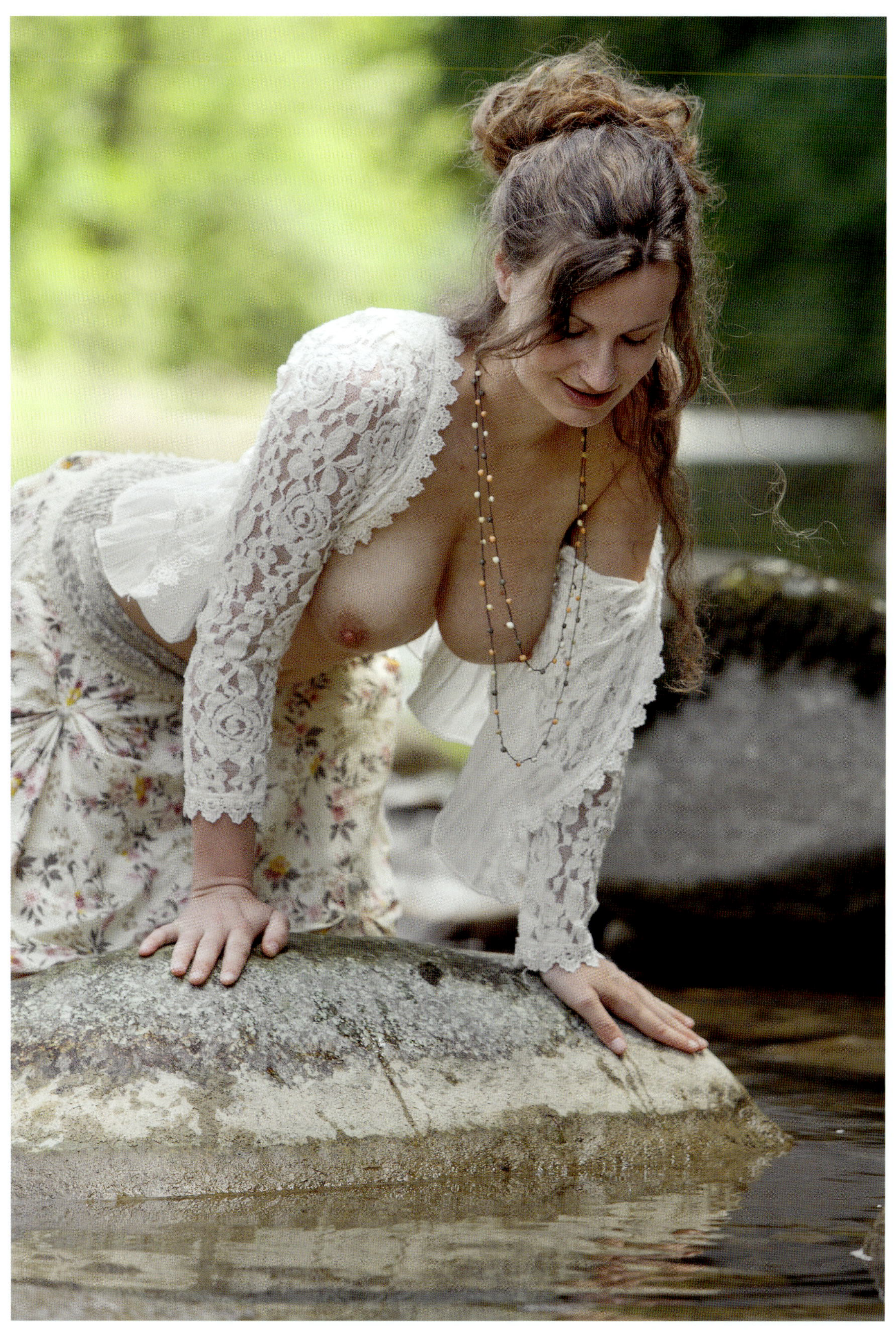

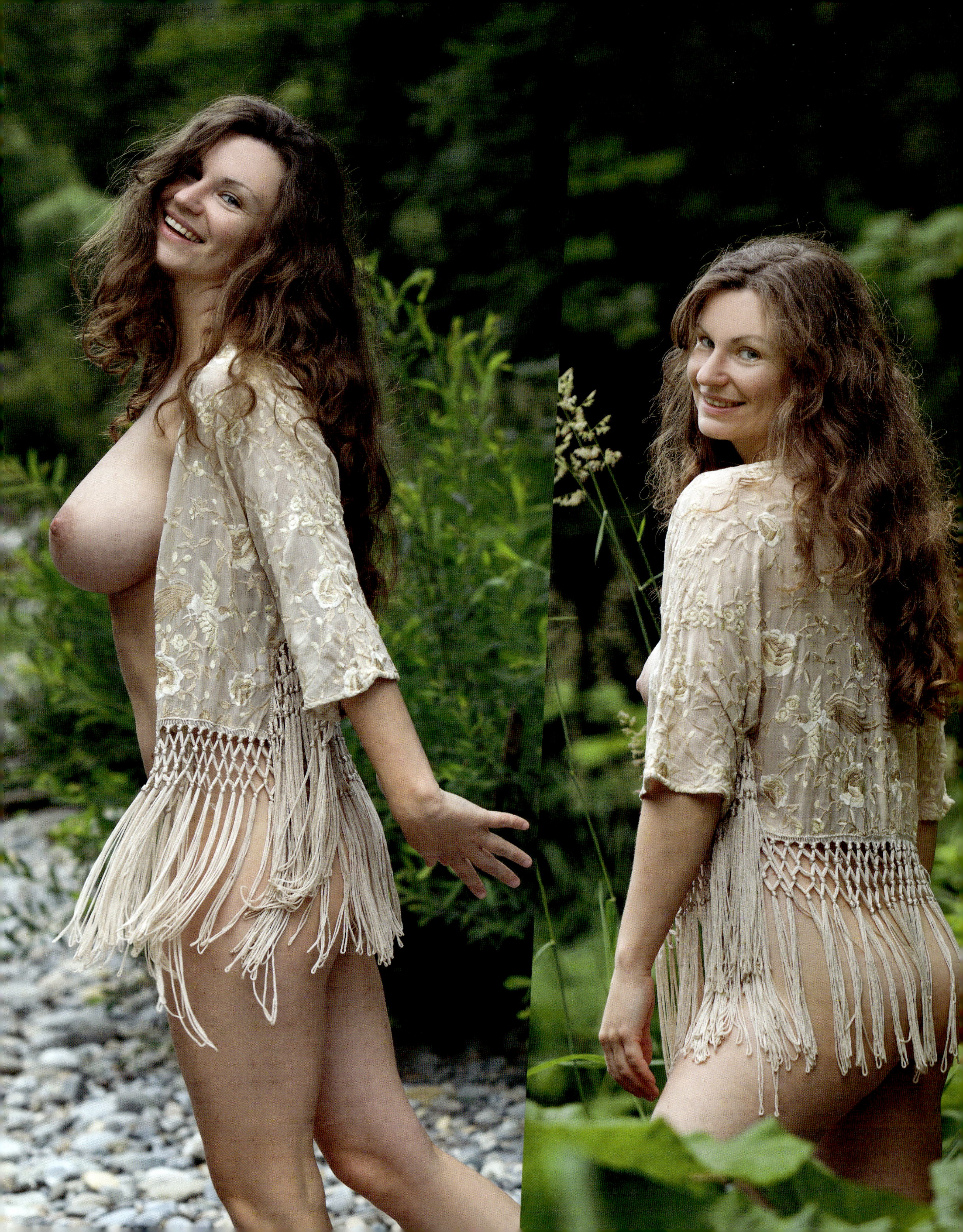

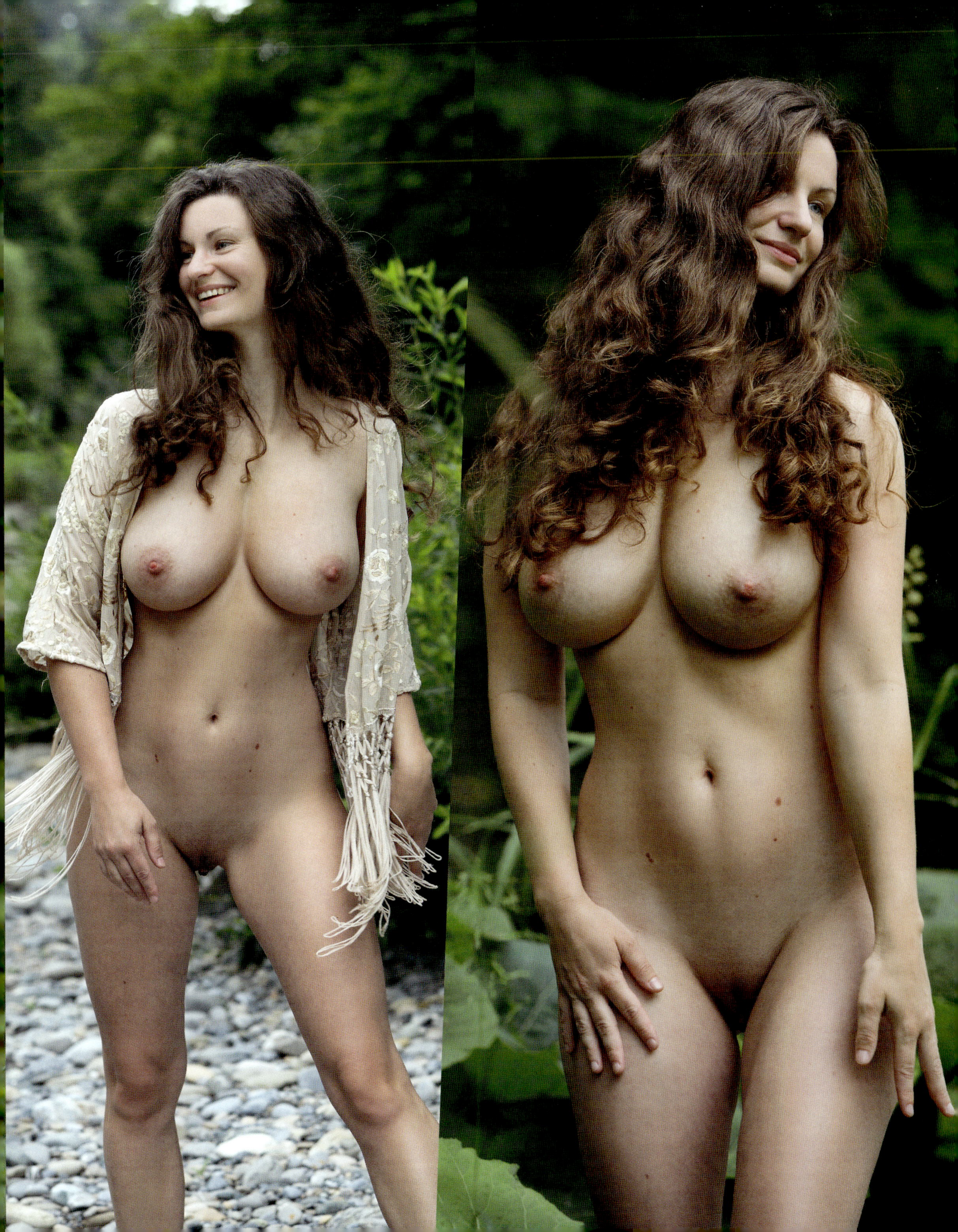

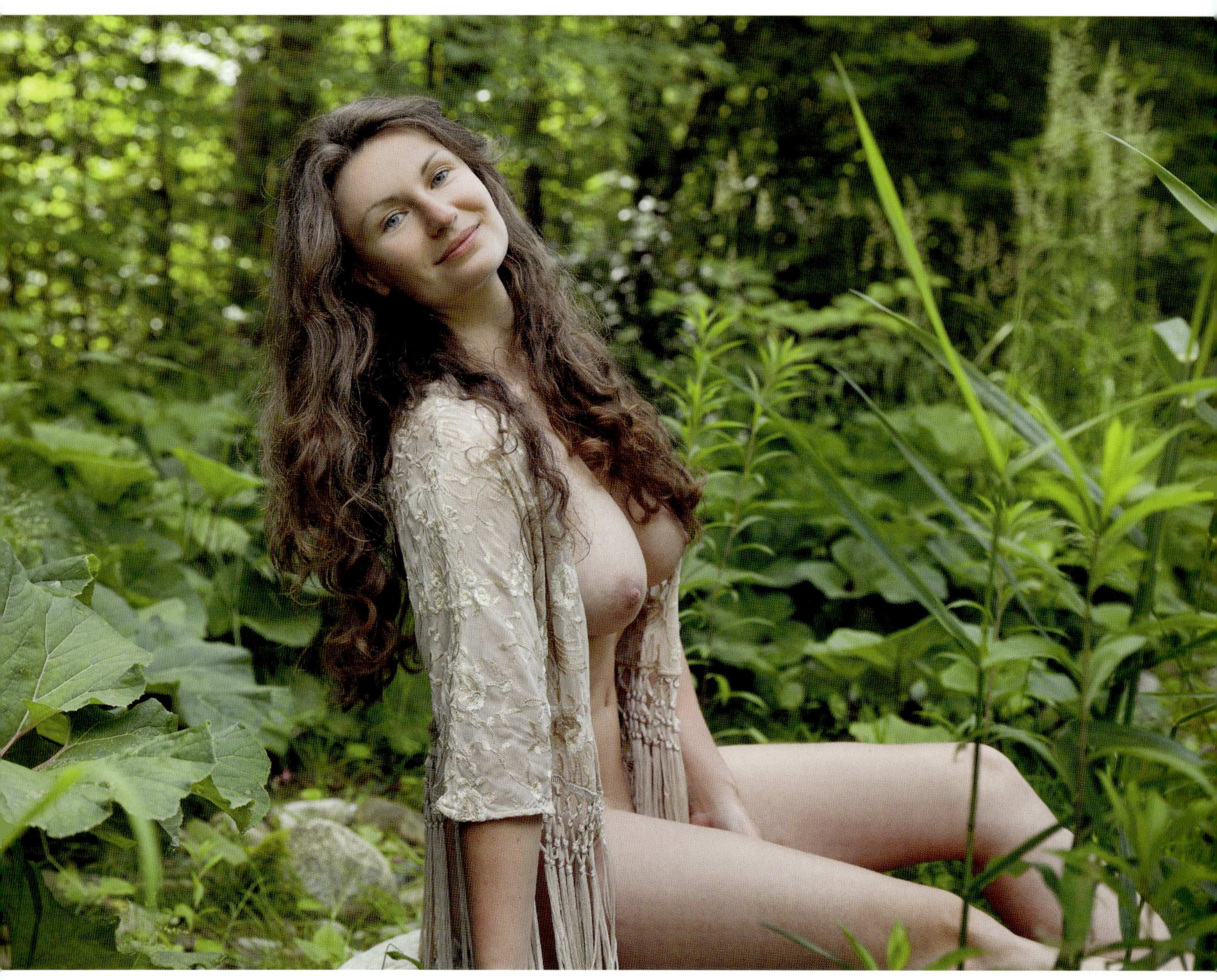

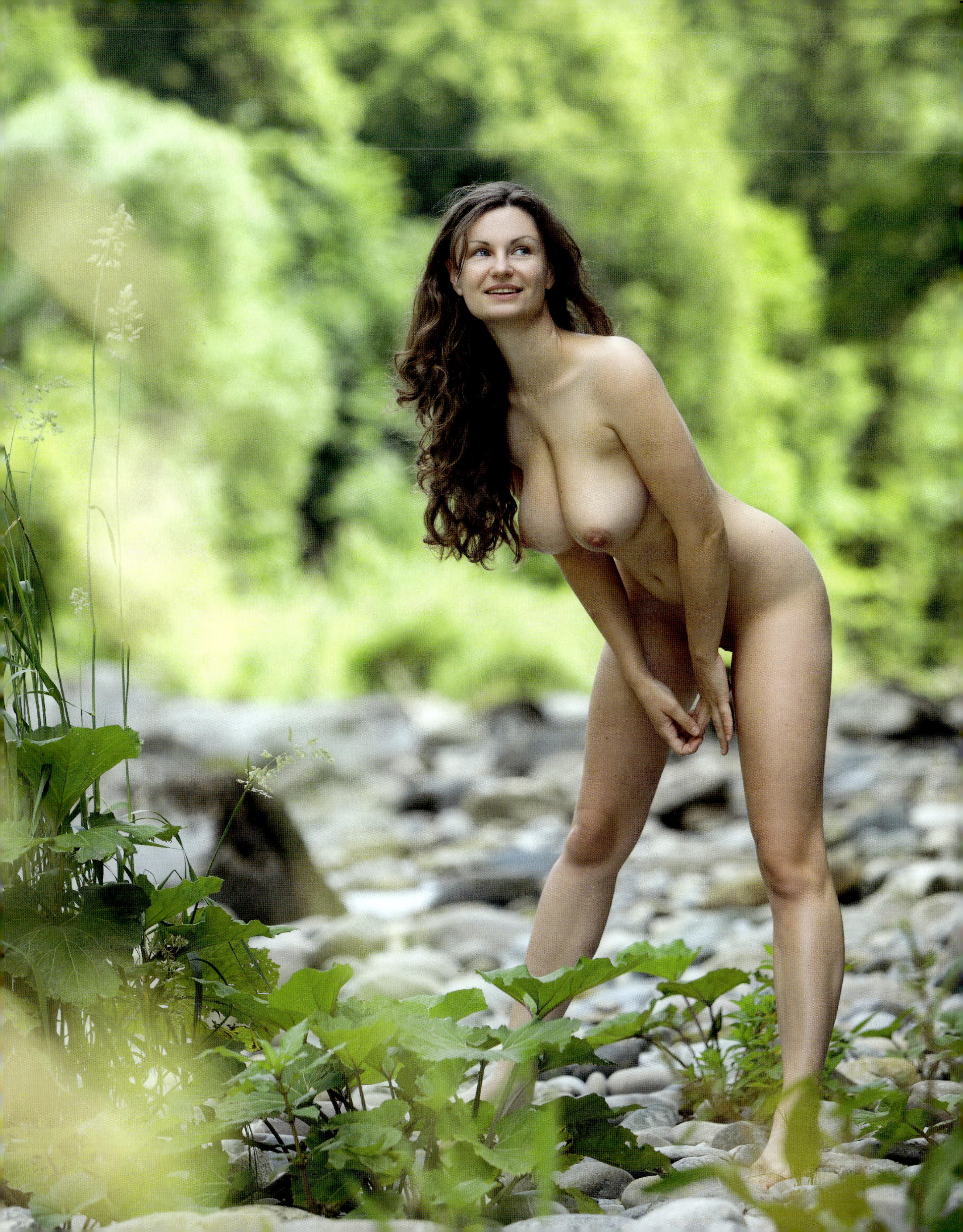

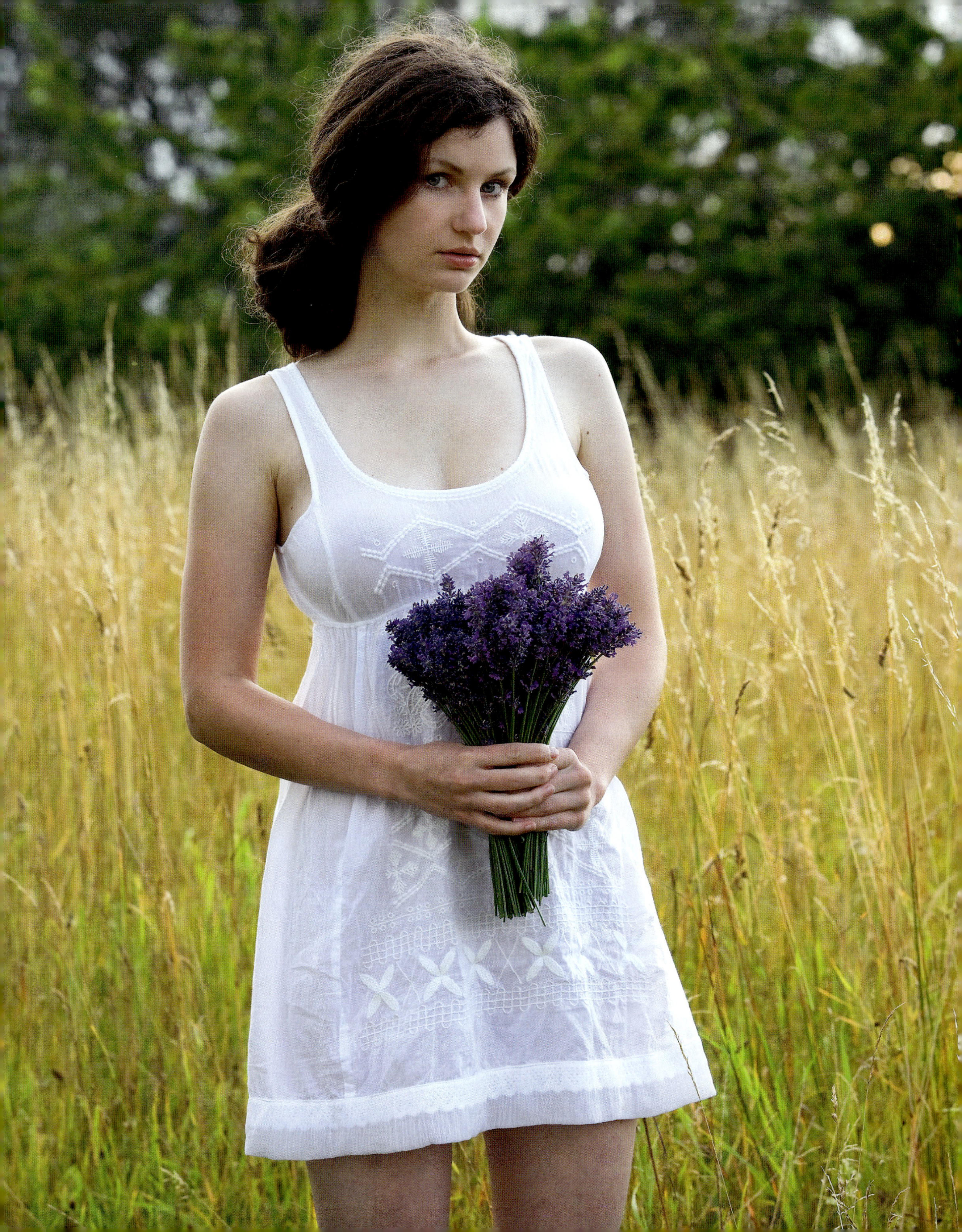

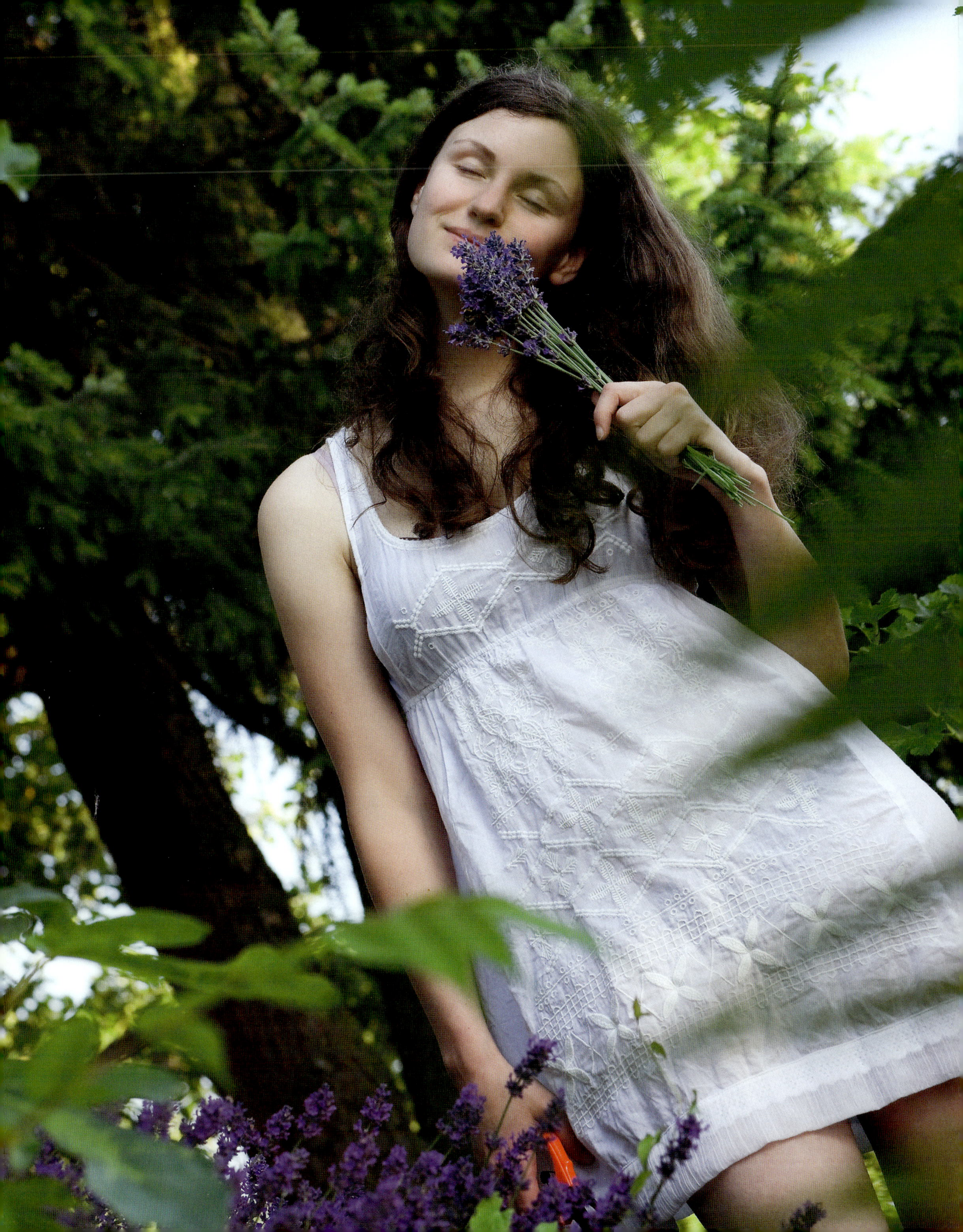

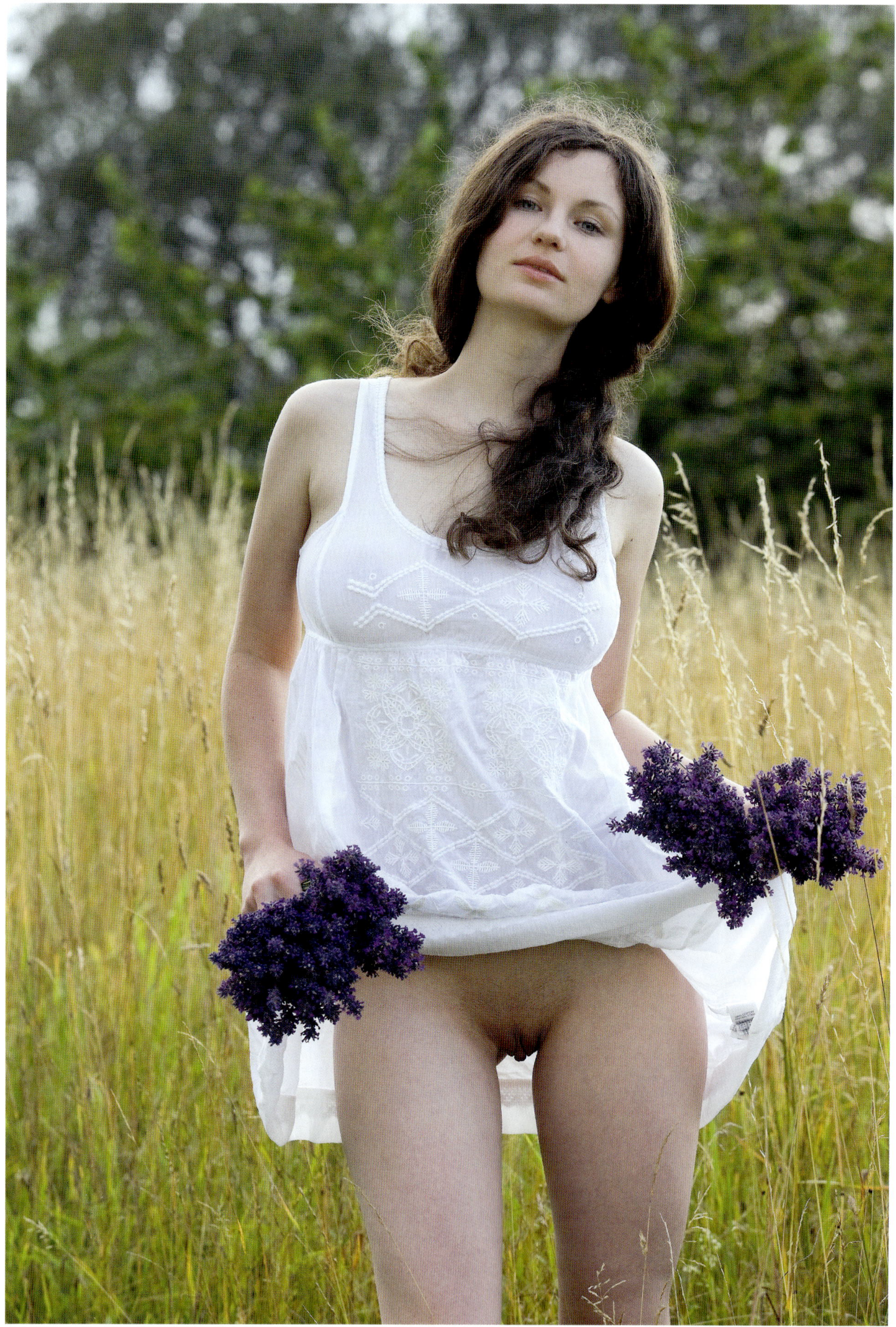

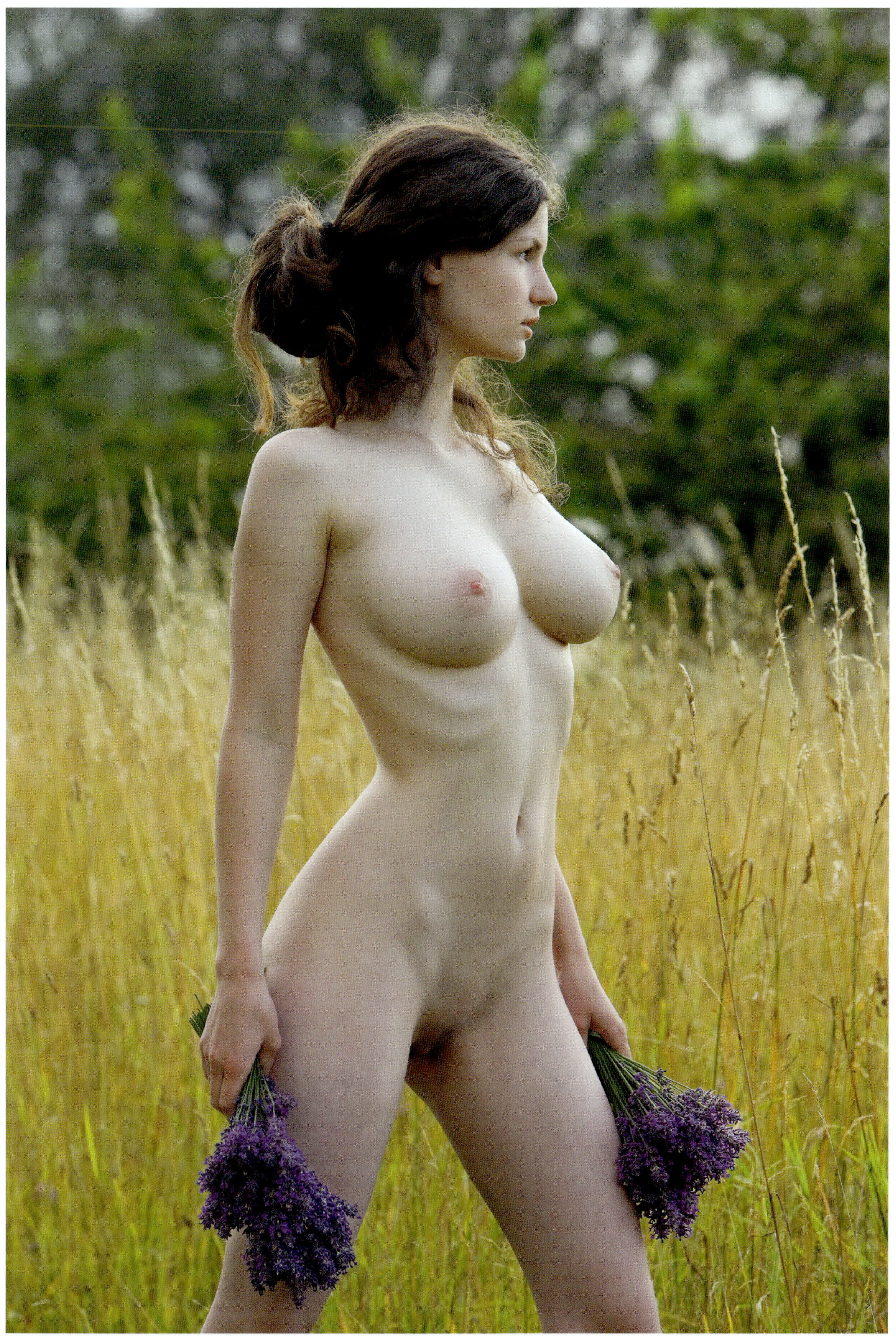

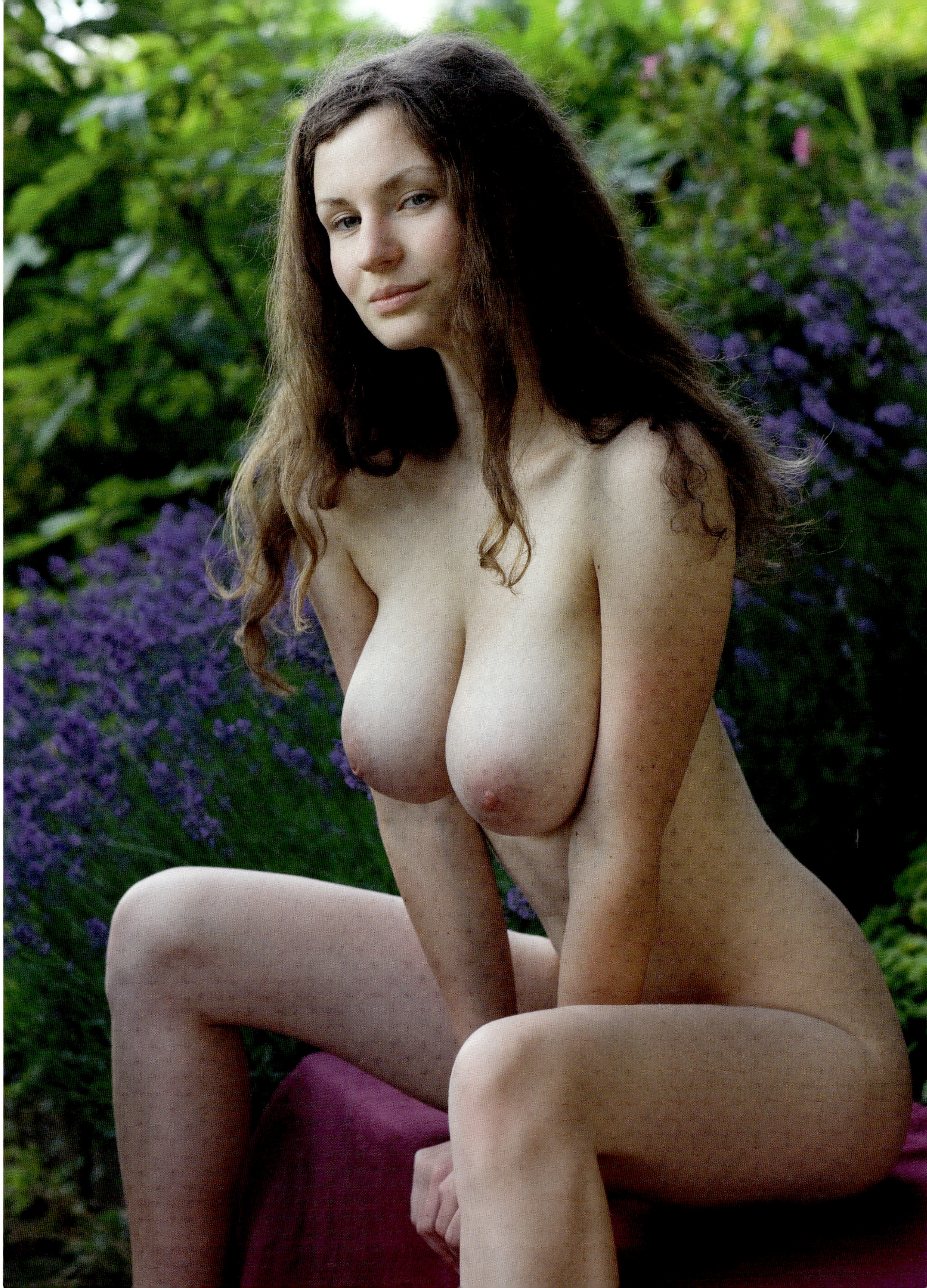

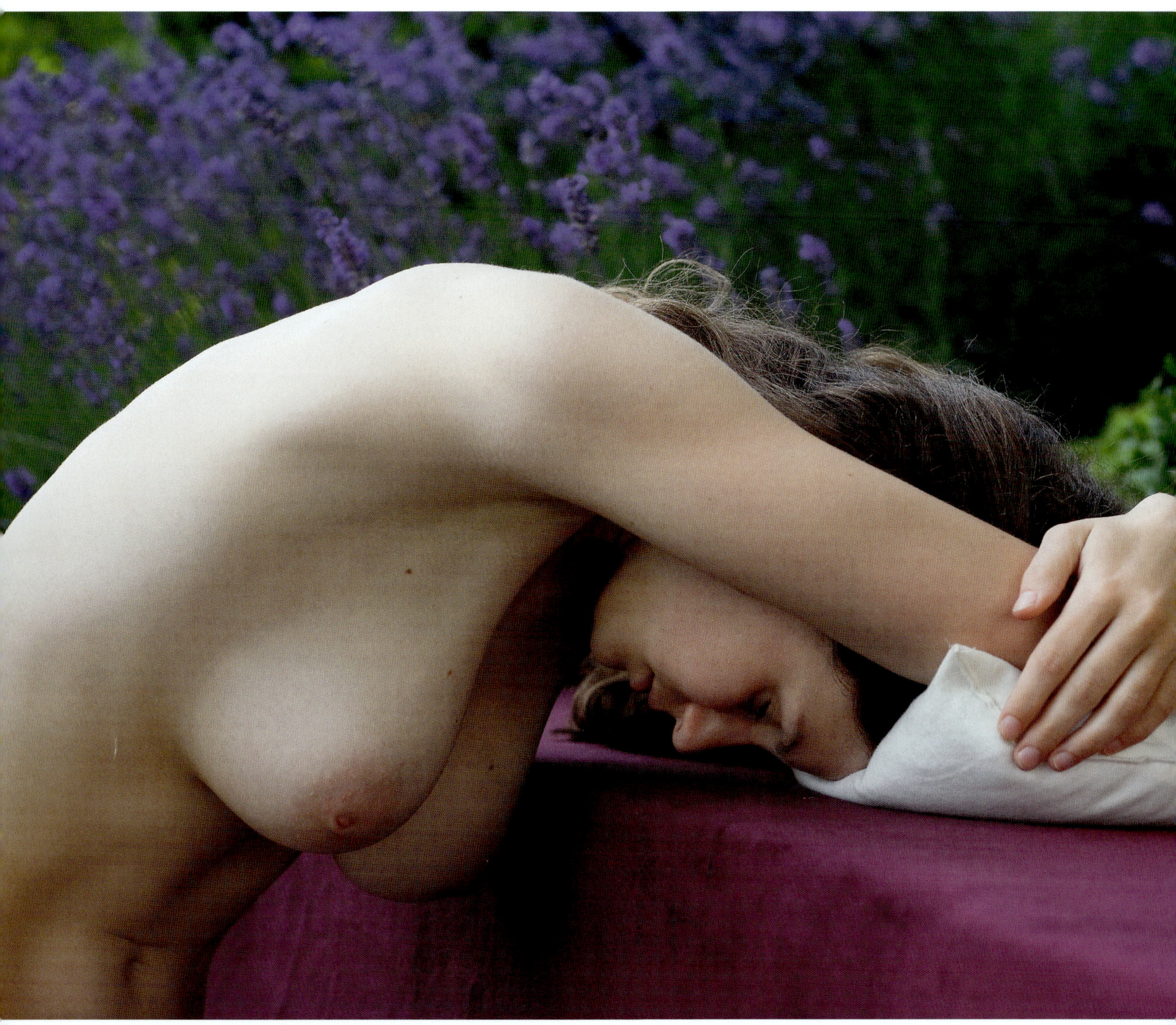

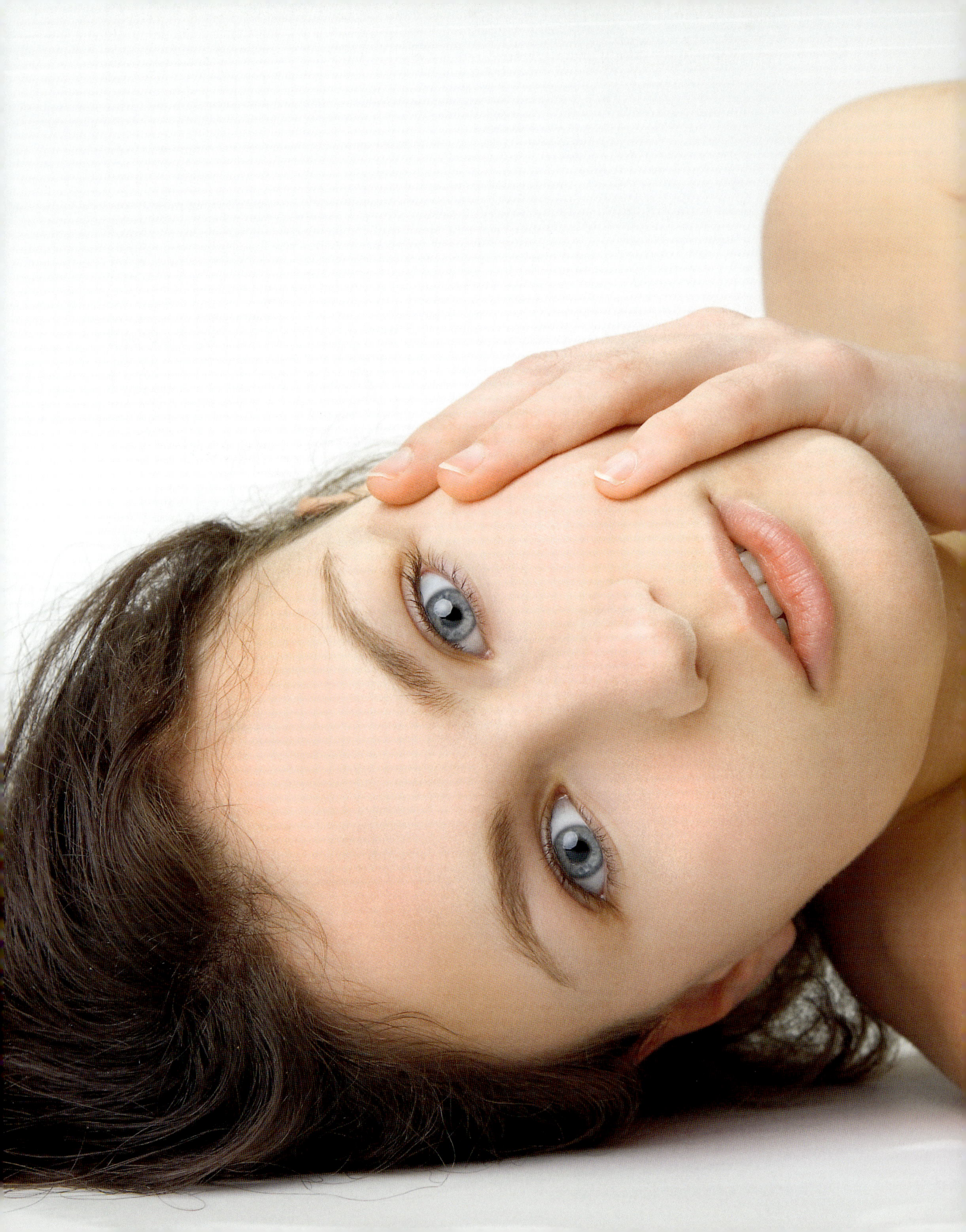

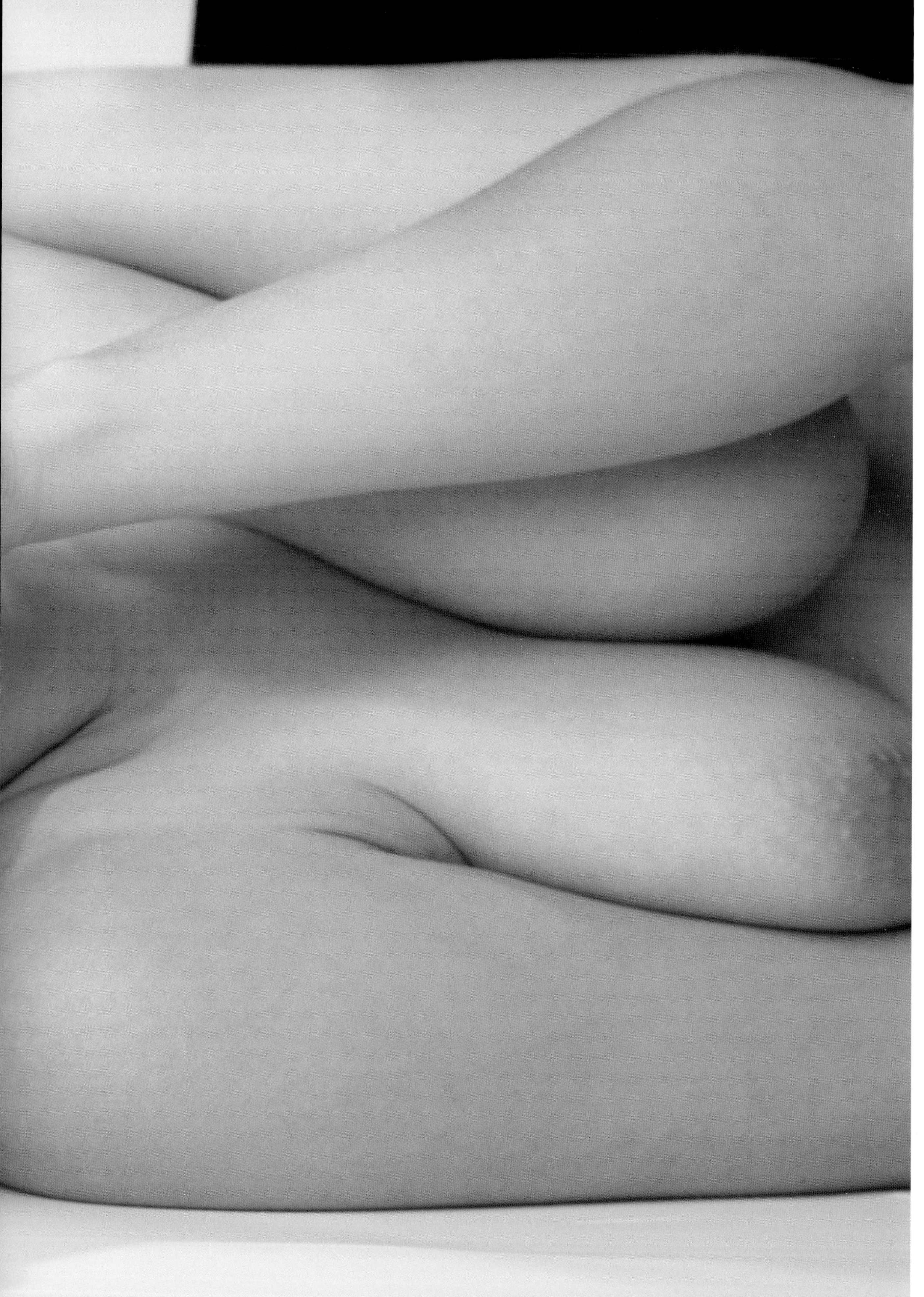

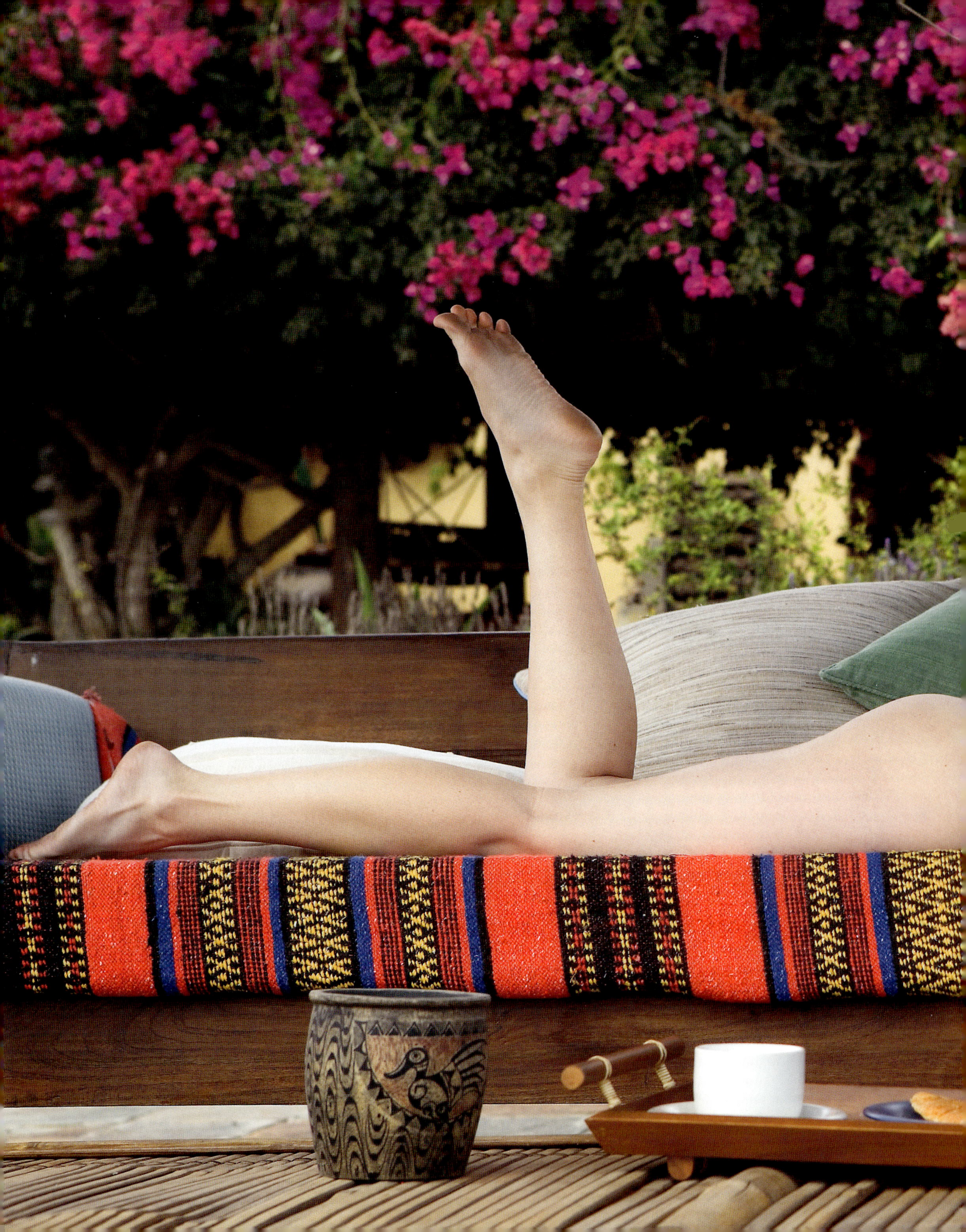

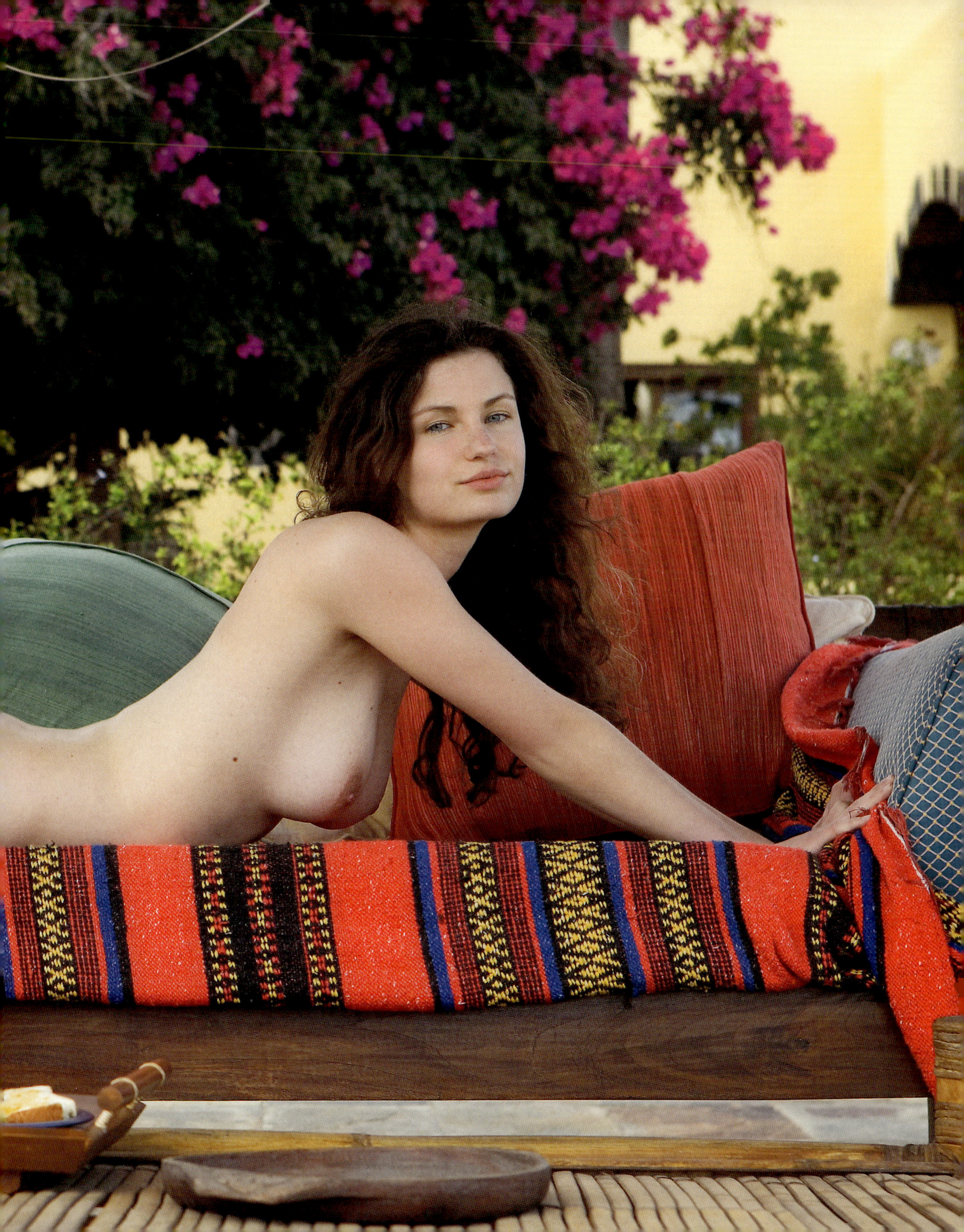

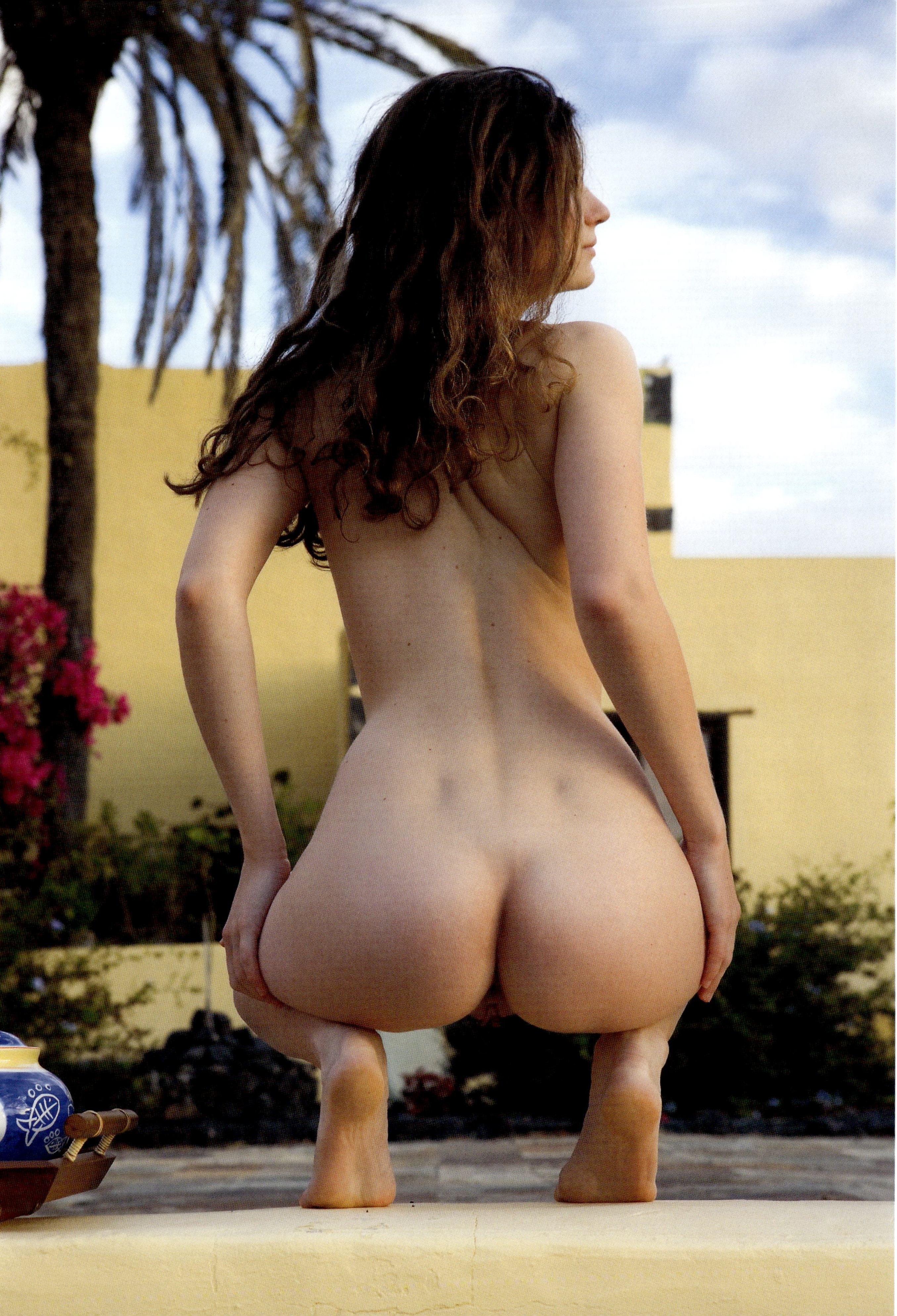

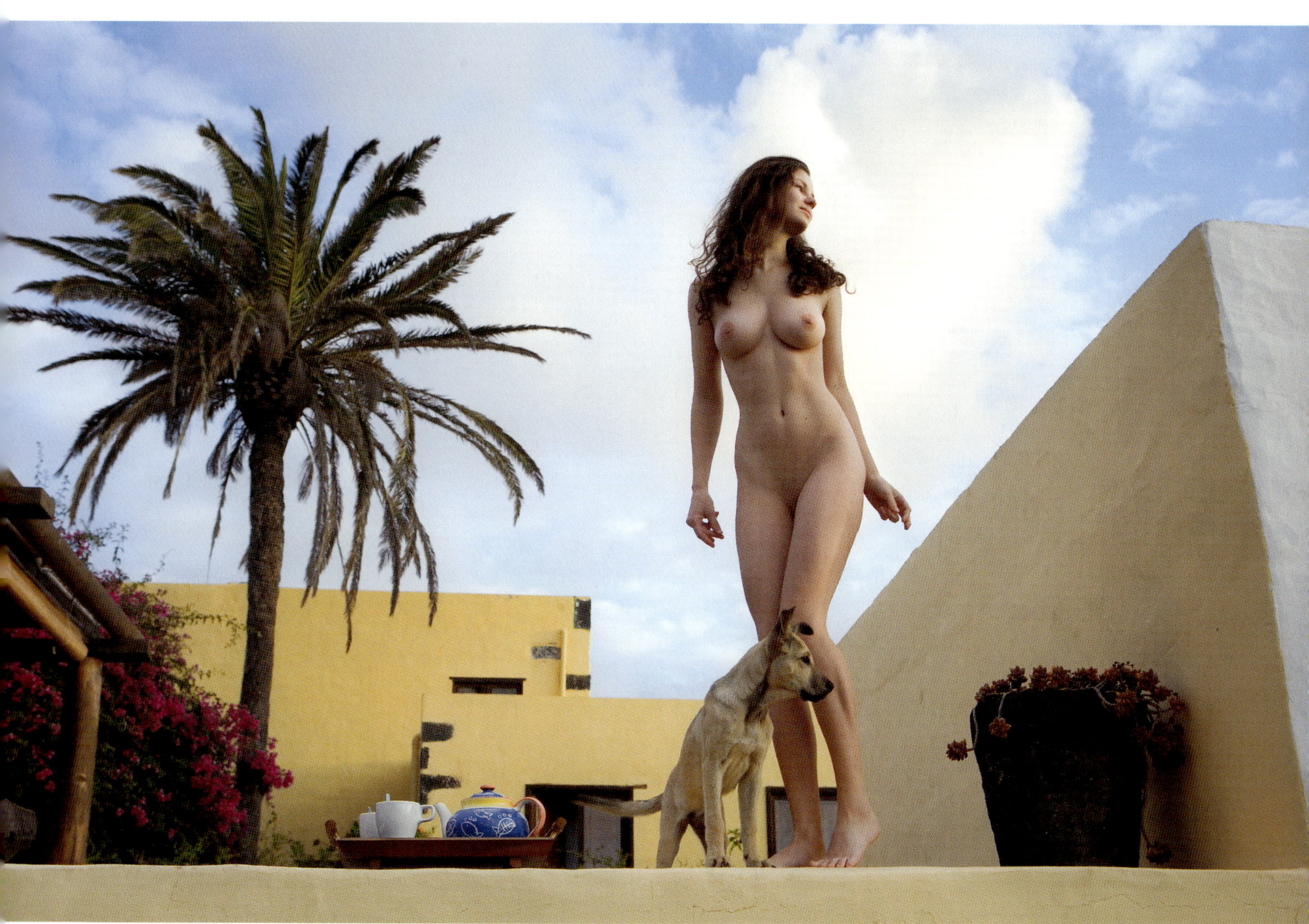

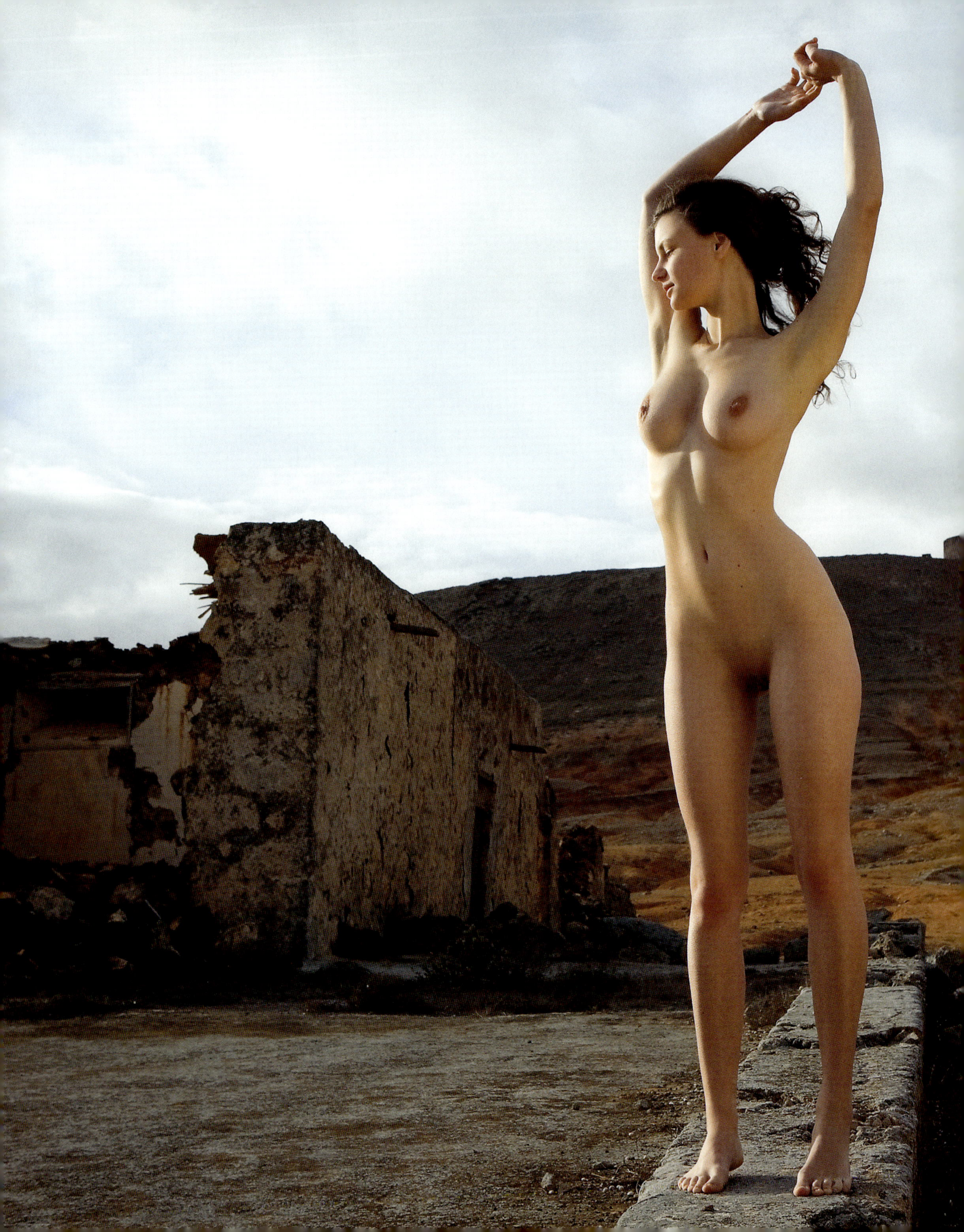

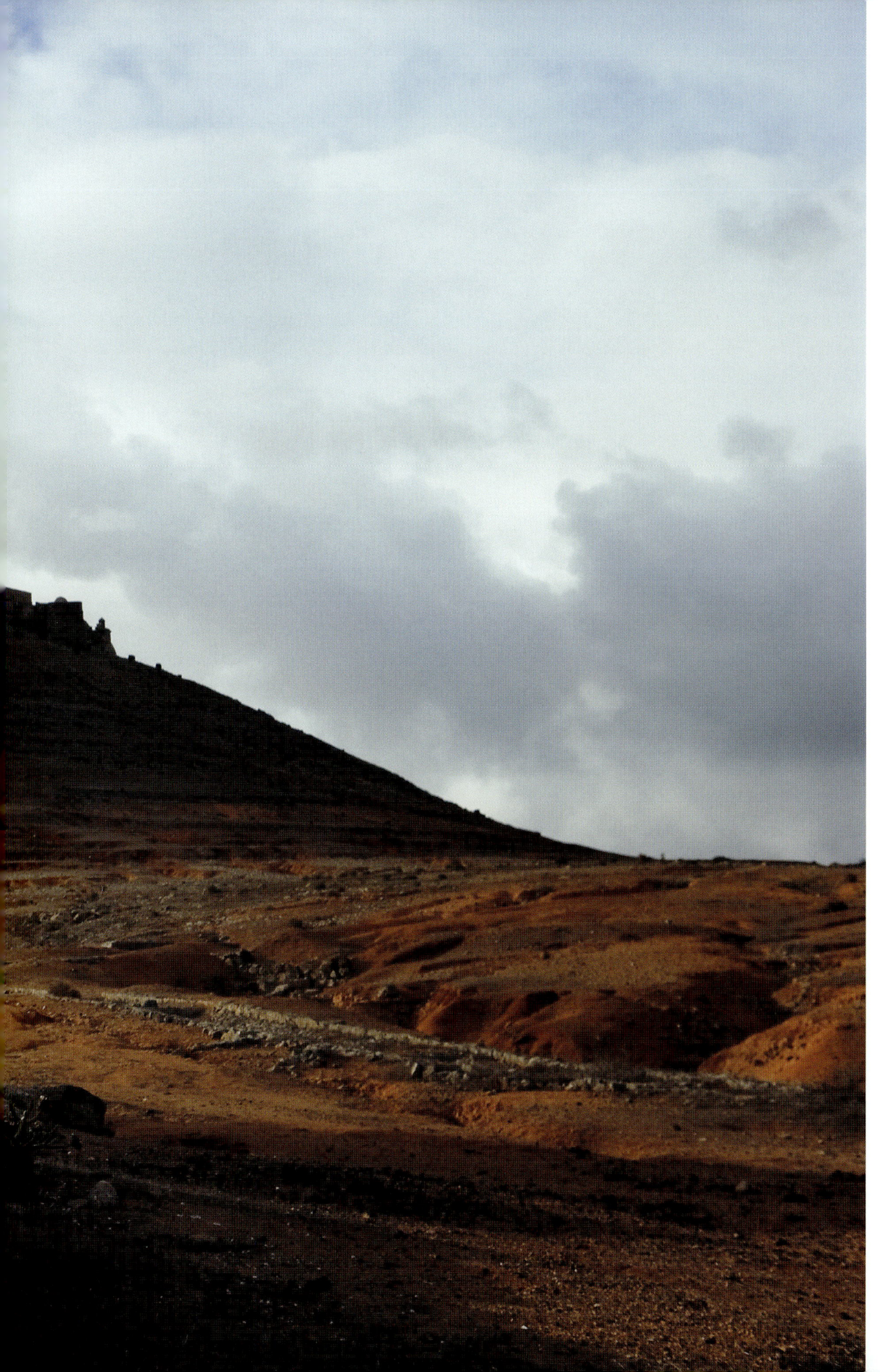

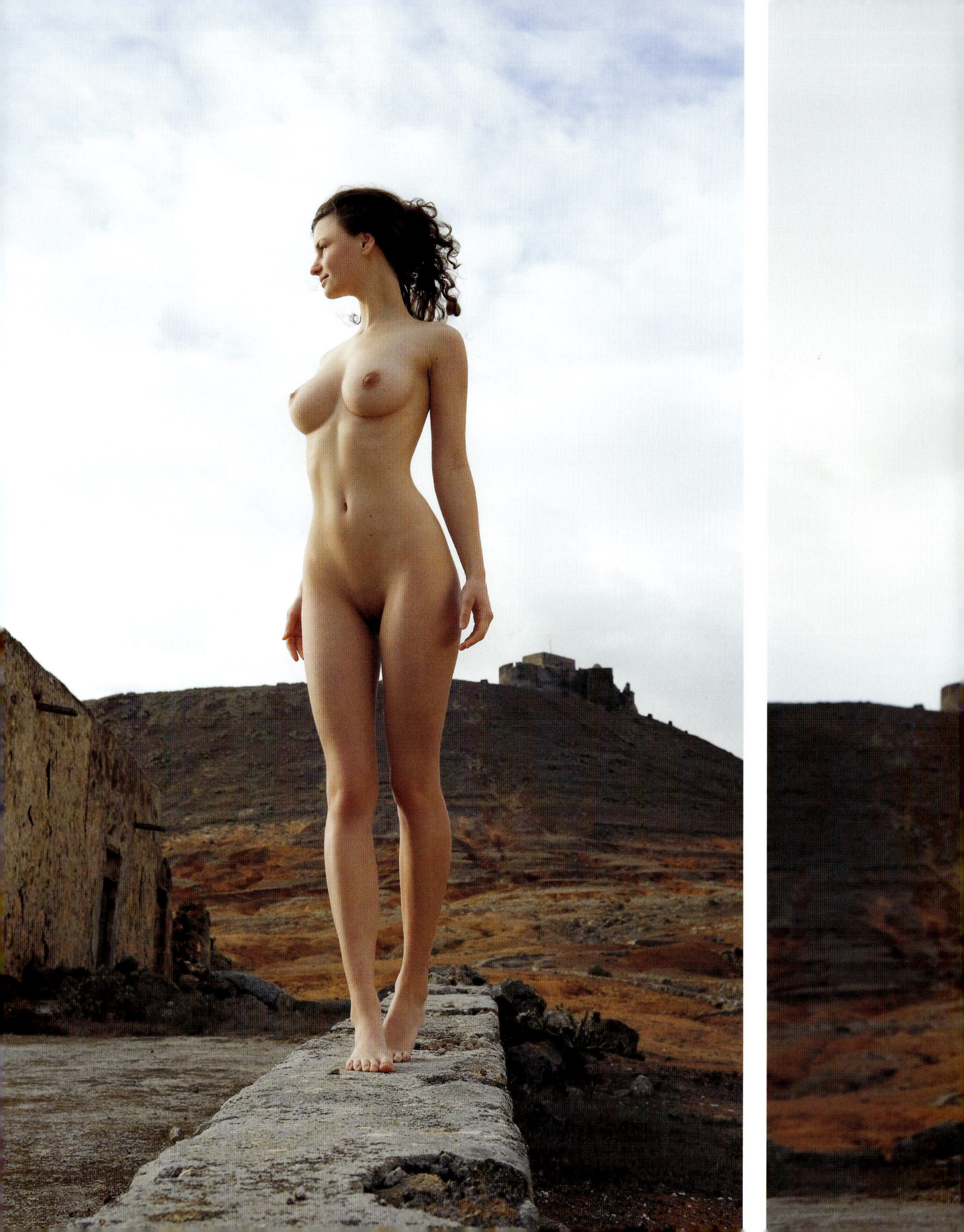

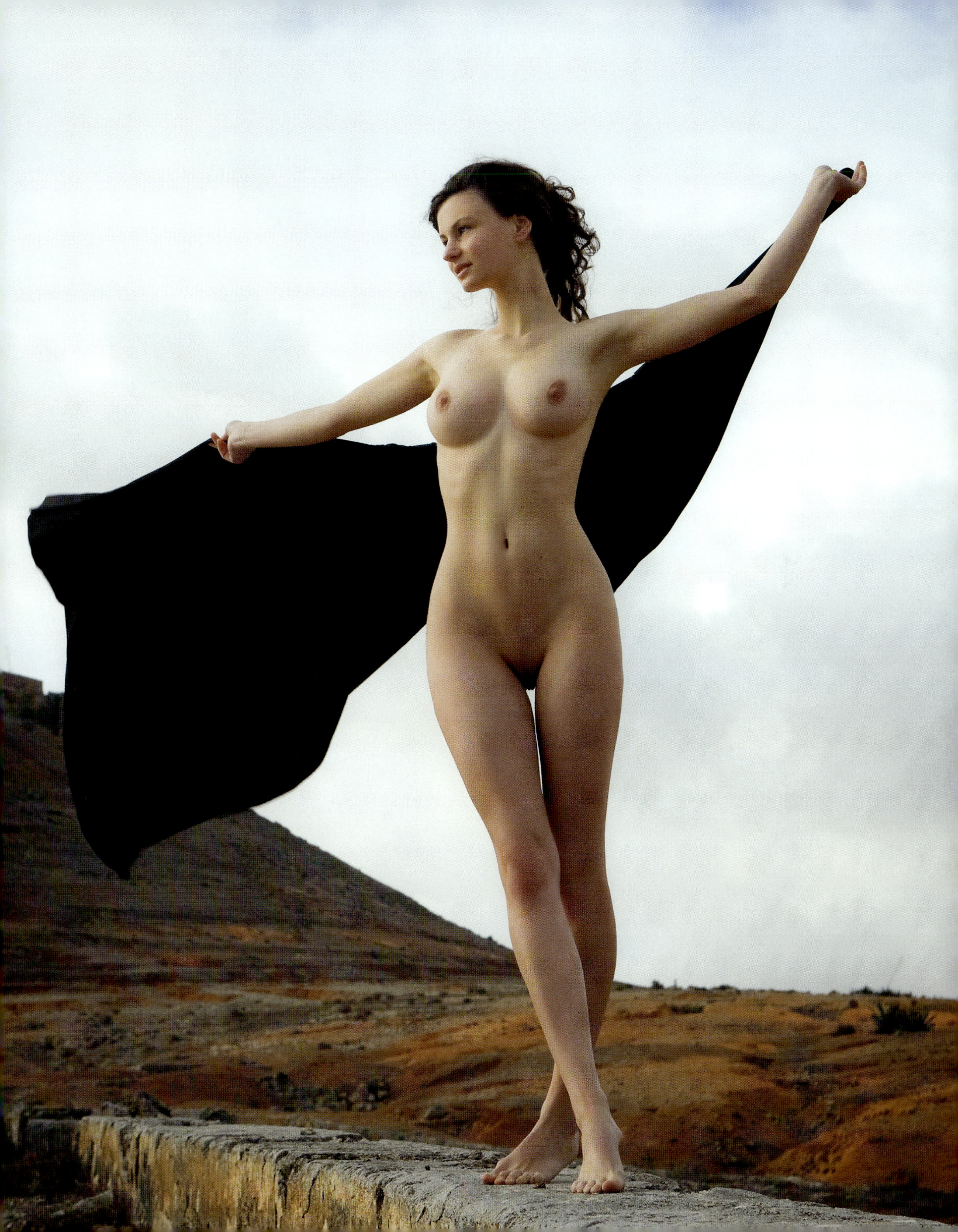

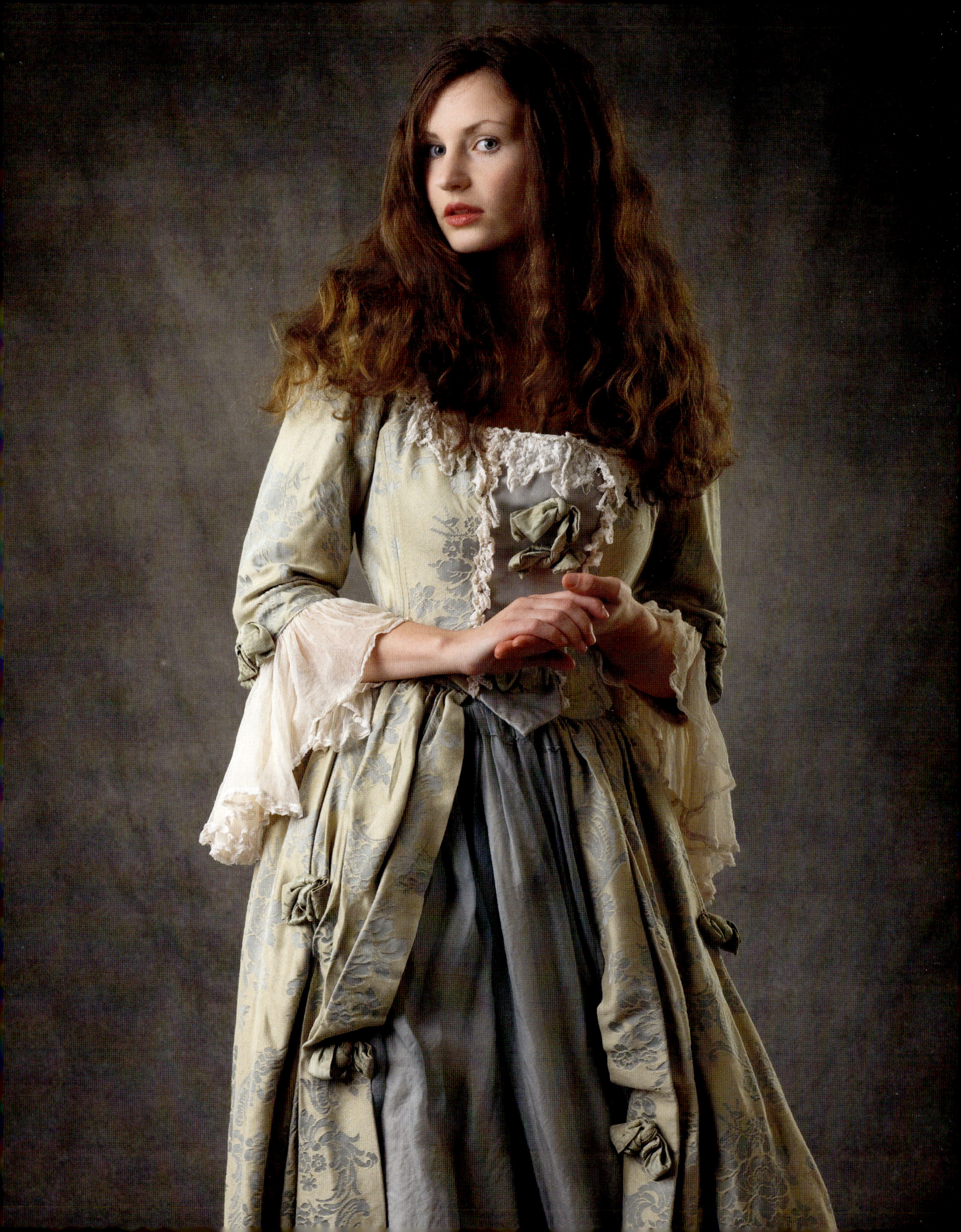

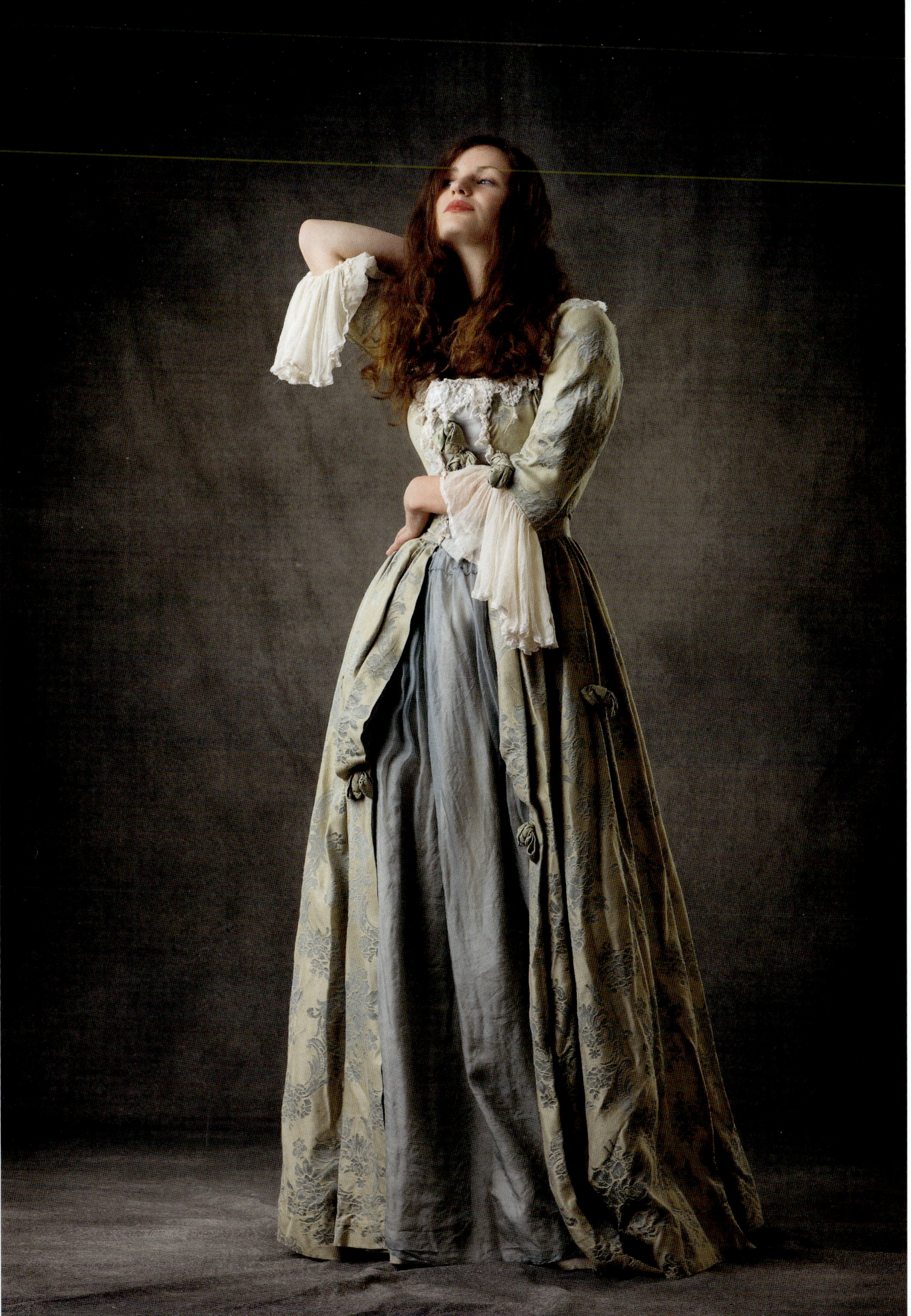

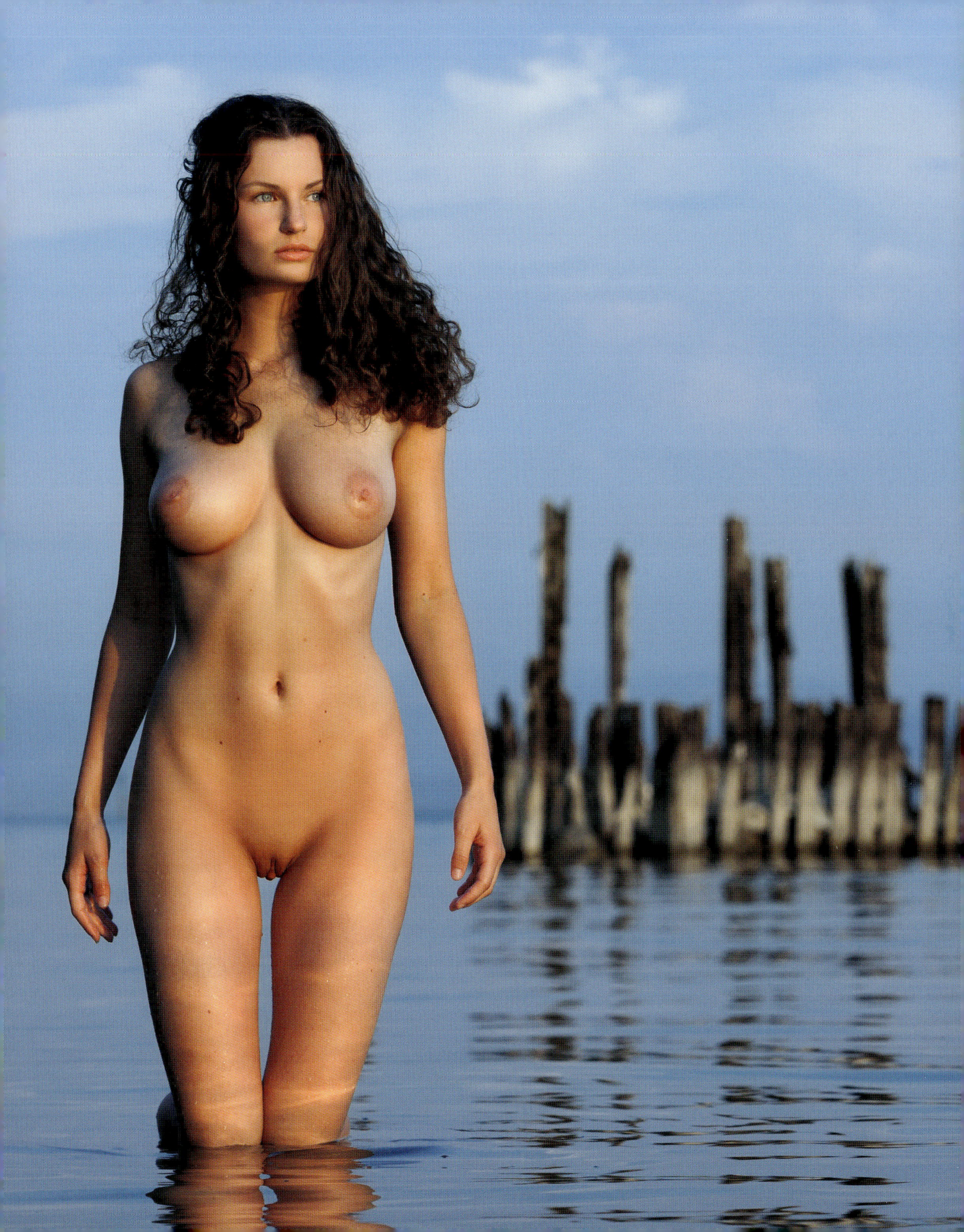

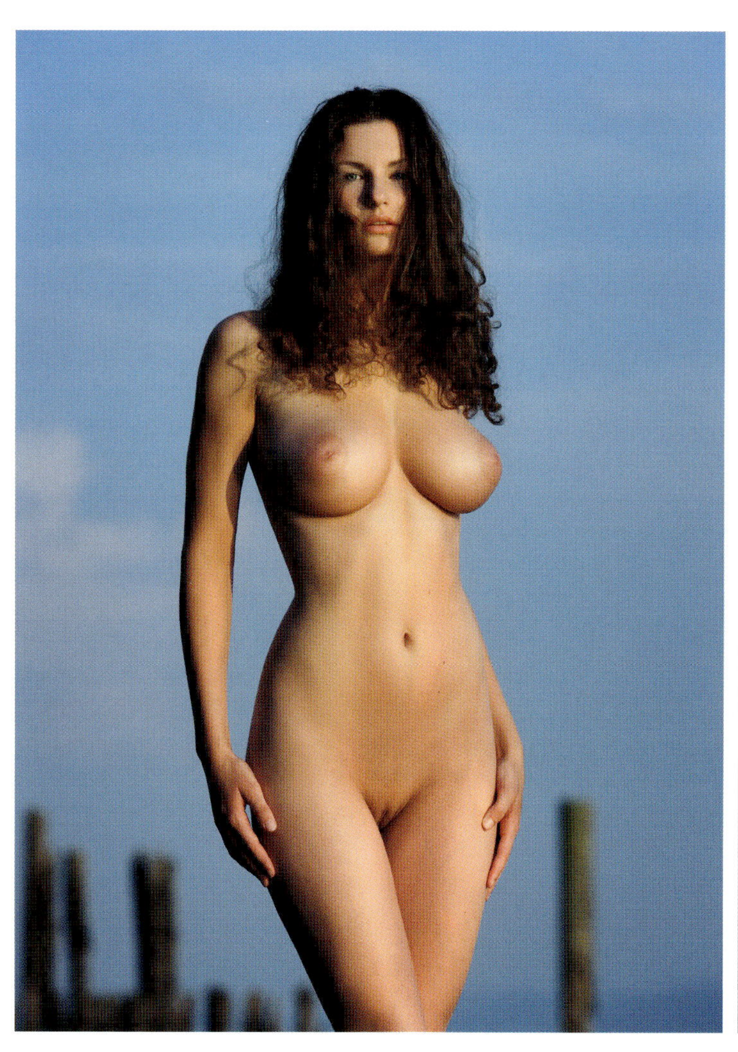

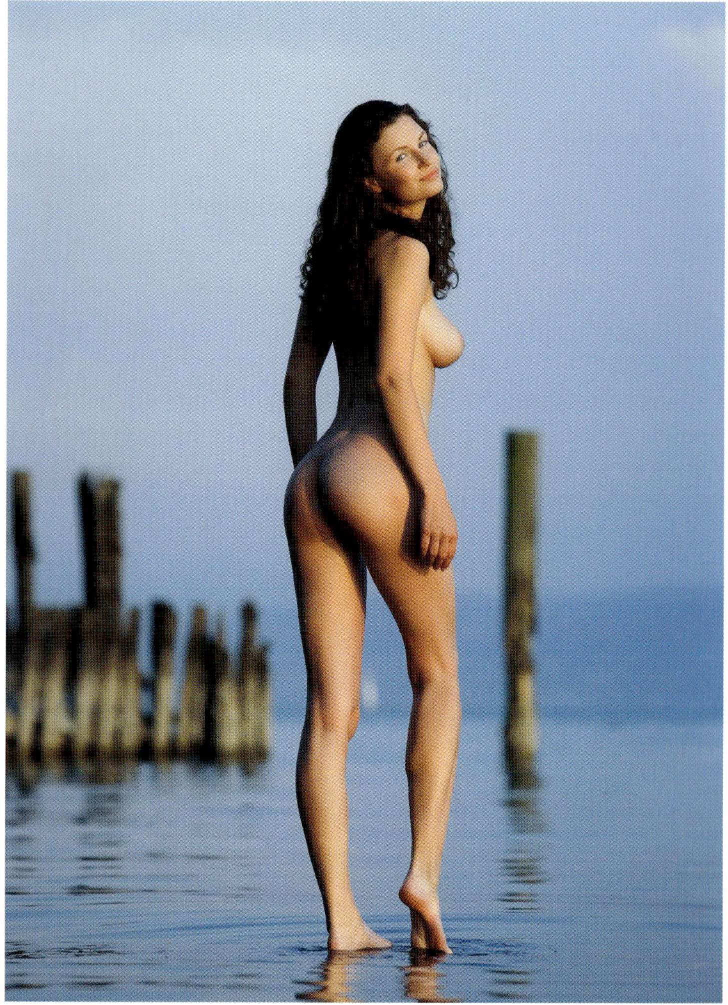

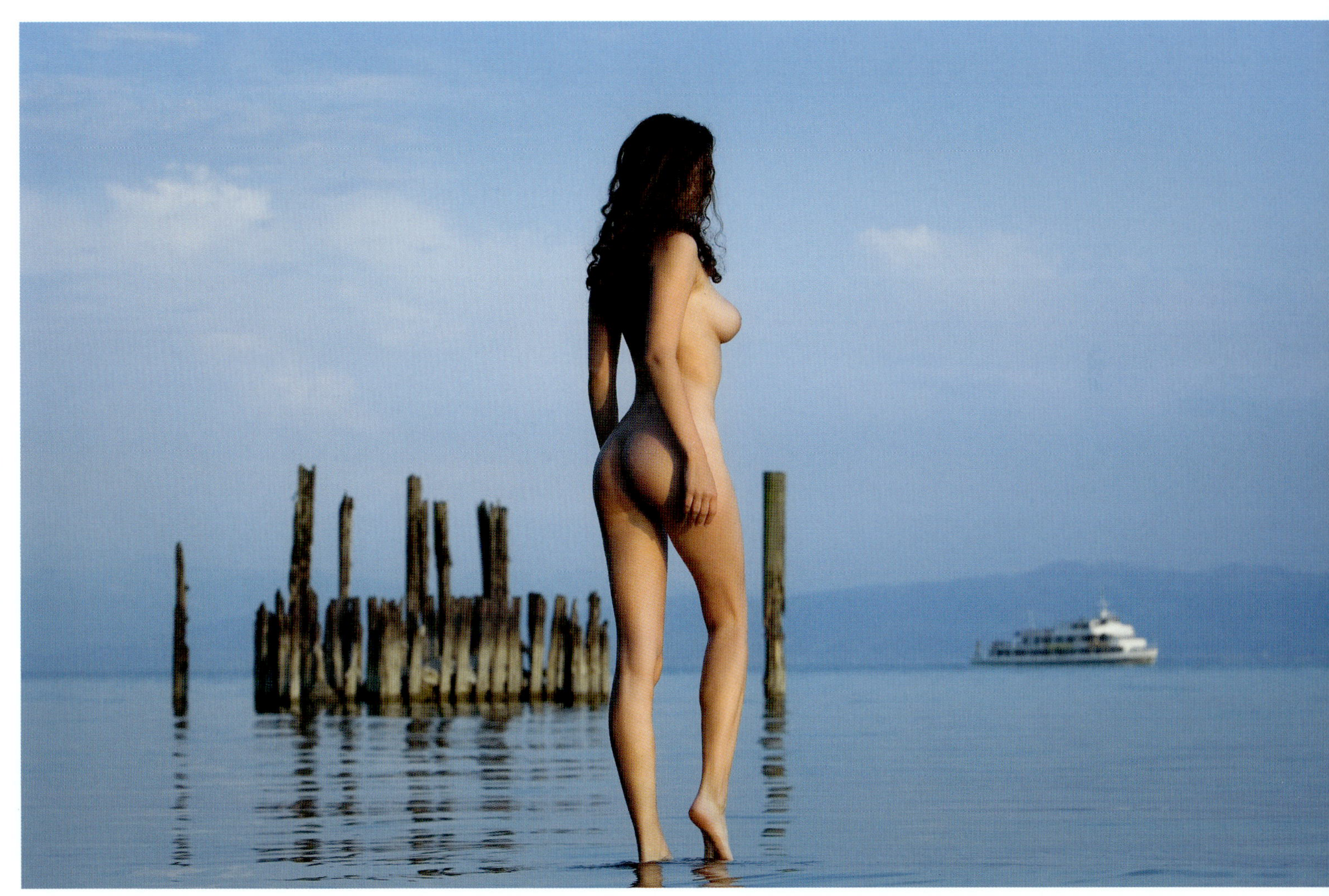

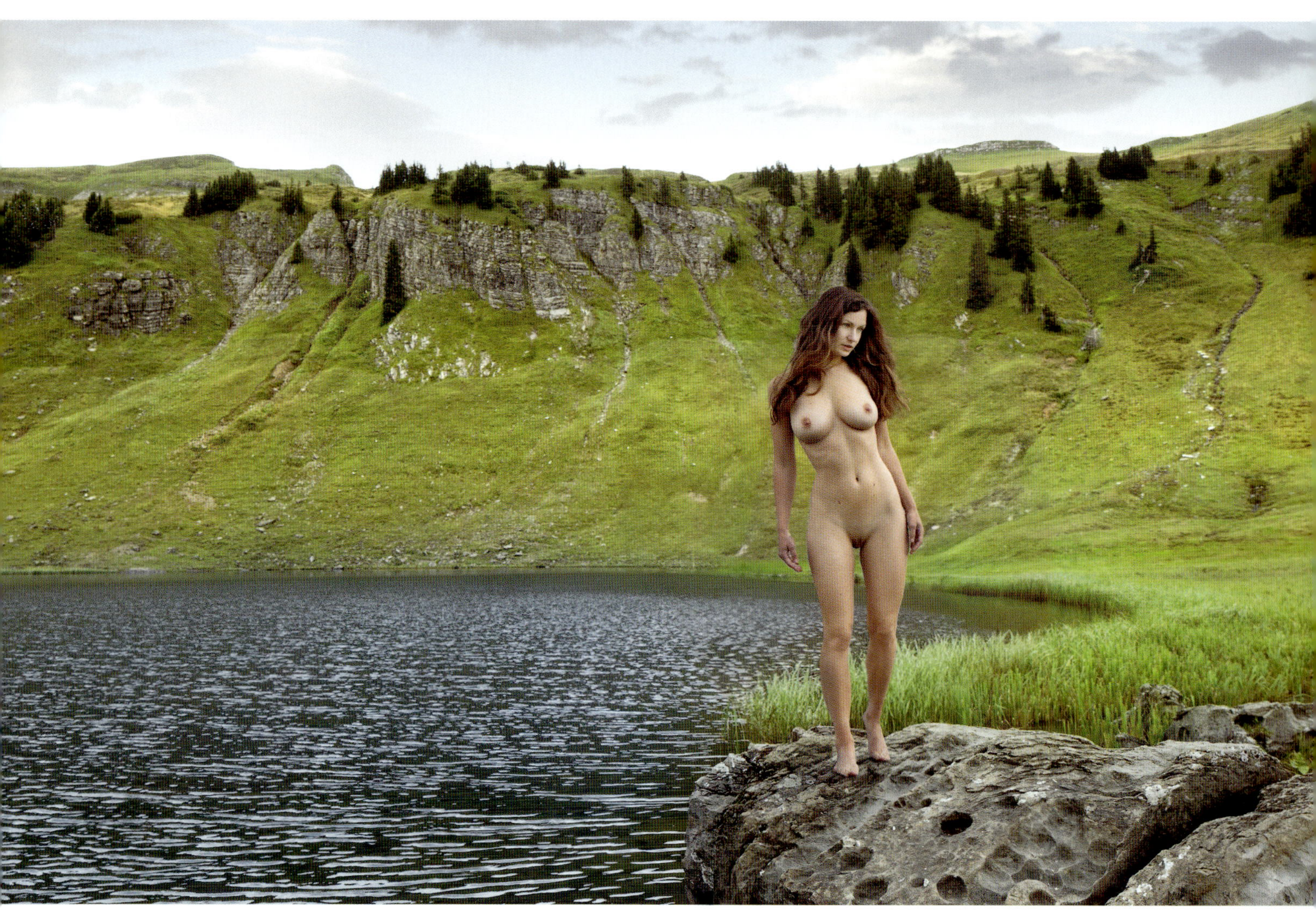

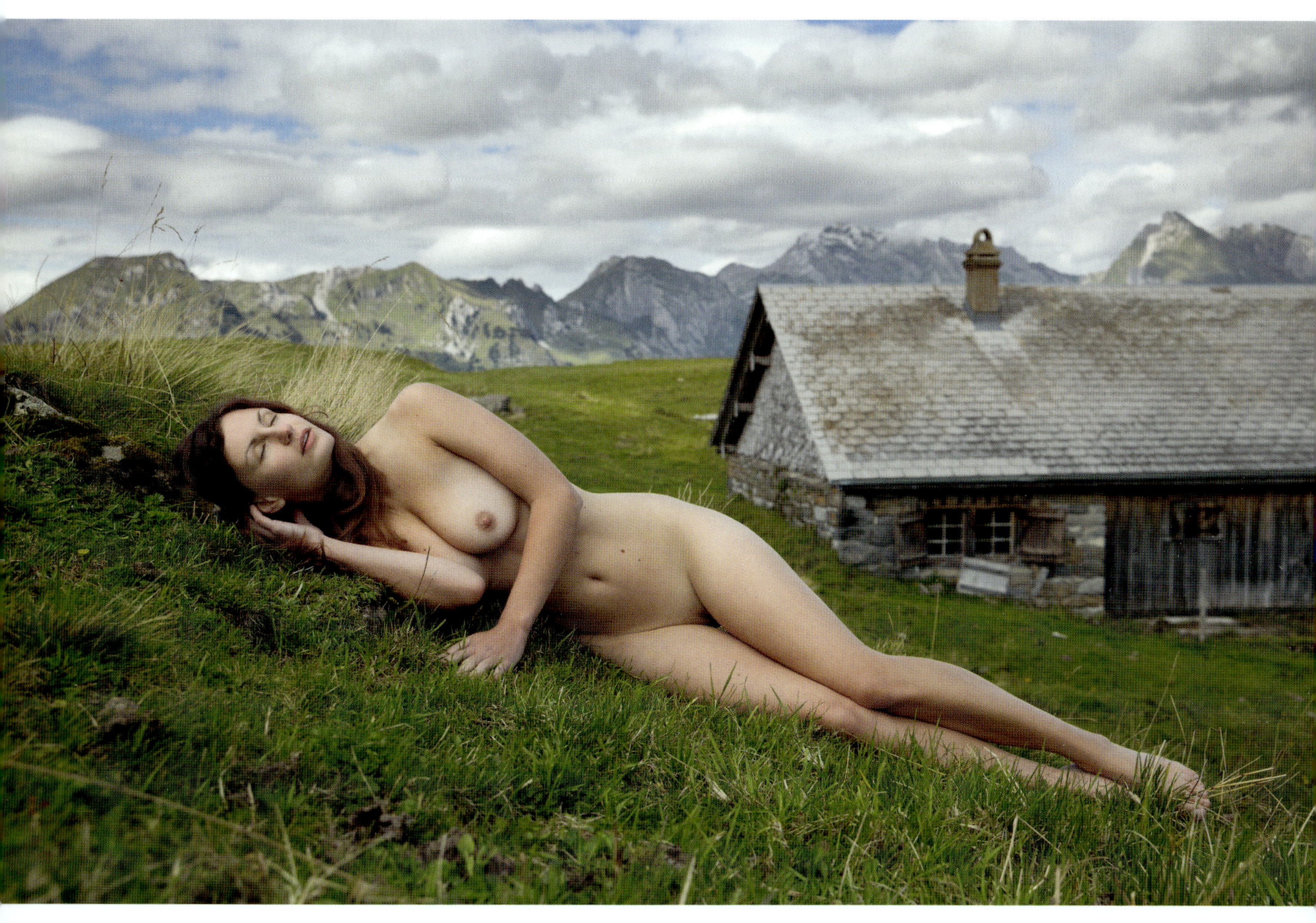

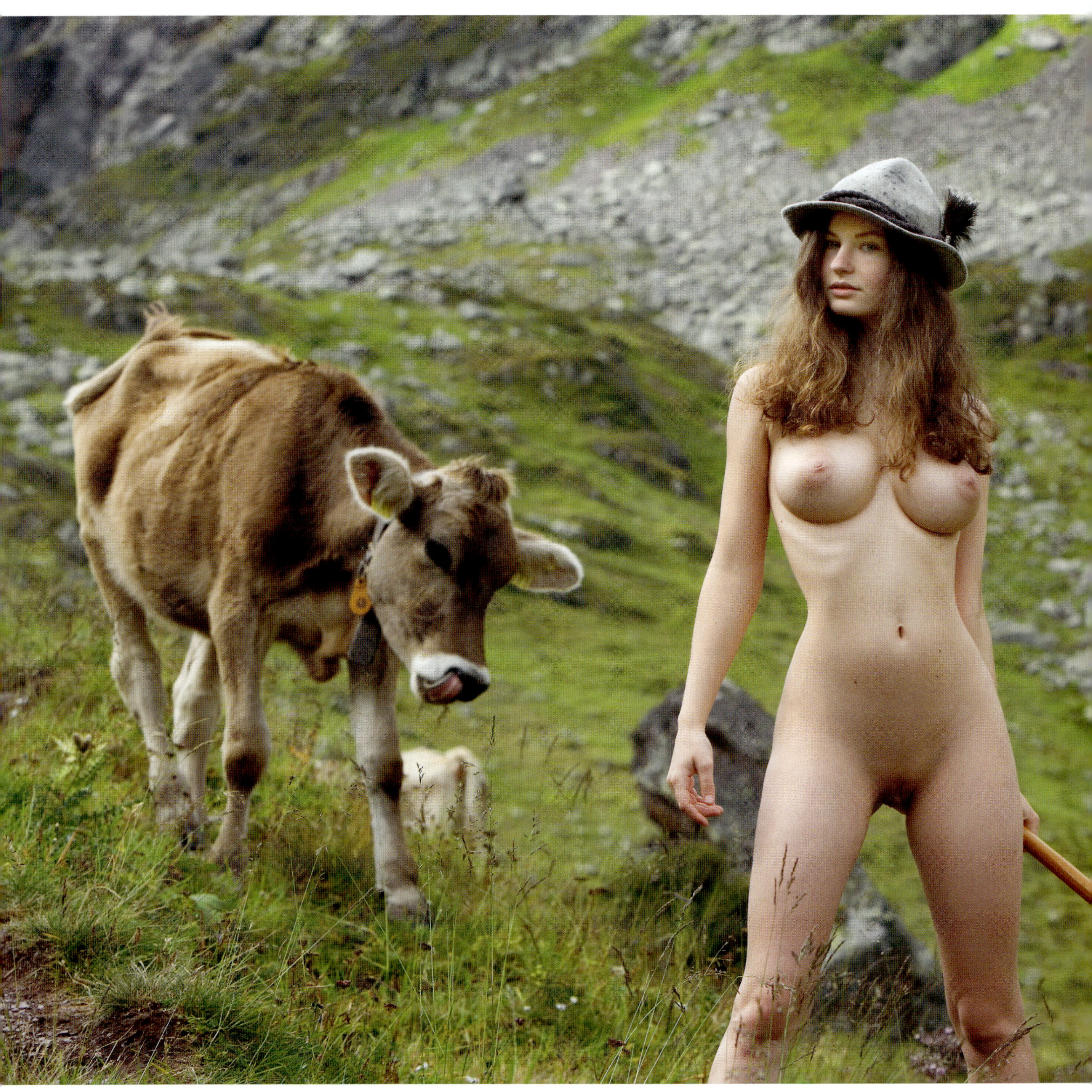

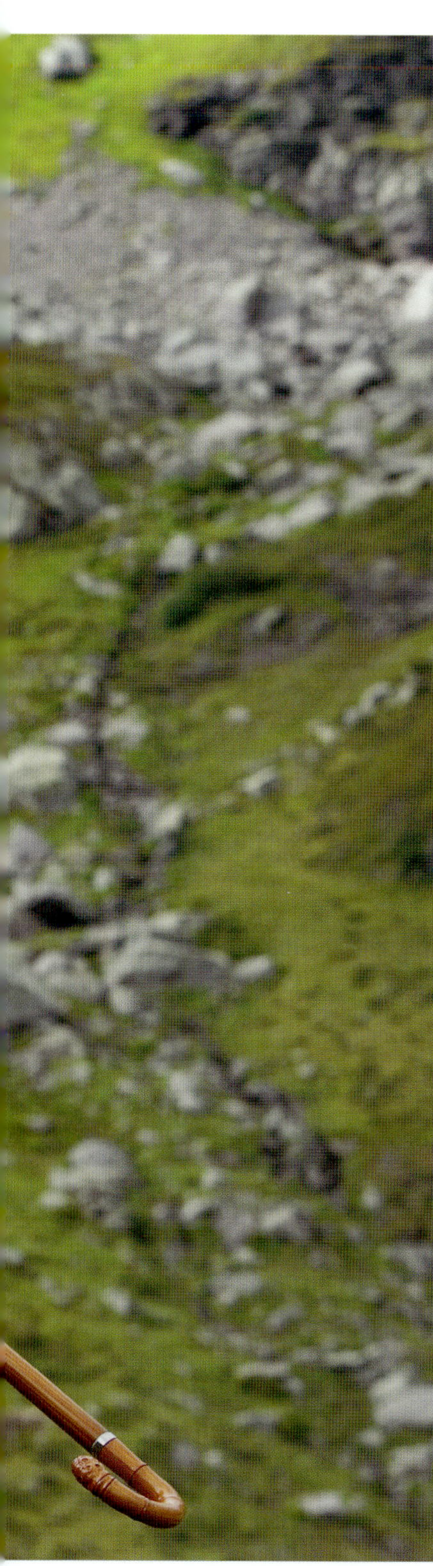

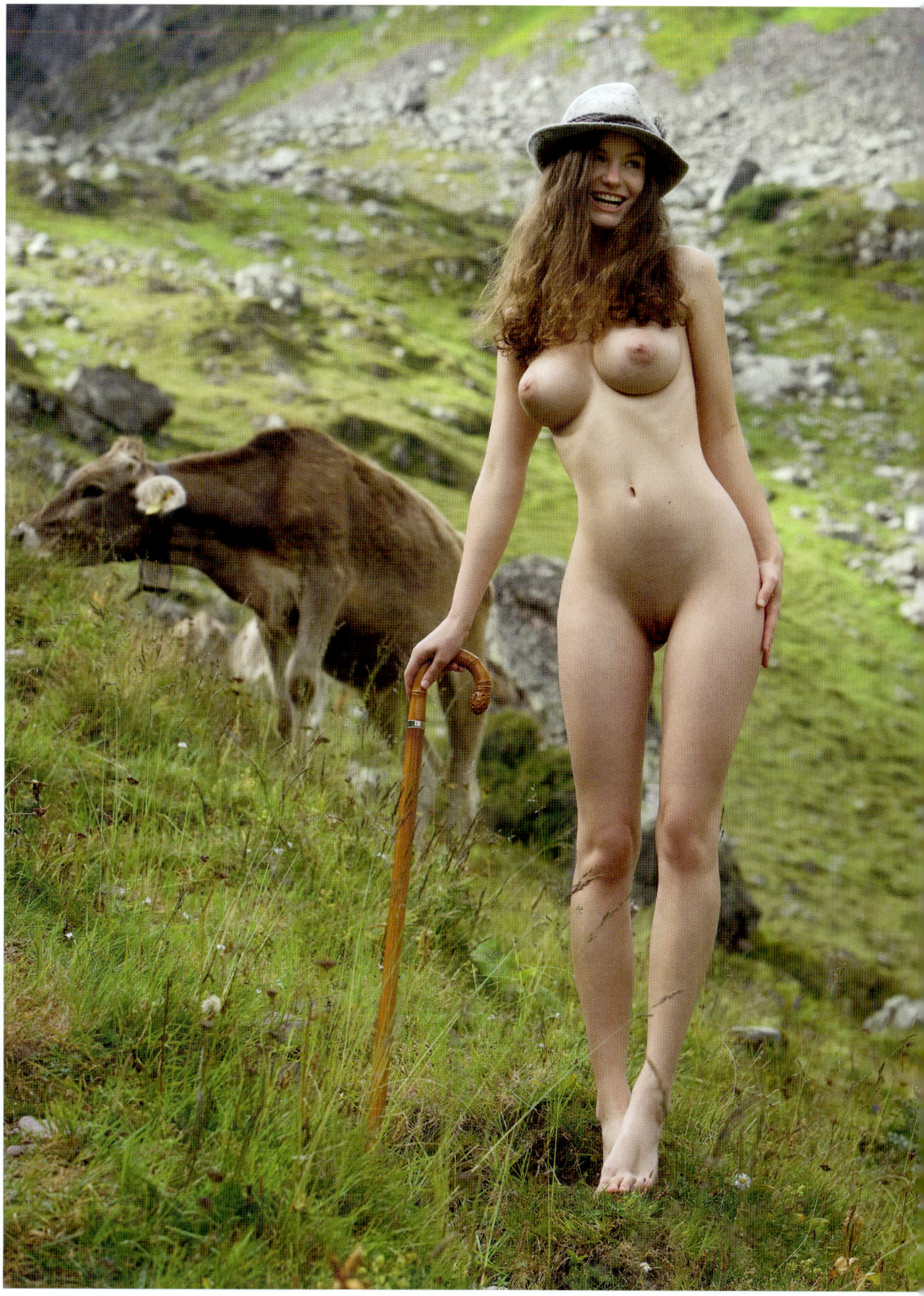

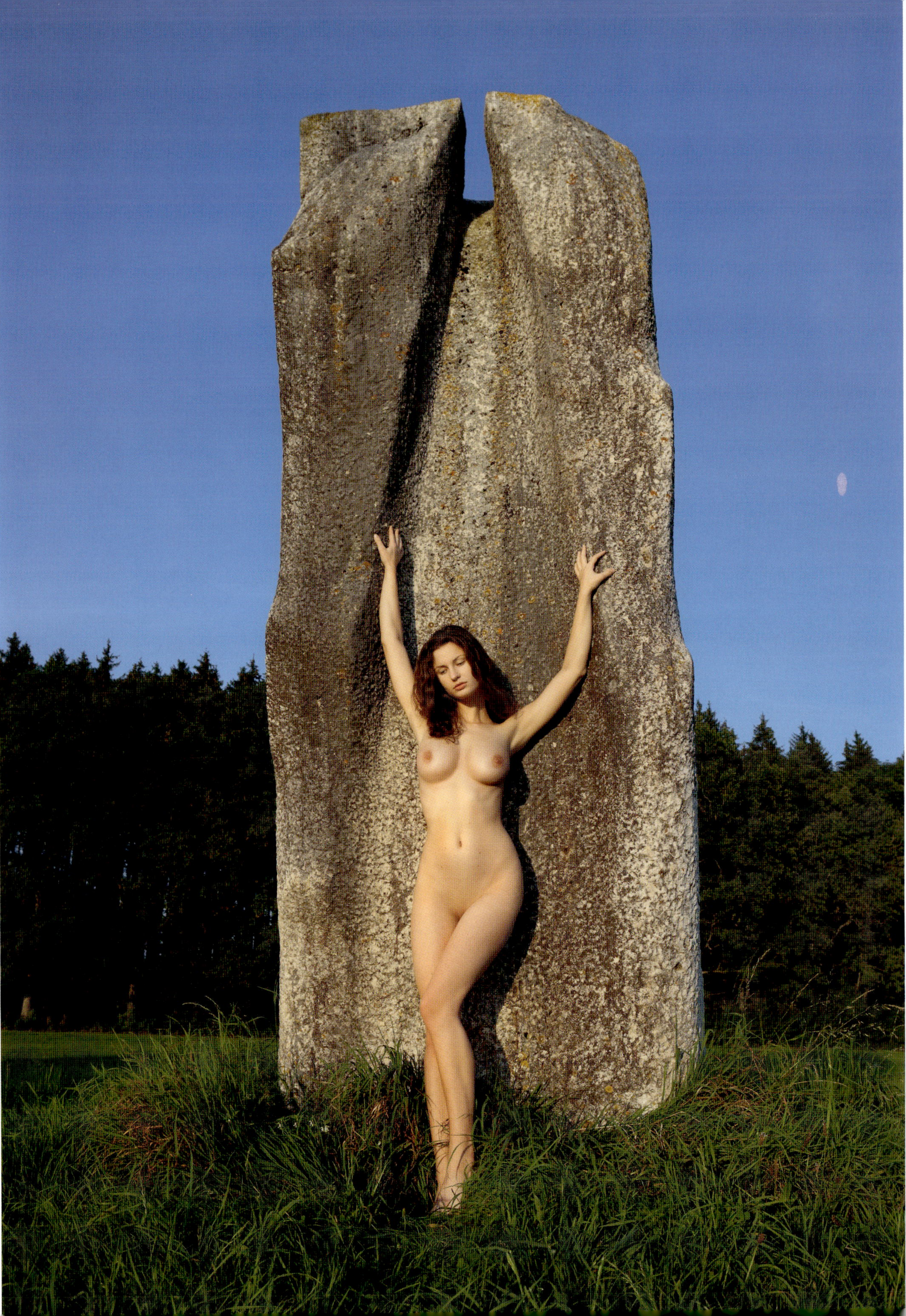

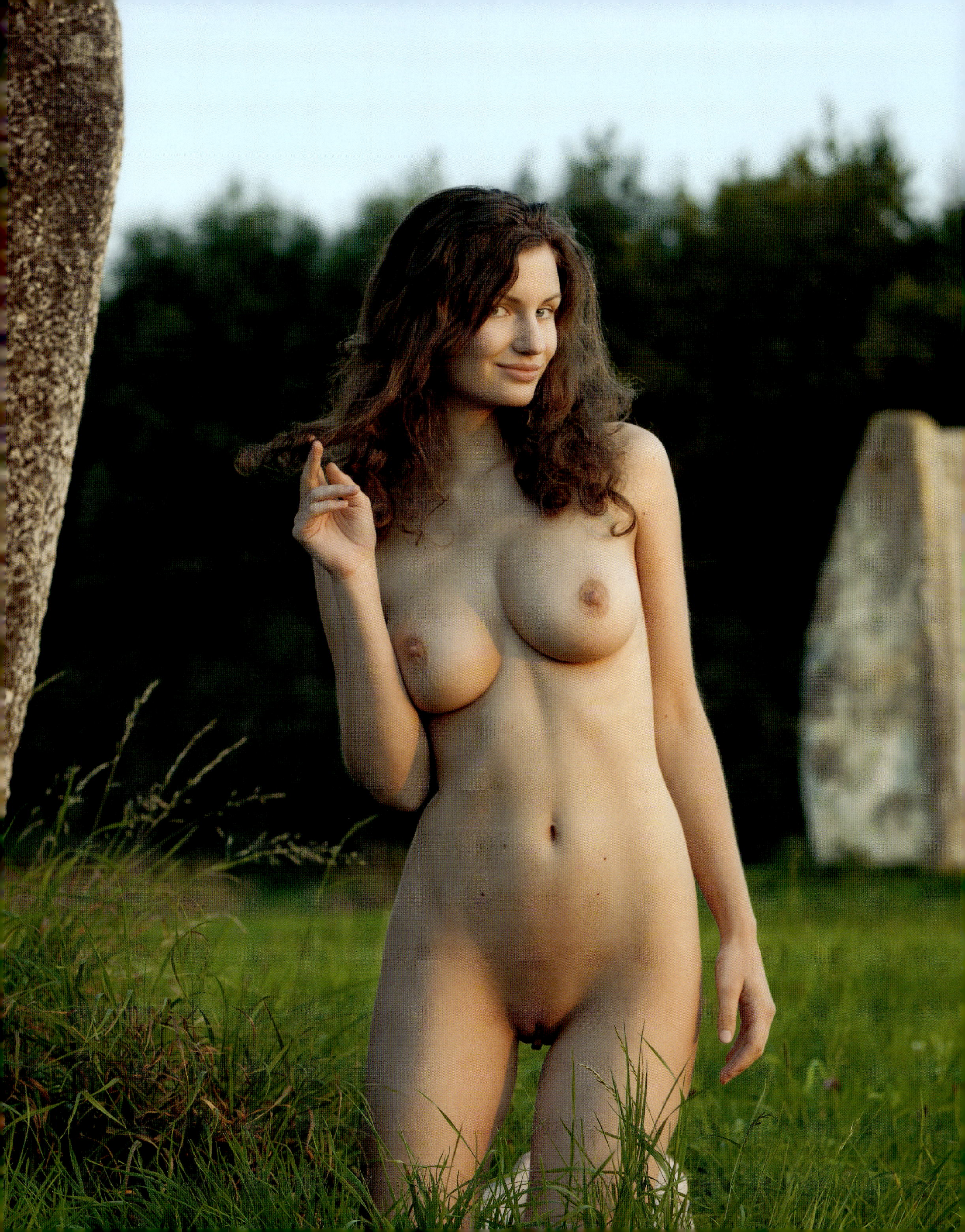

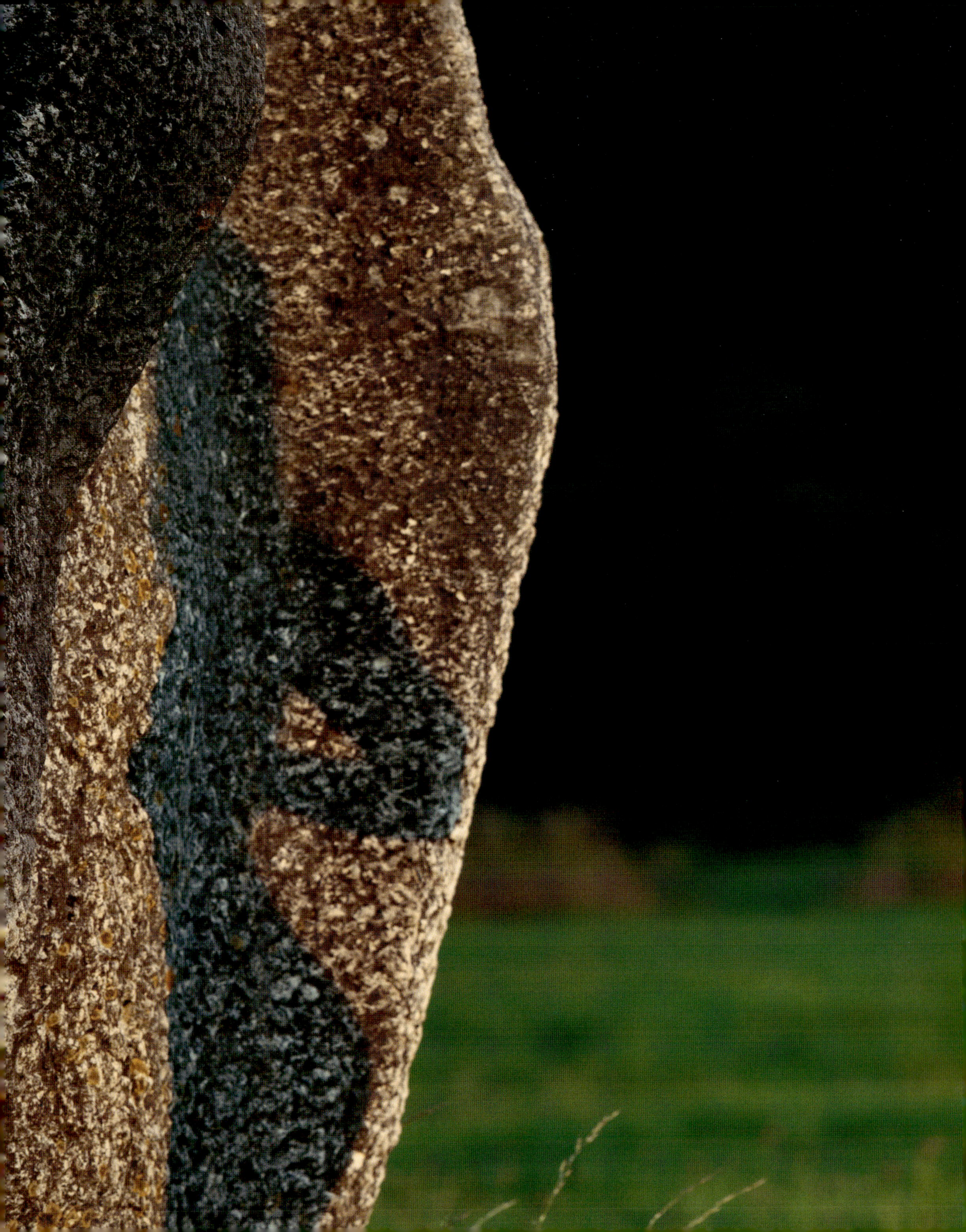

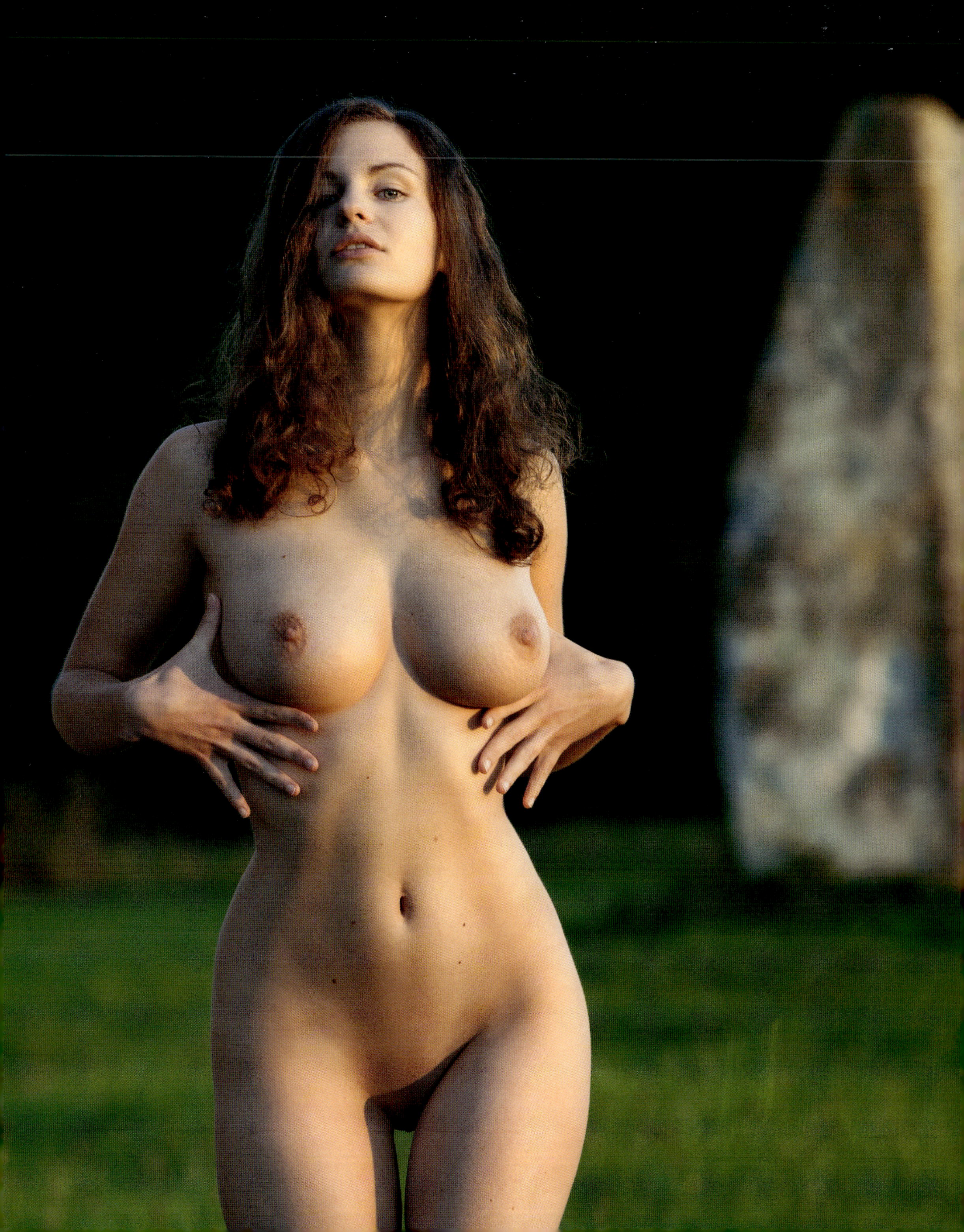

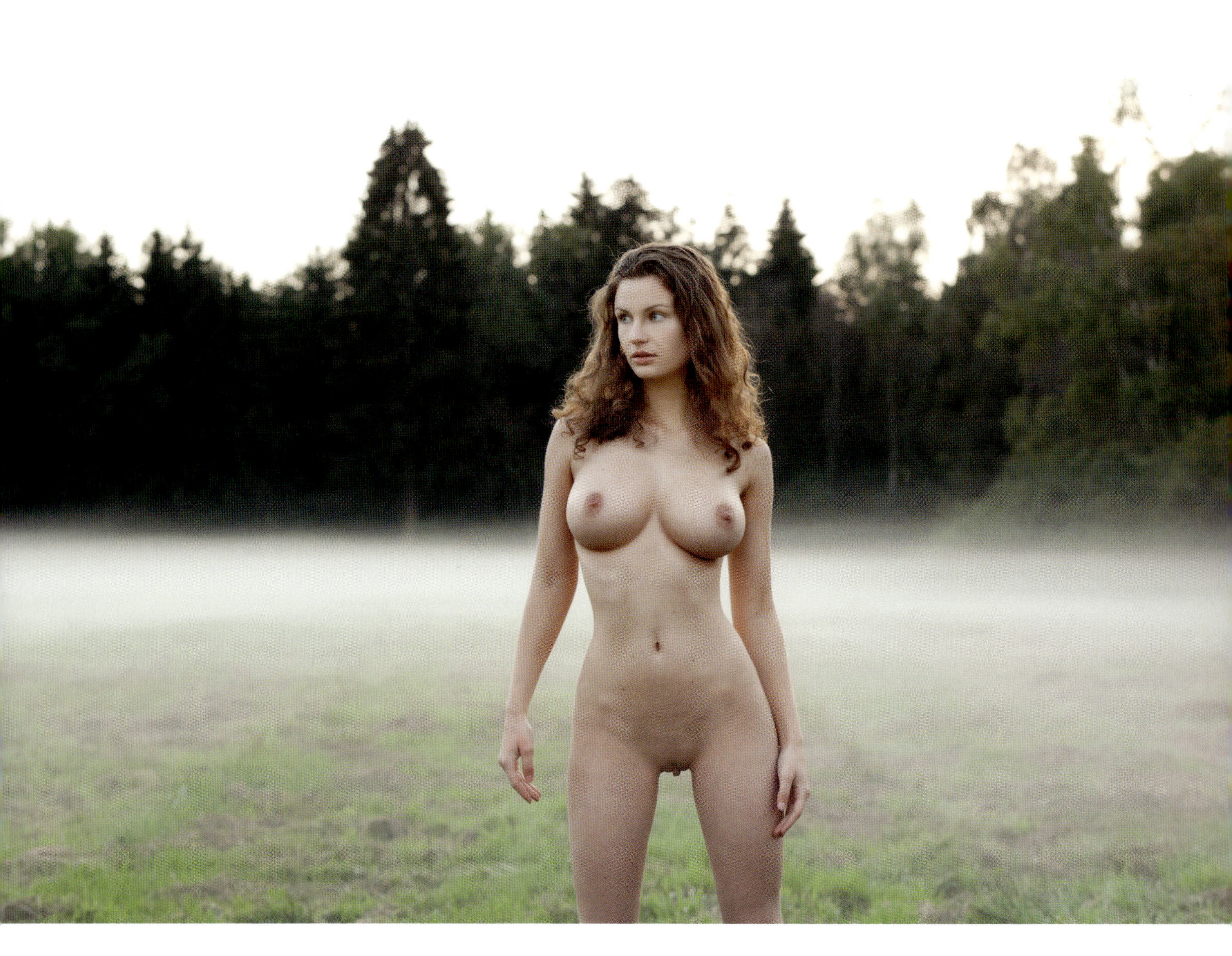

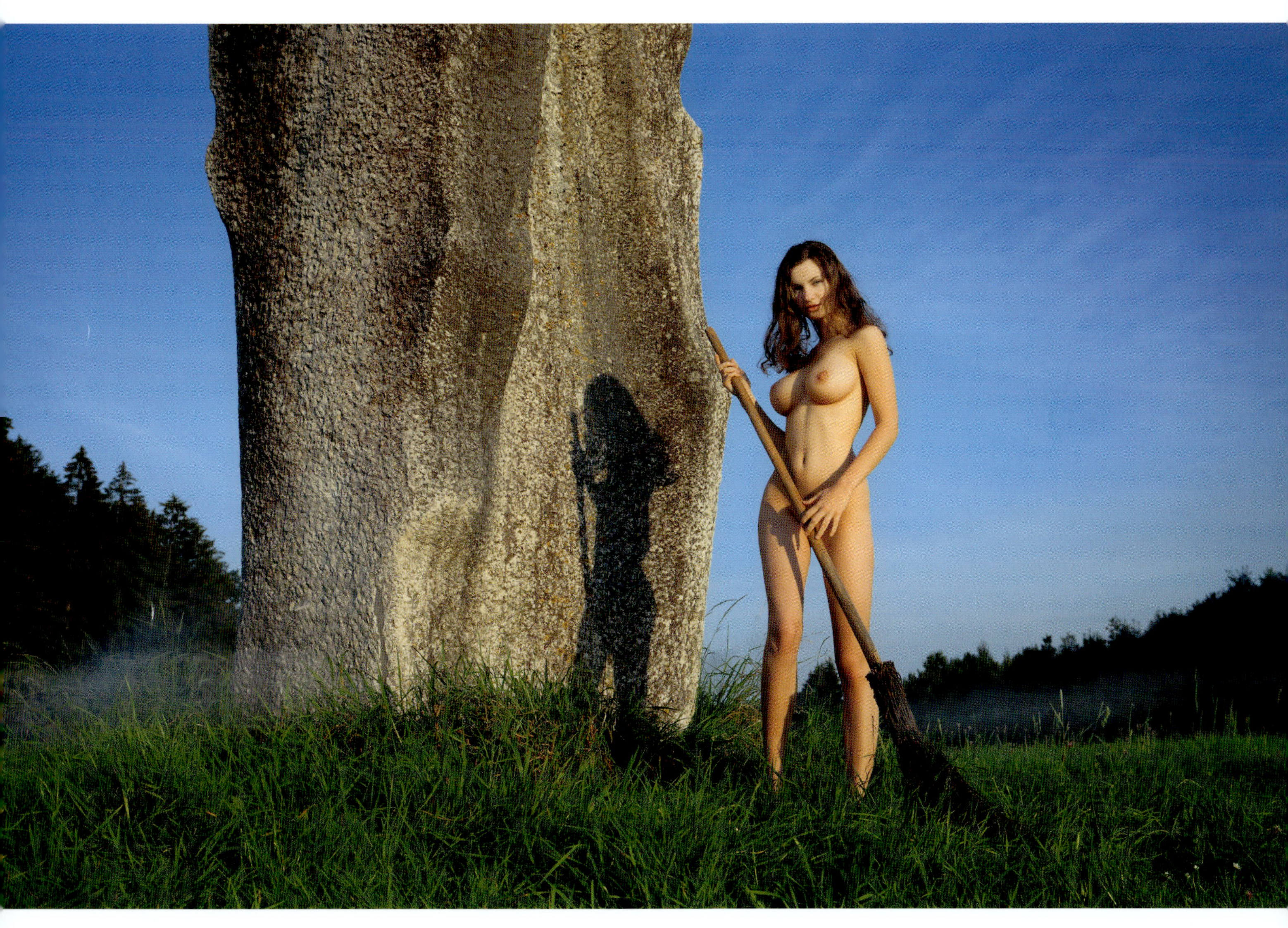

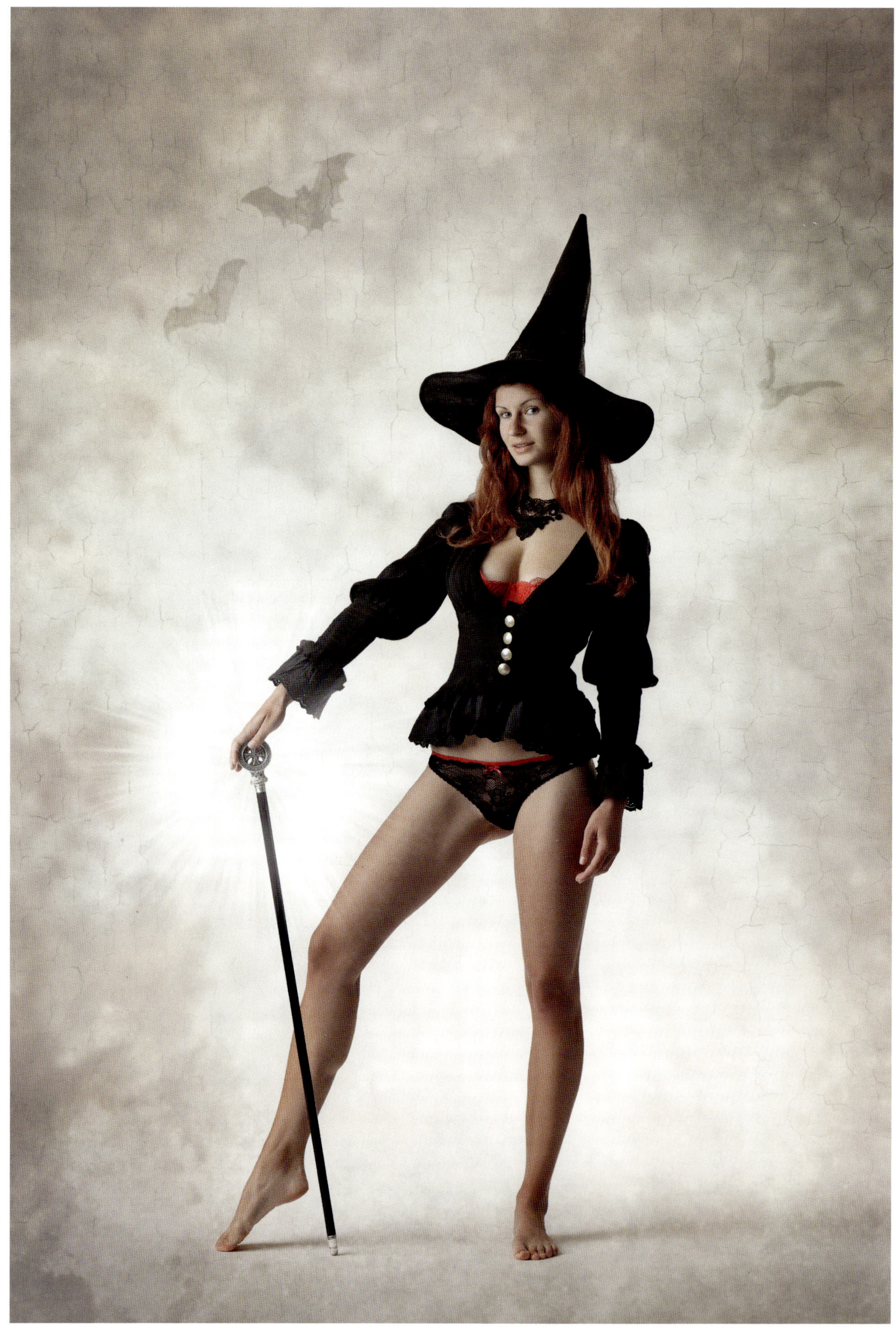

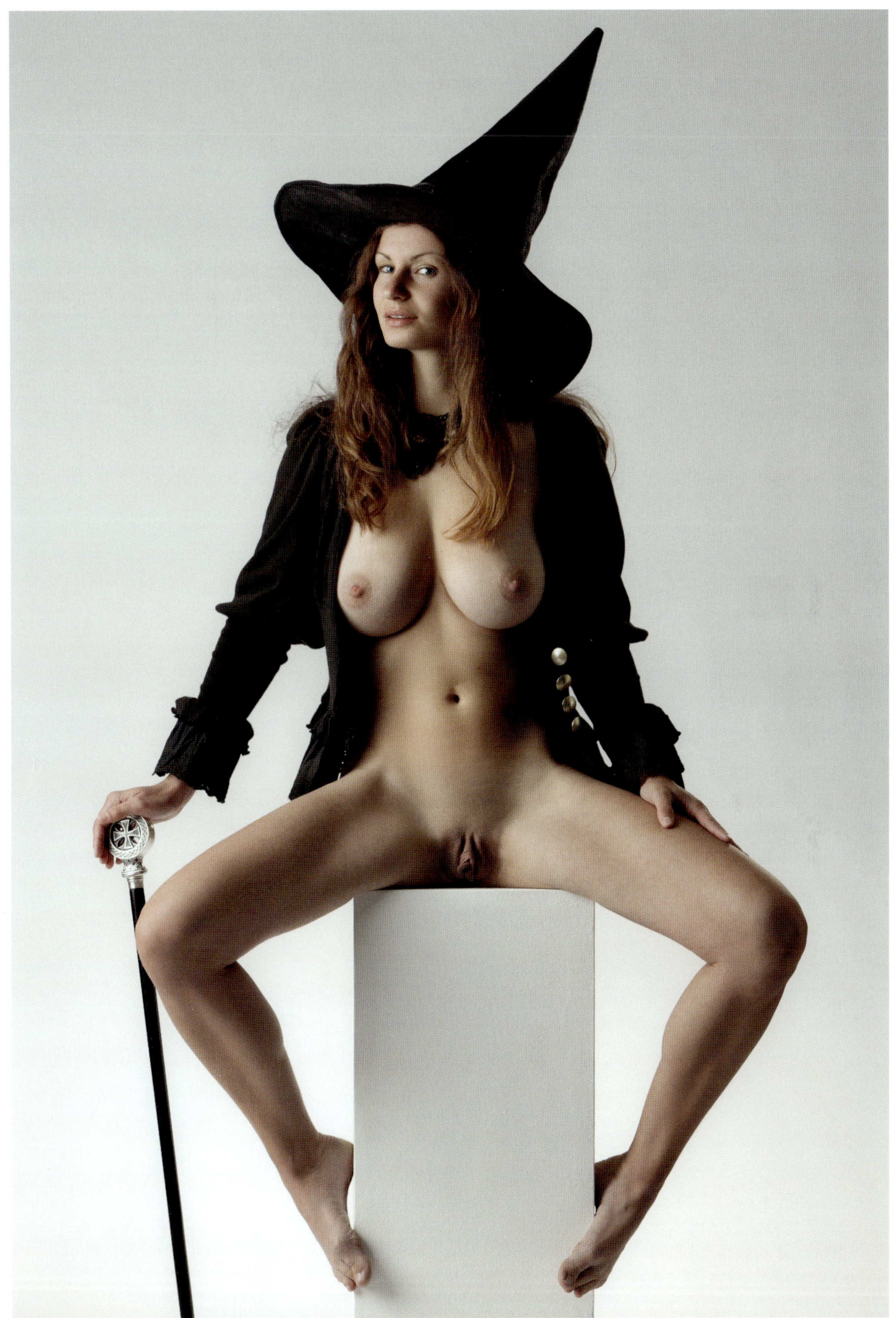

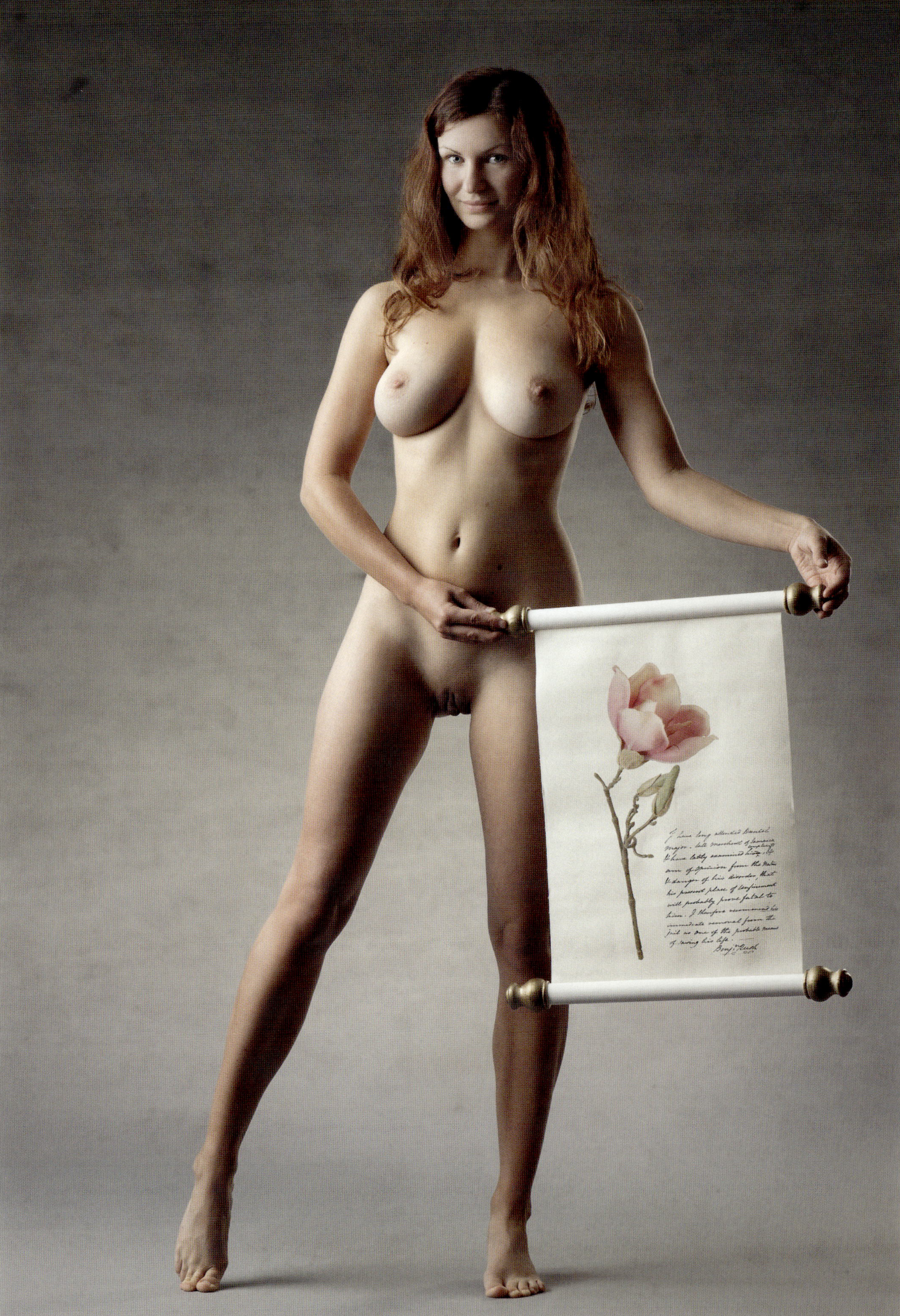

I have long attended Daniel
his present place of confinement
will probably prove fatal to
immediate removal from the
jail as one of the probable means
of saving his life.

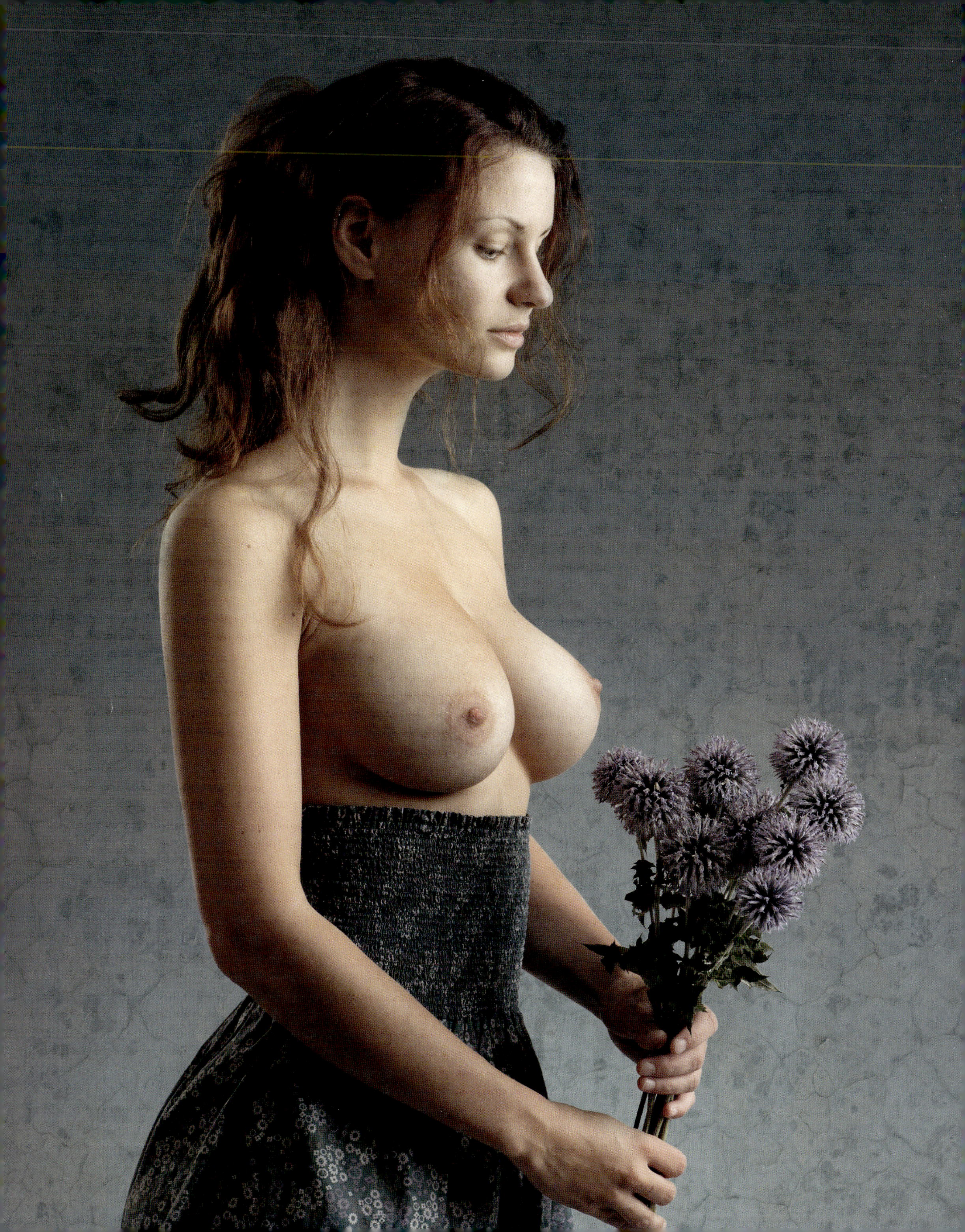

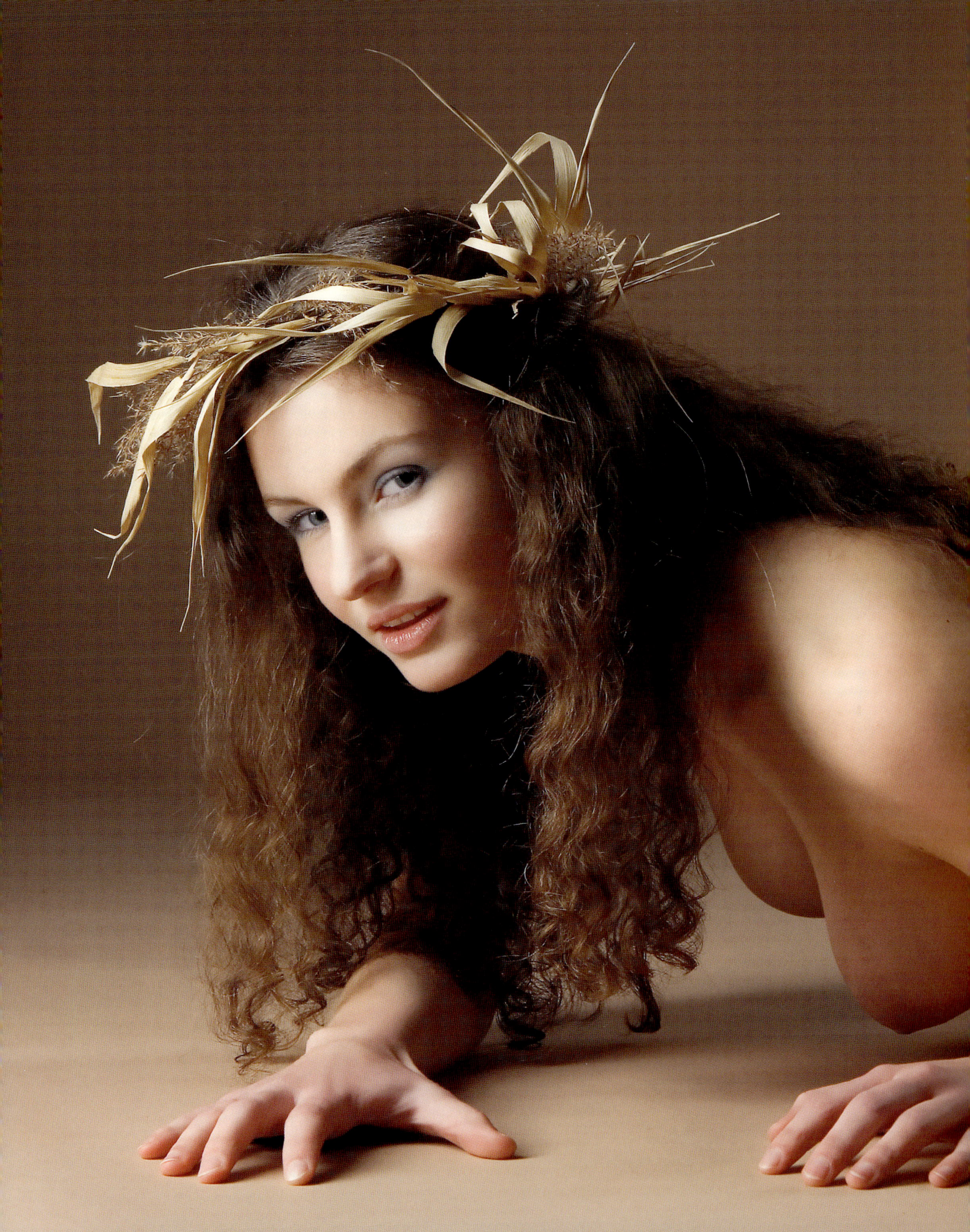

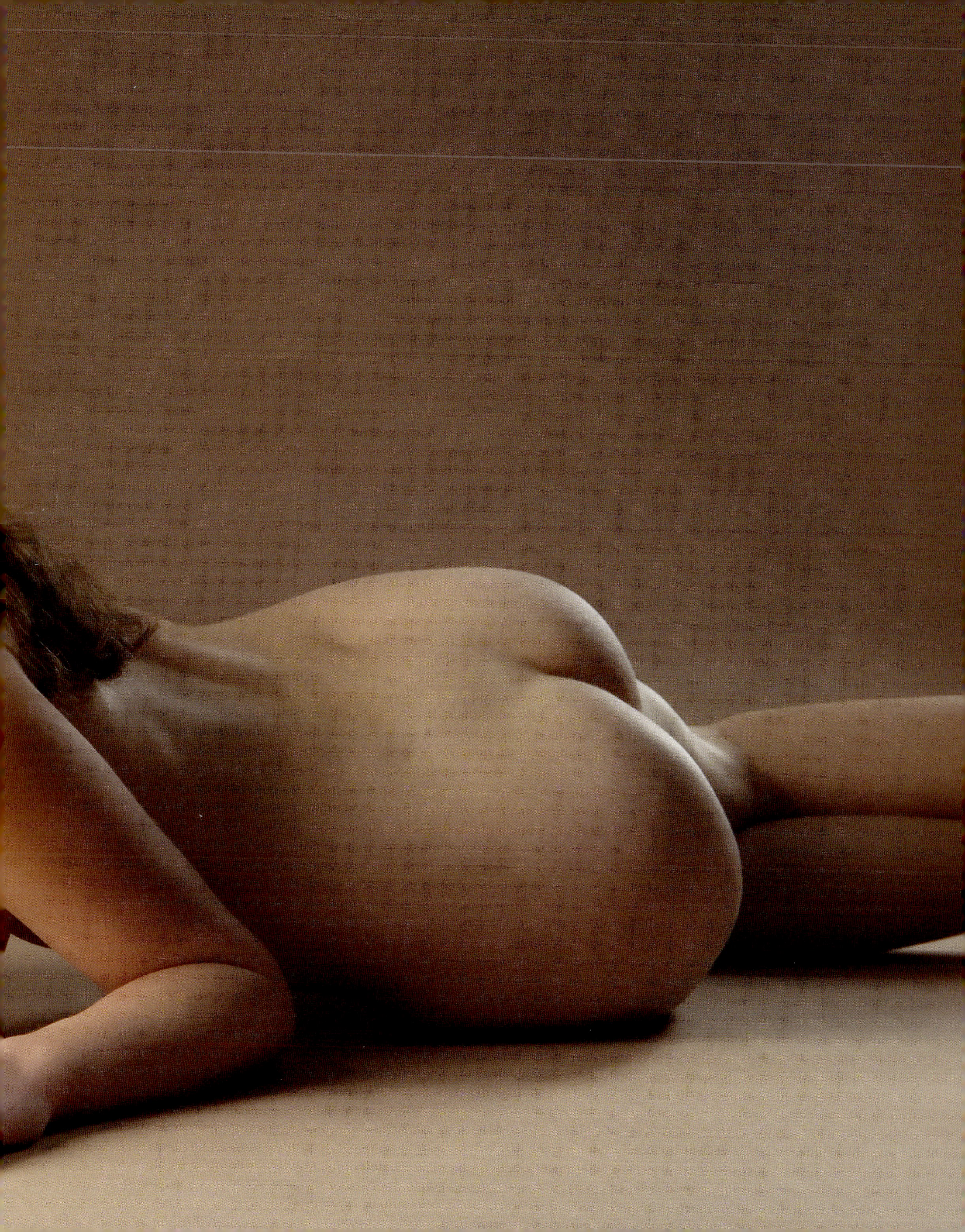

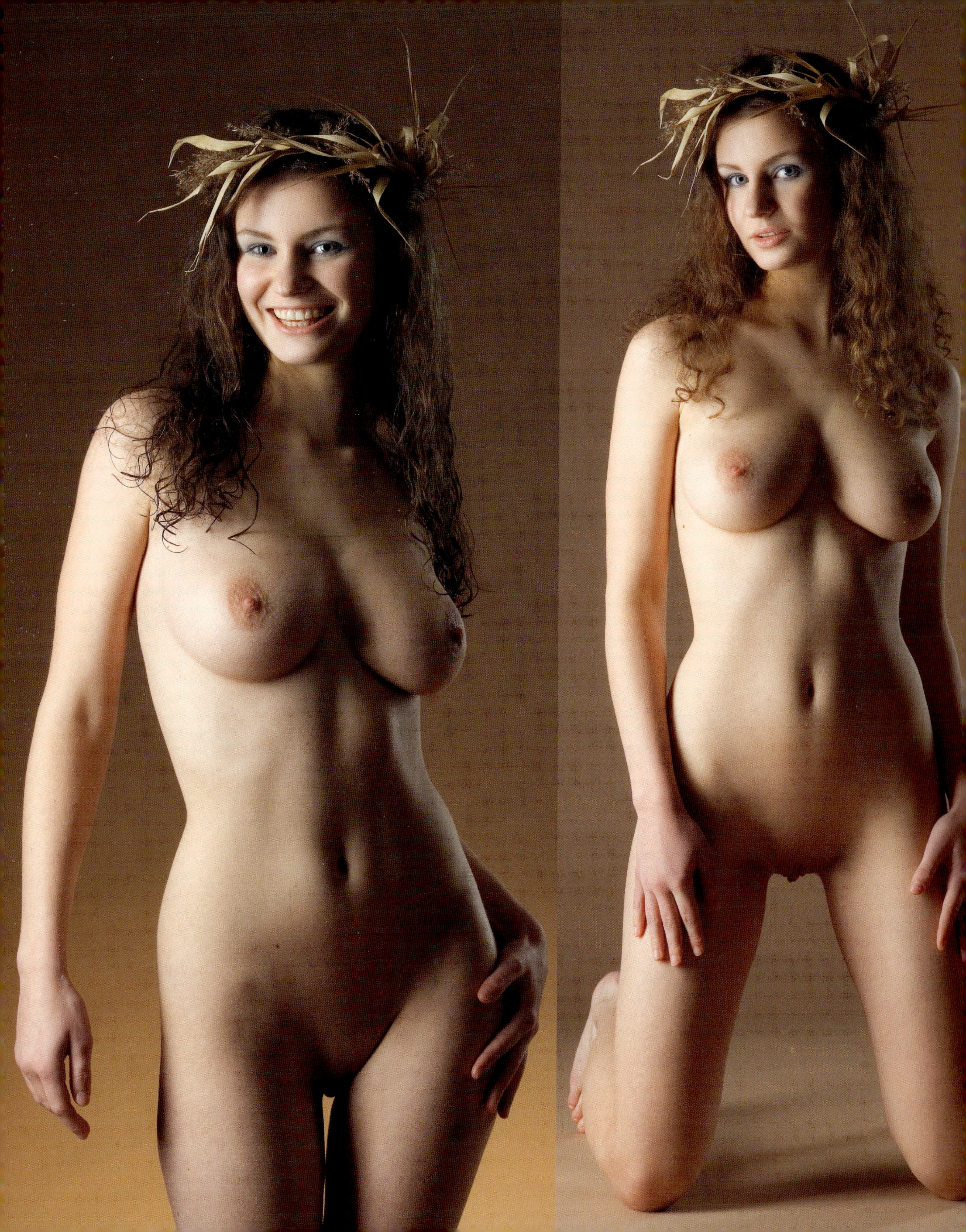

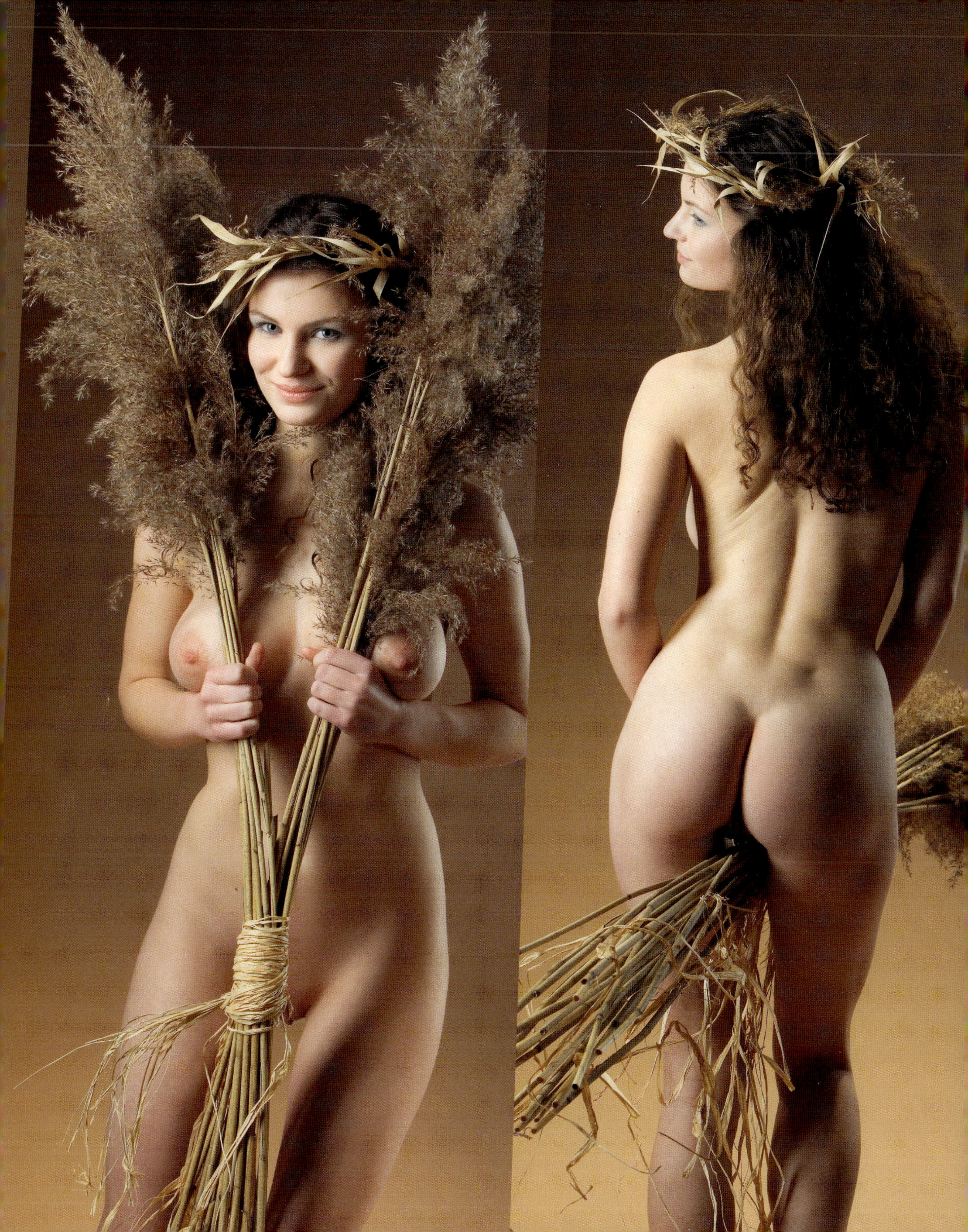

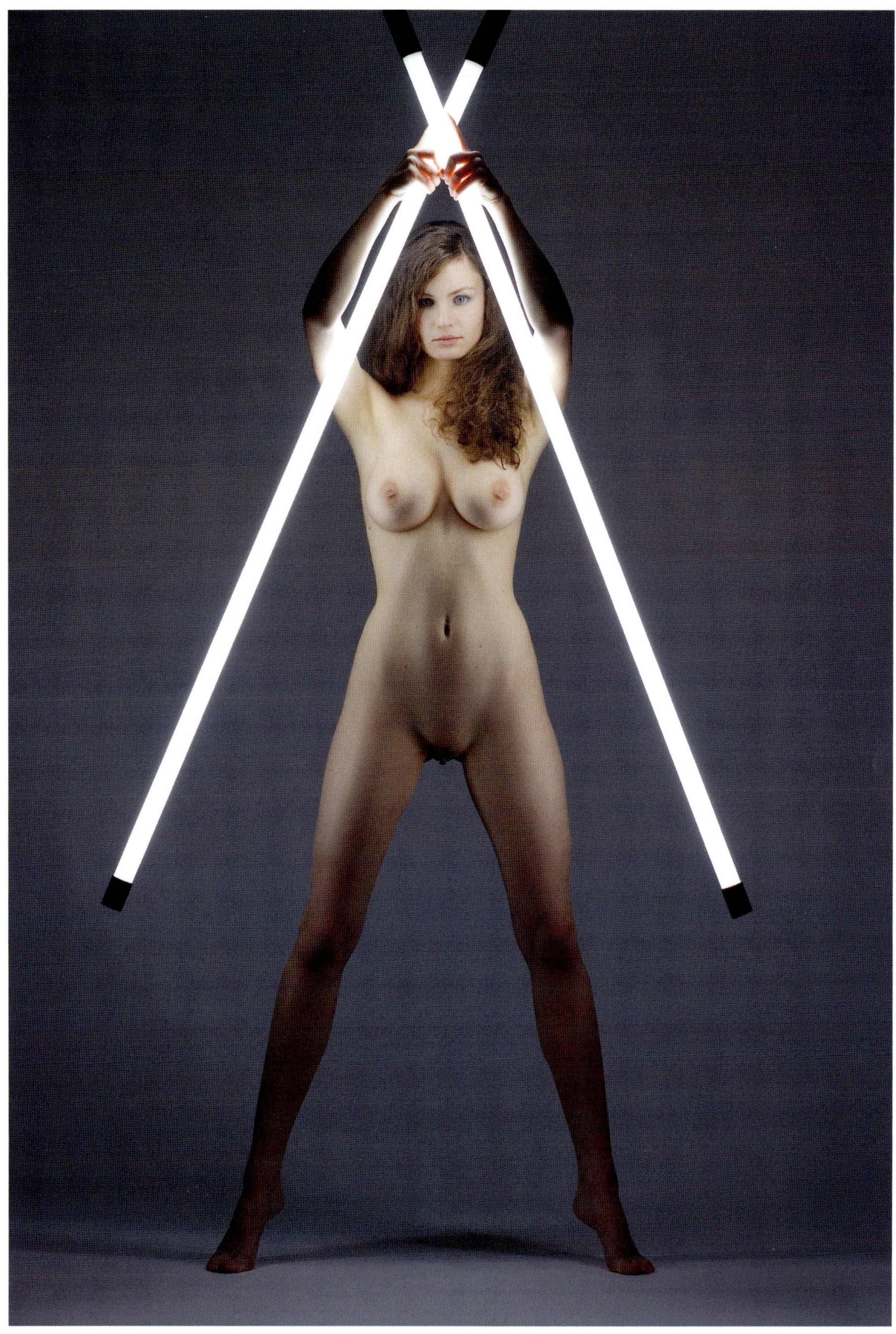

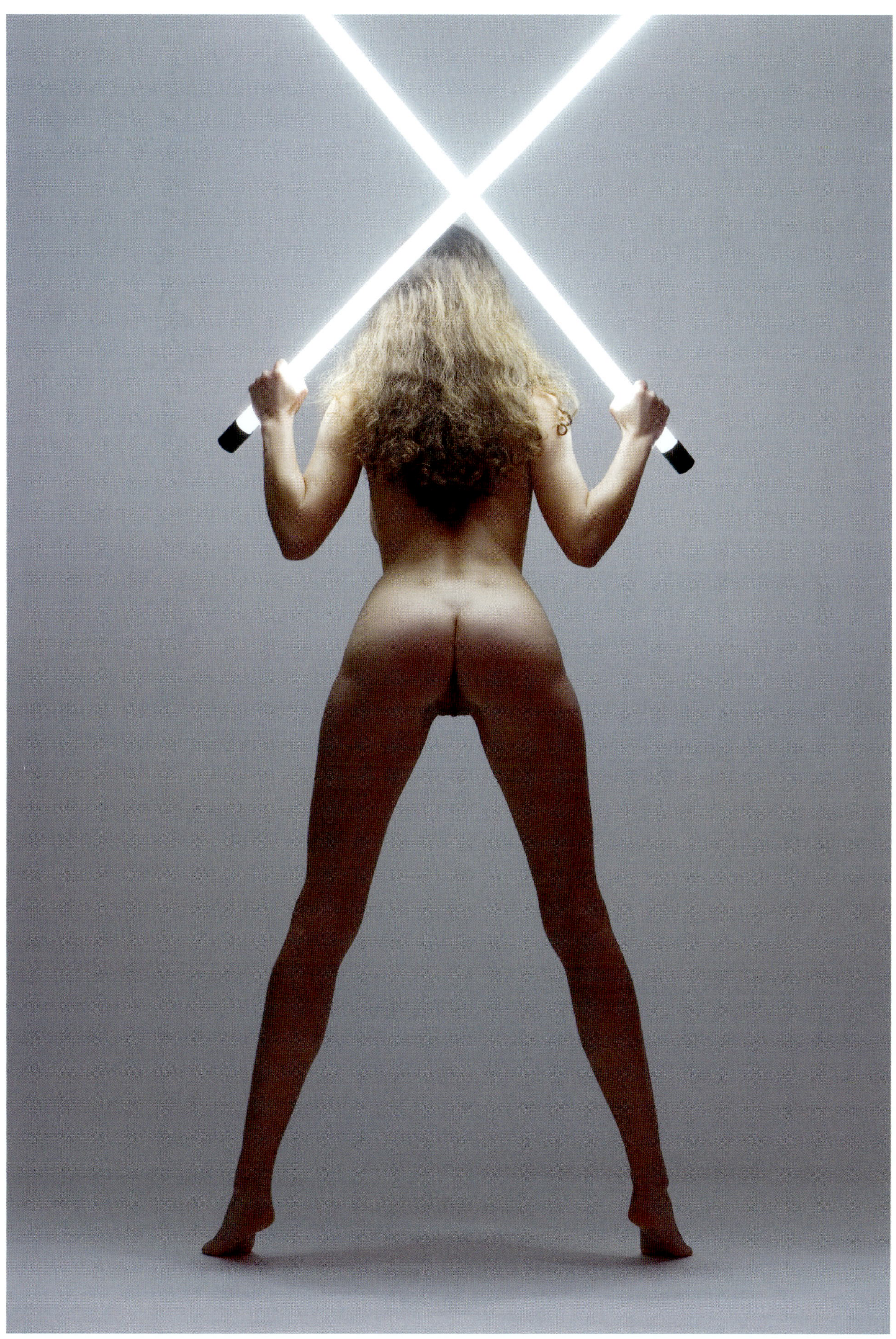

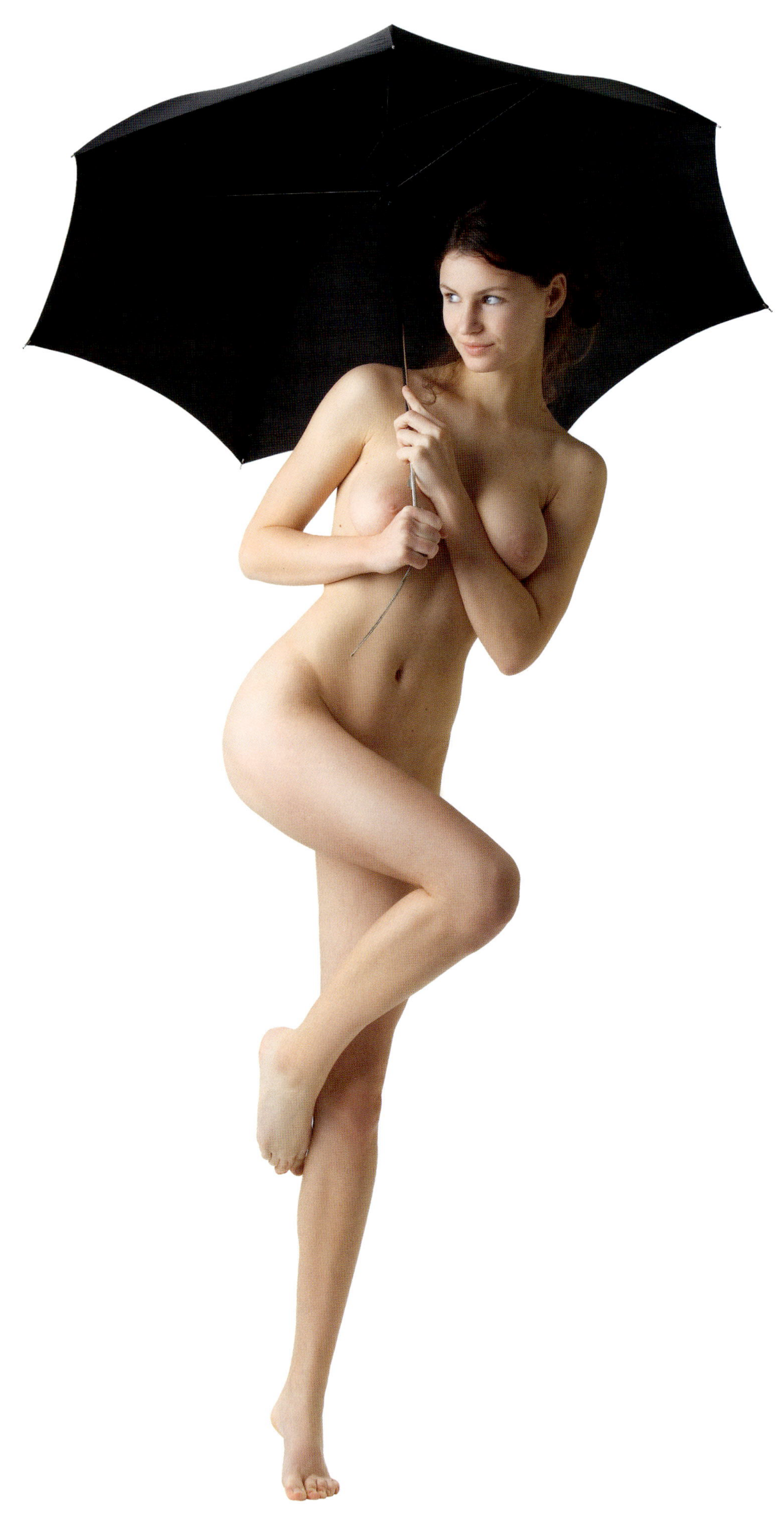

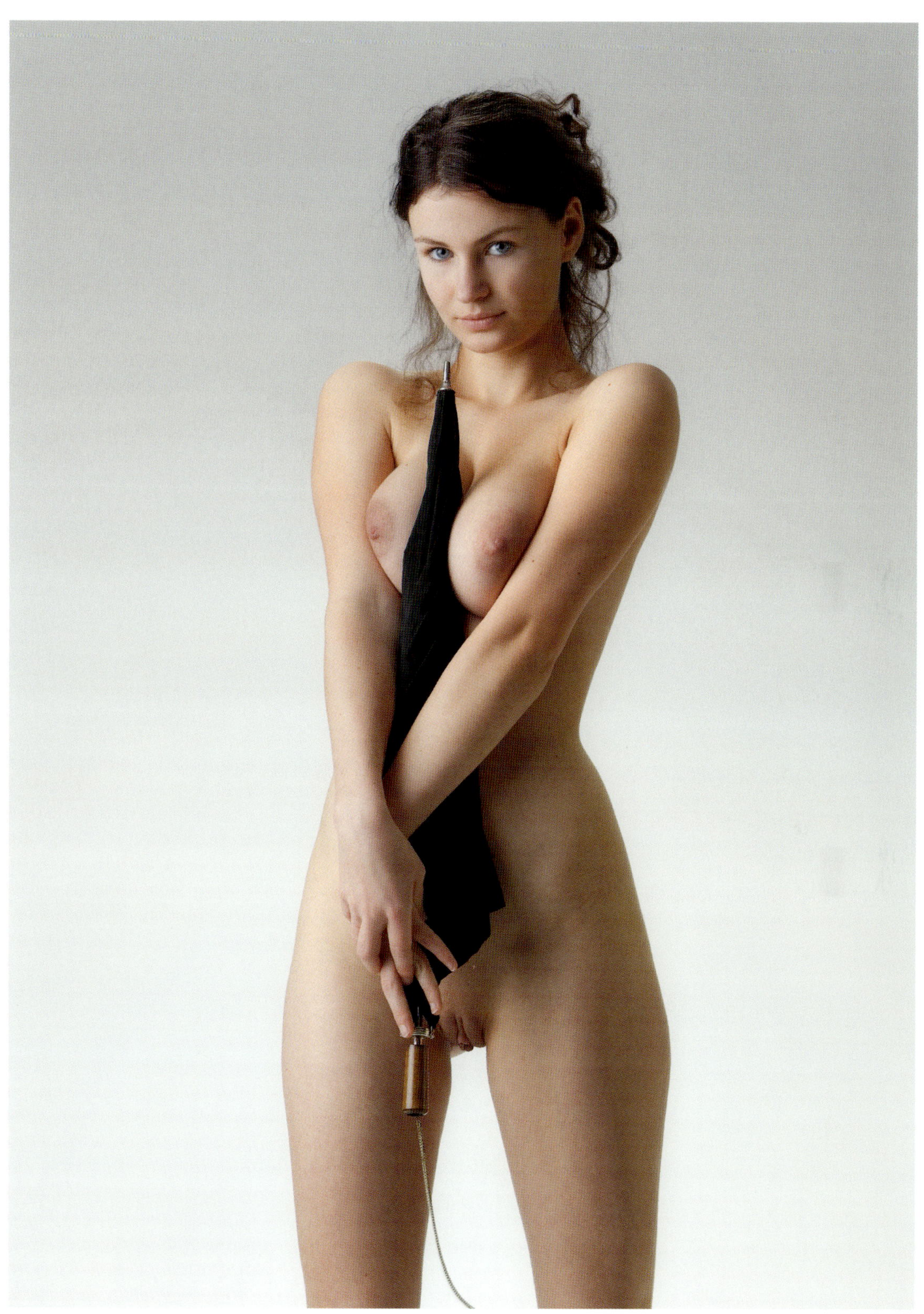

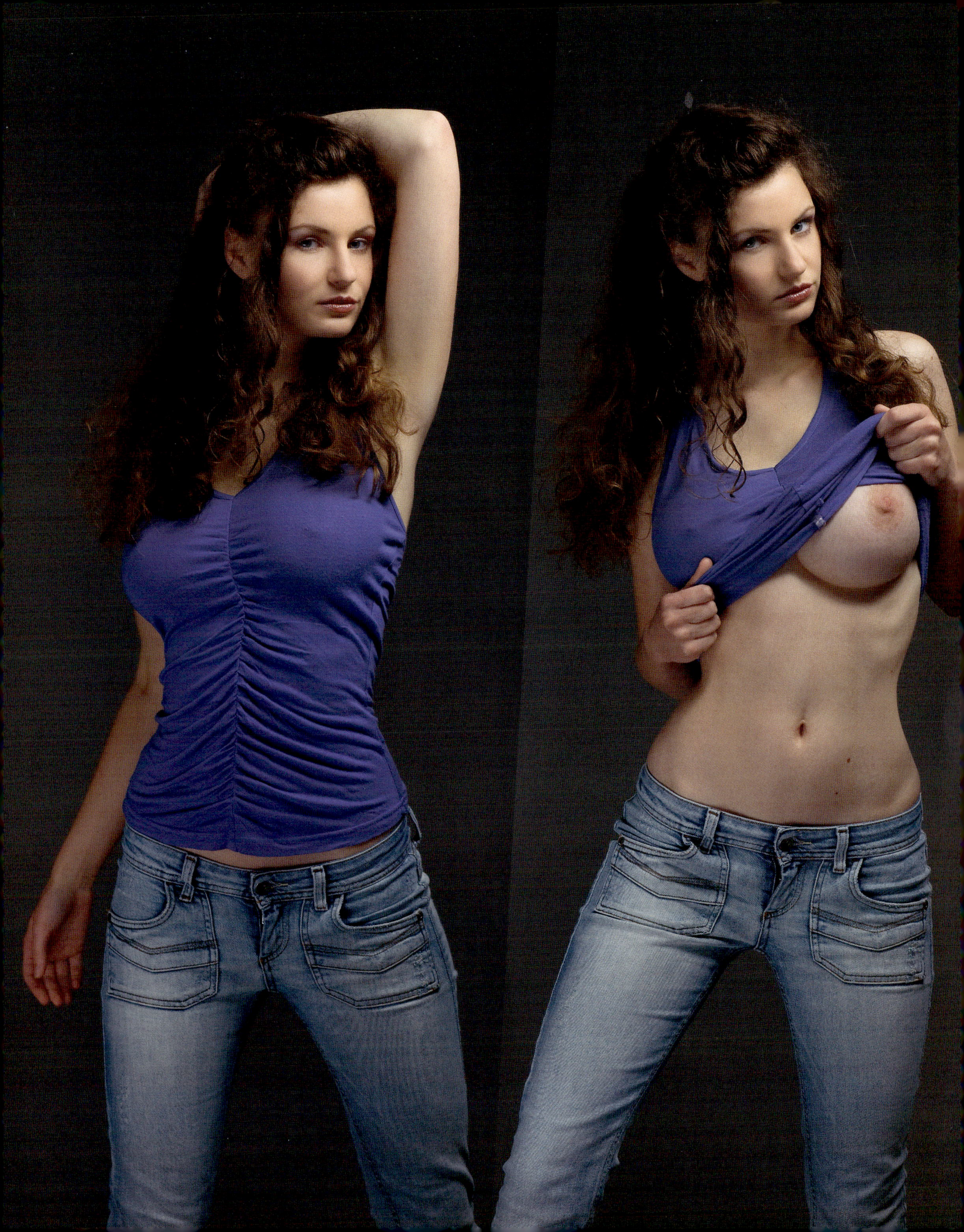

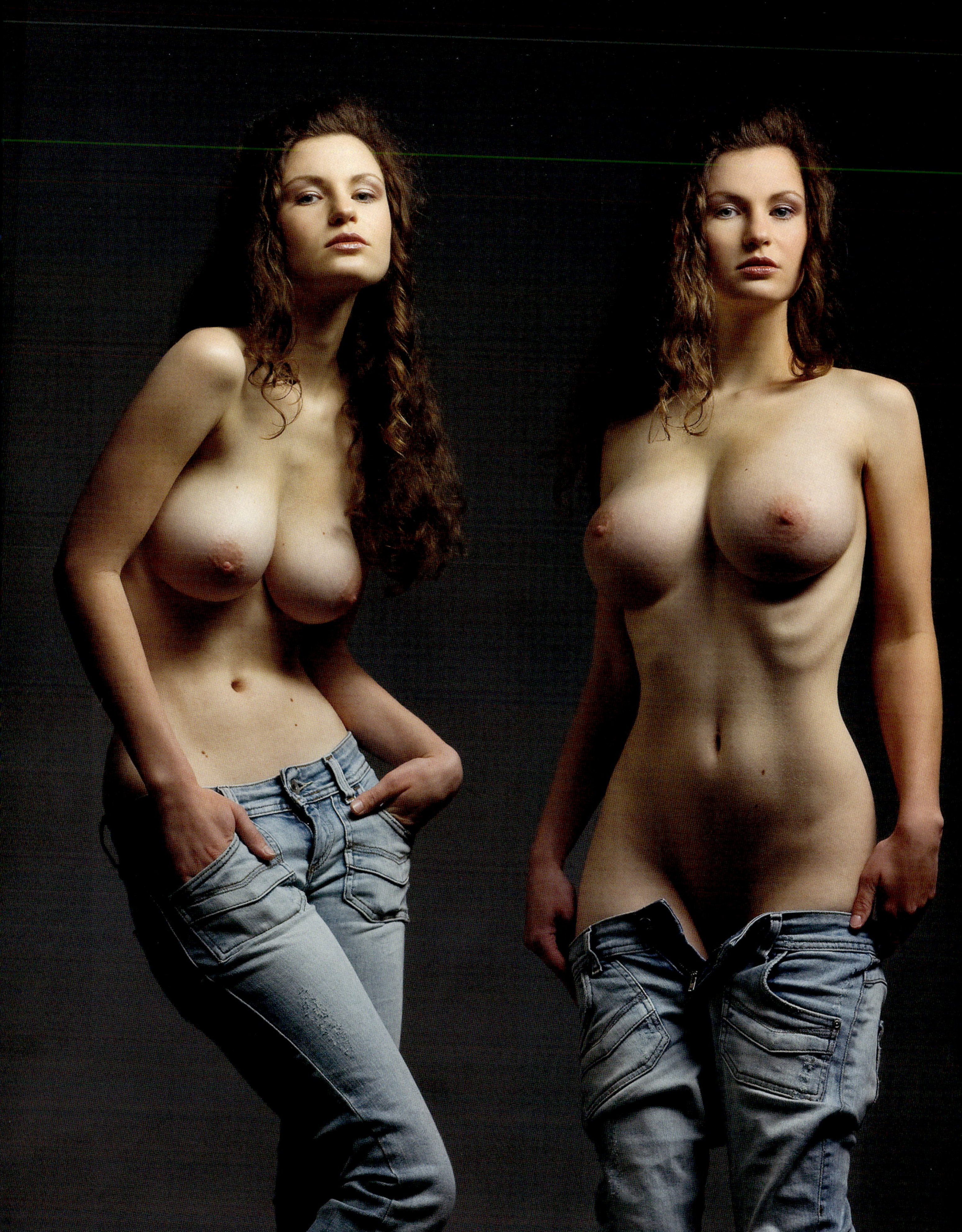

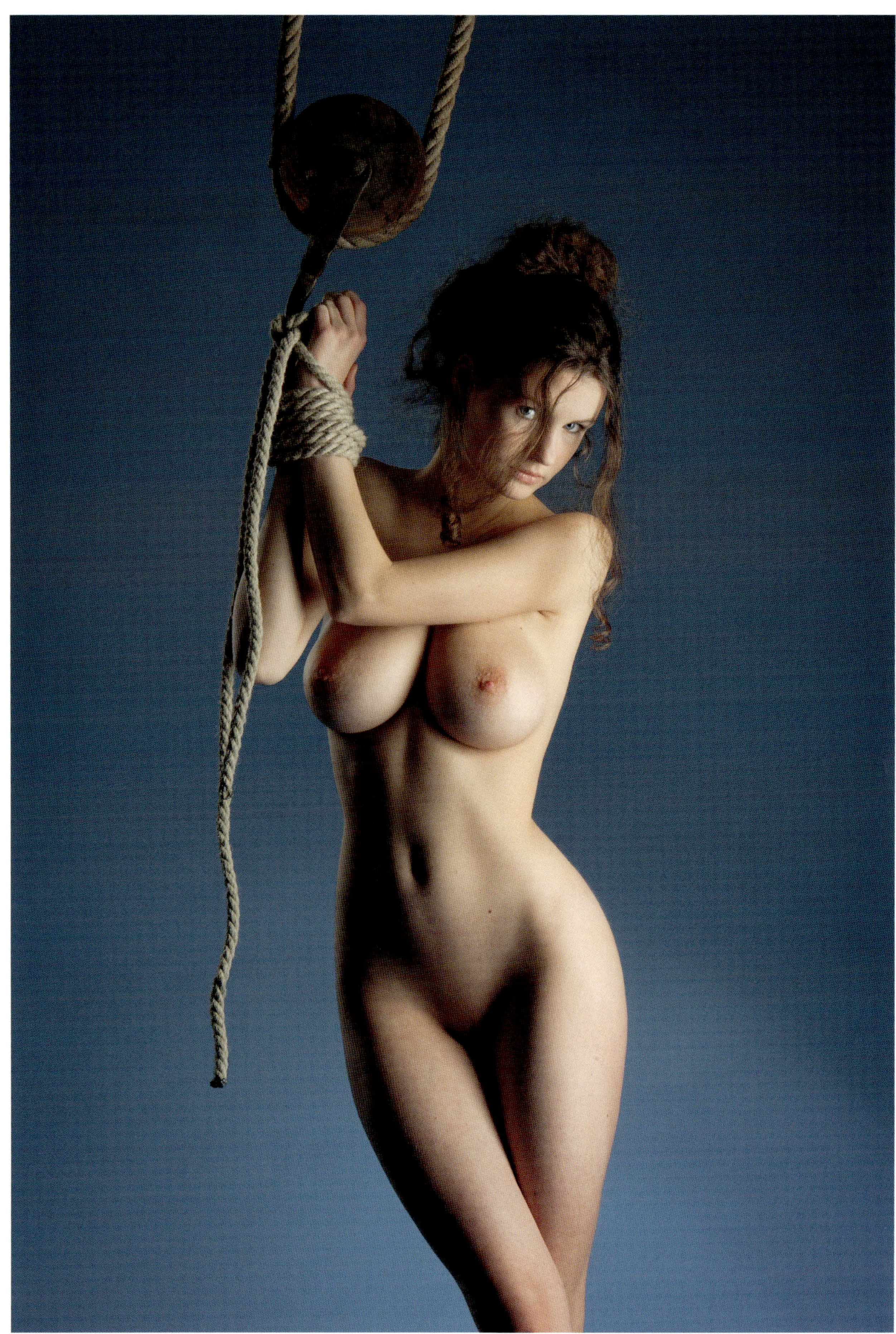

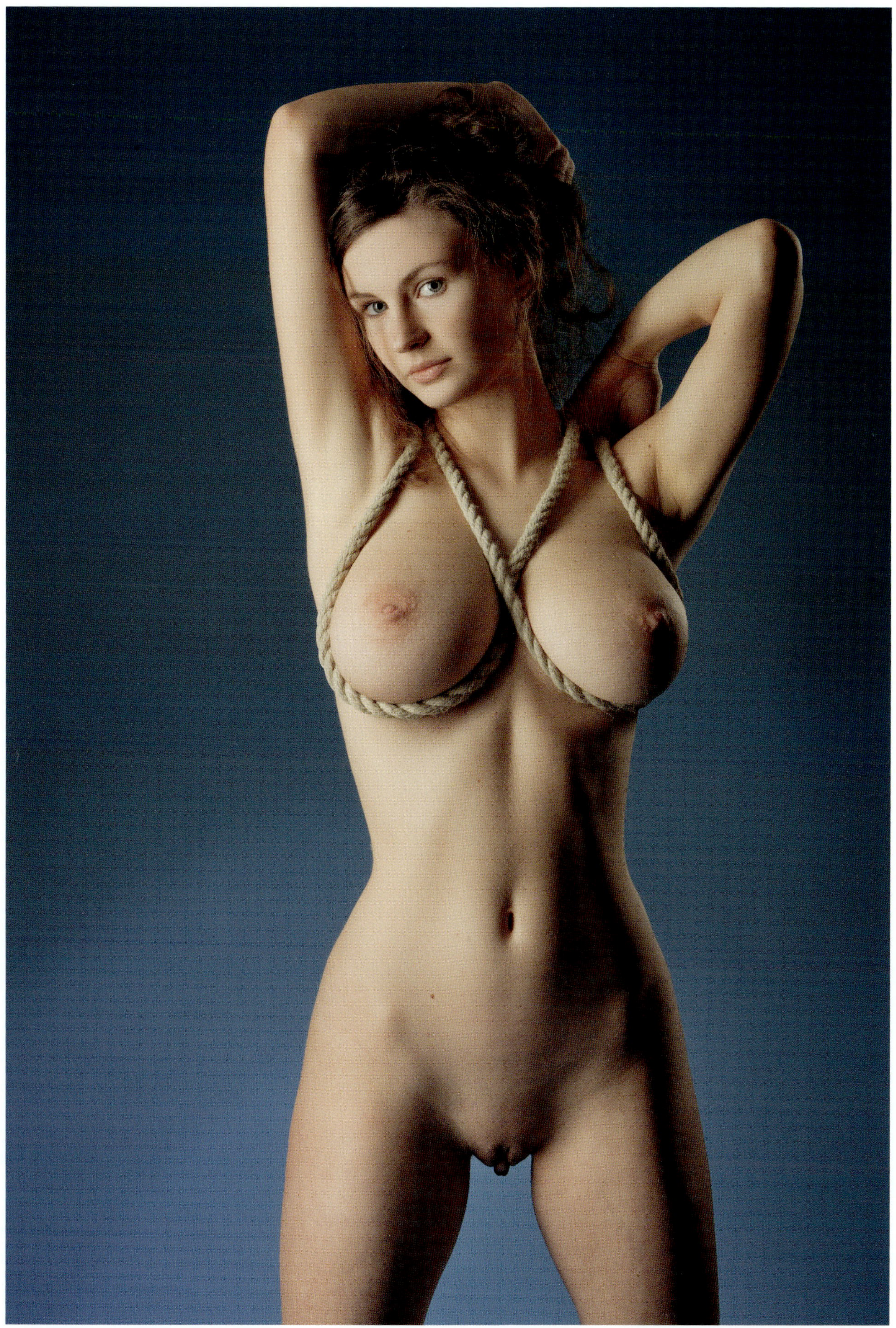

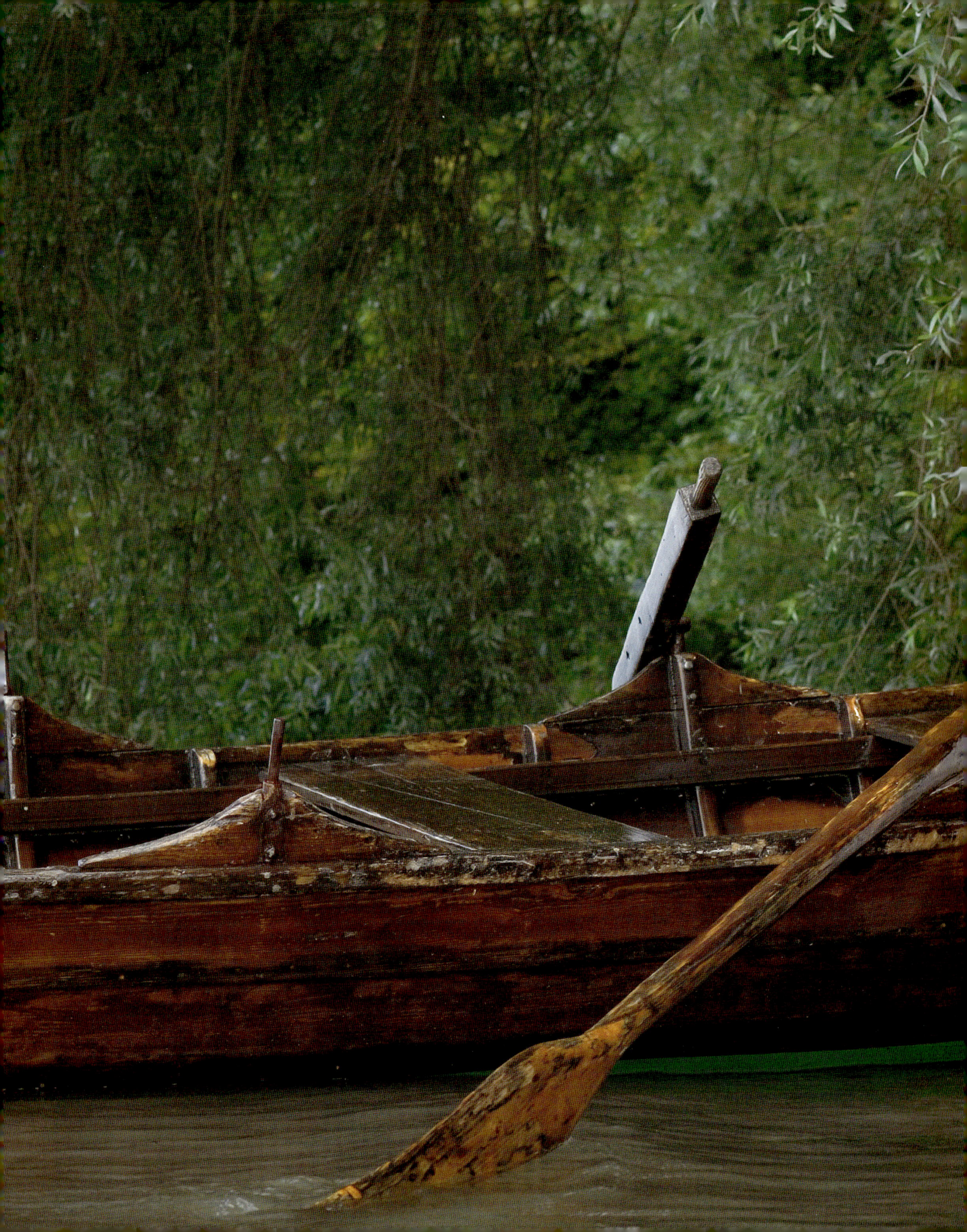

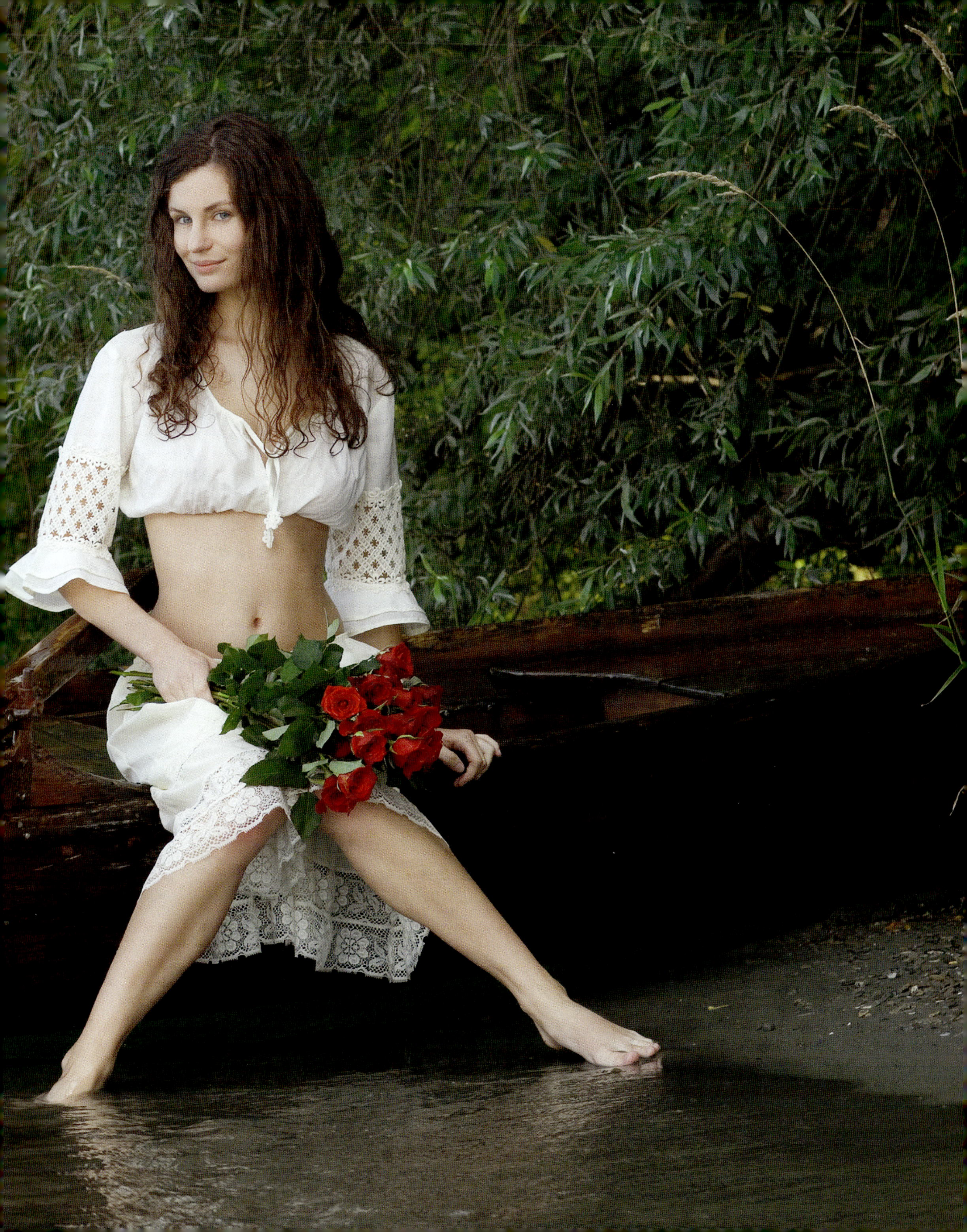

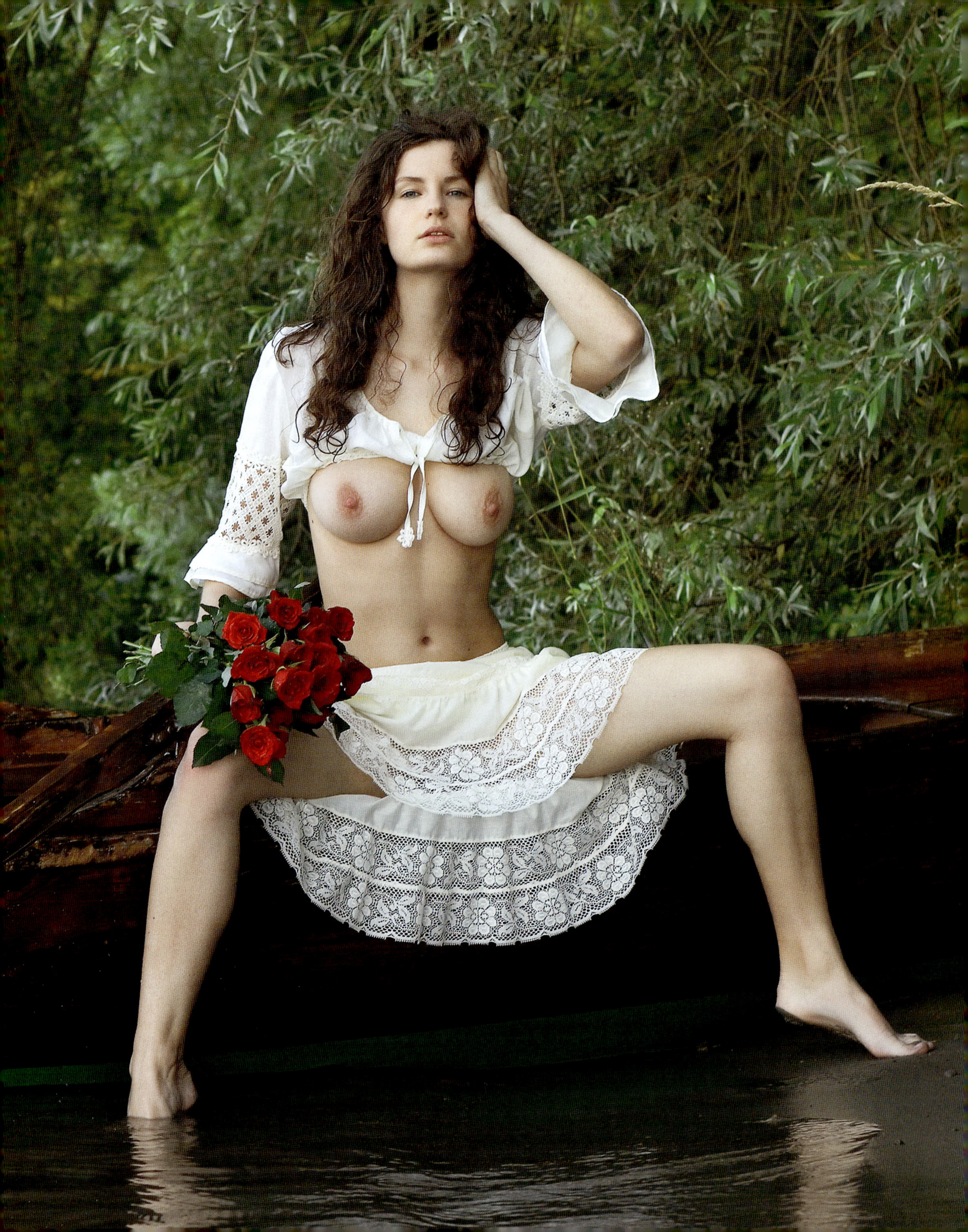

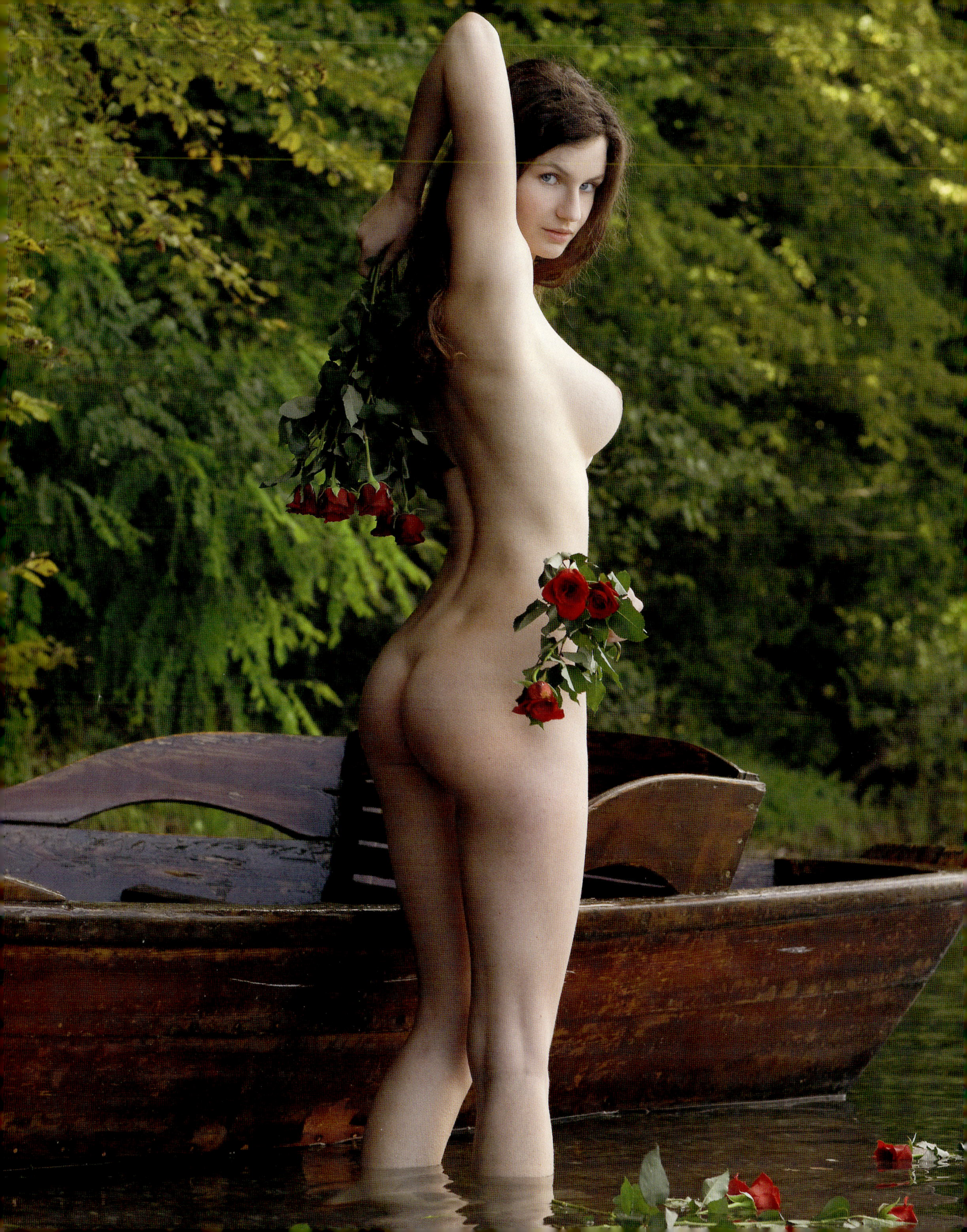

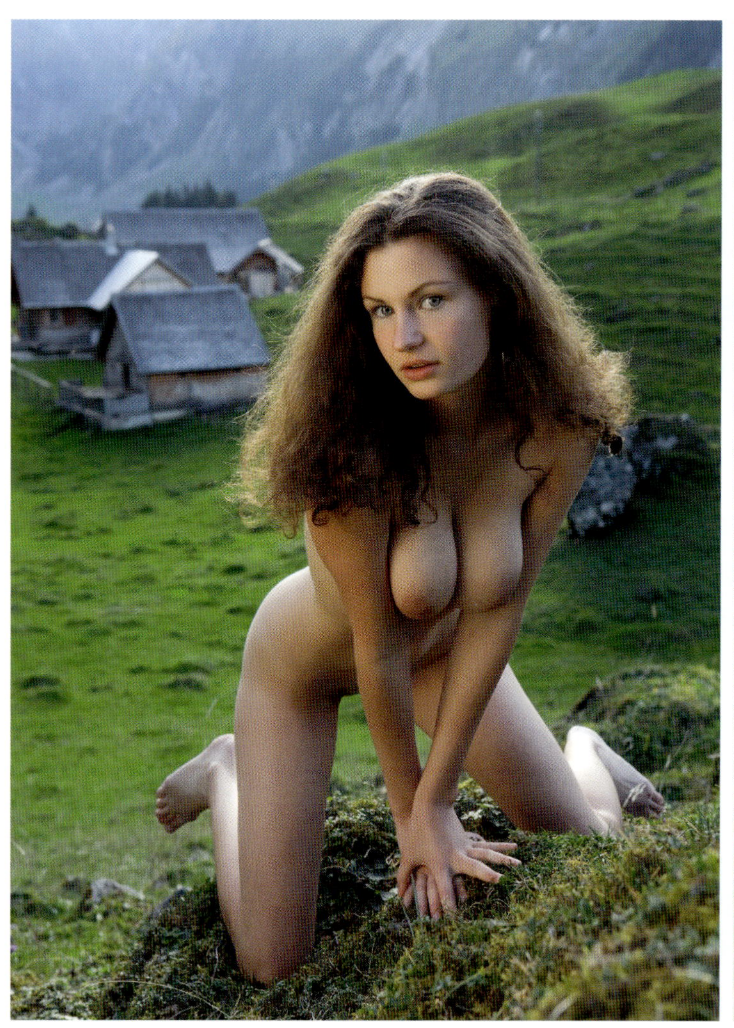

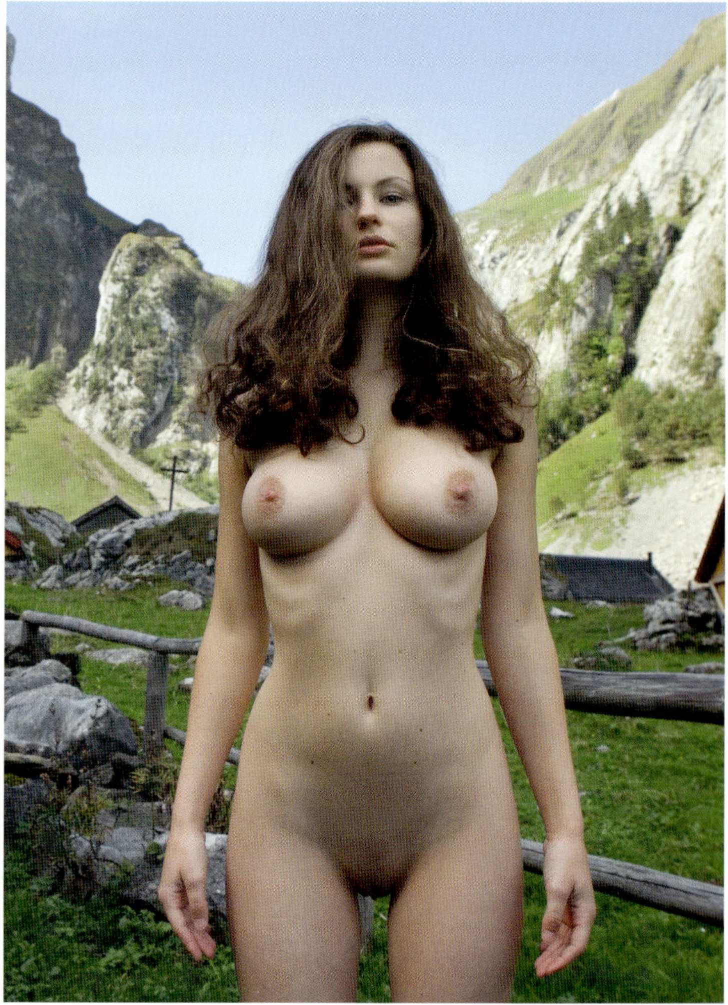

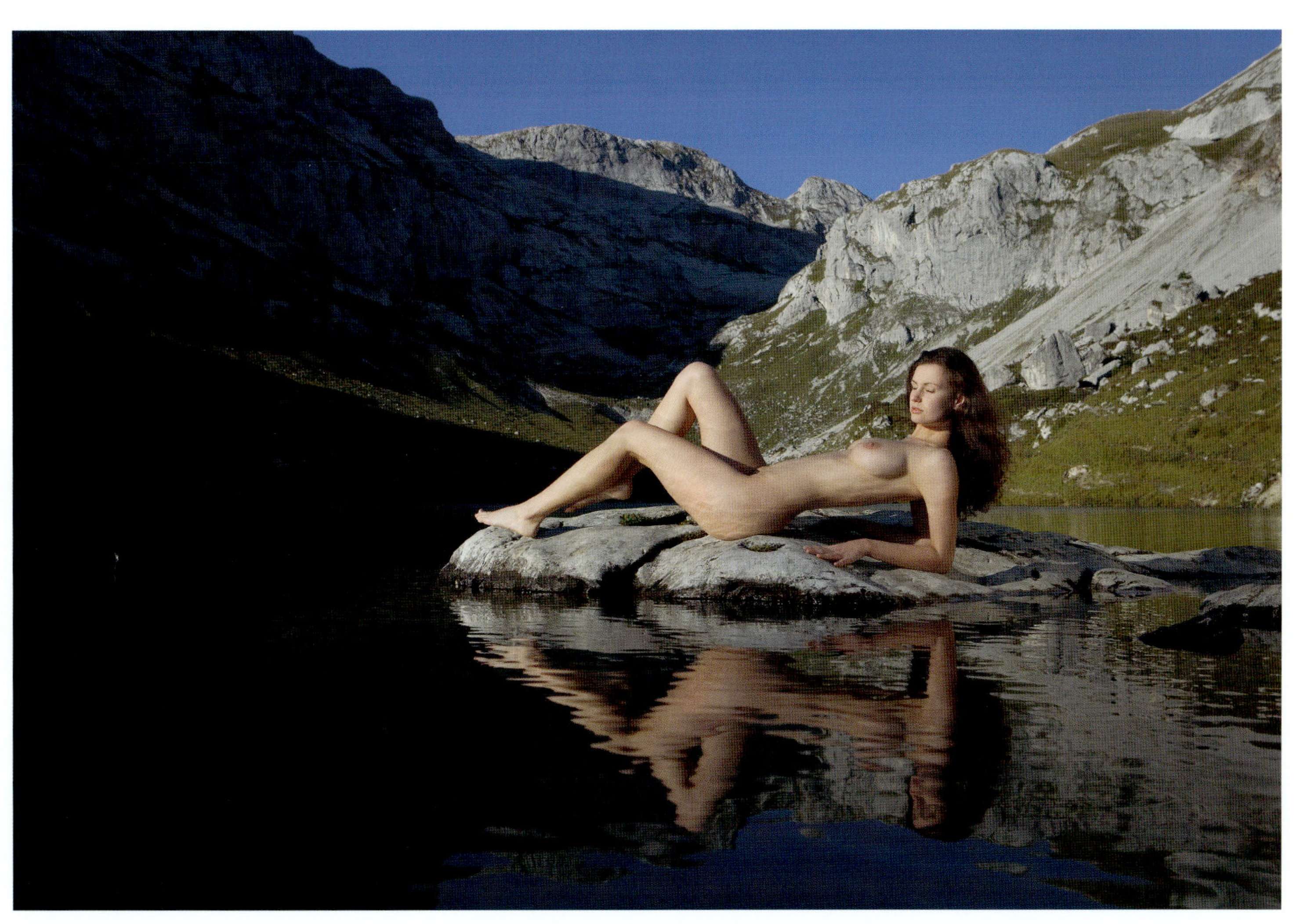

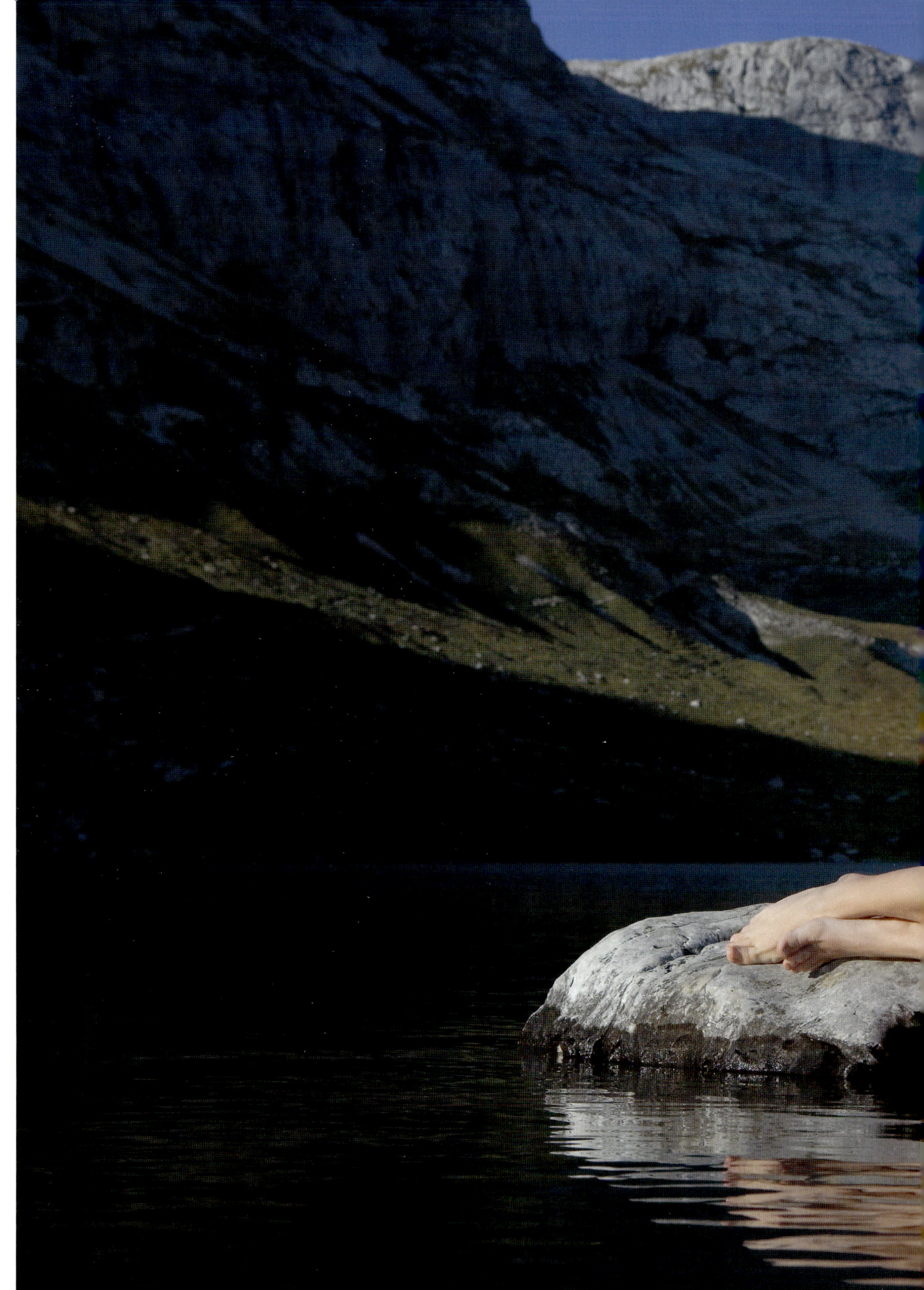

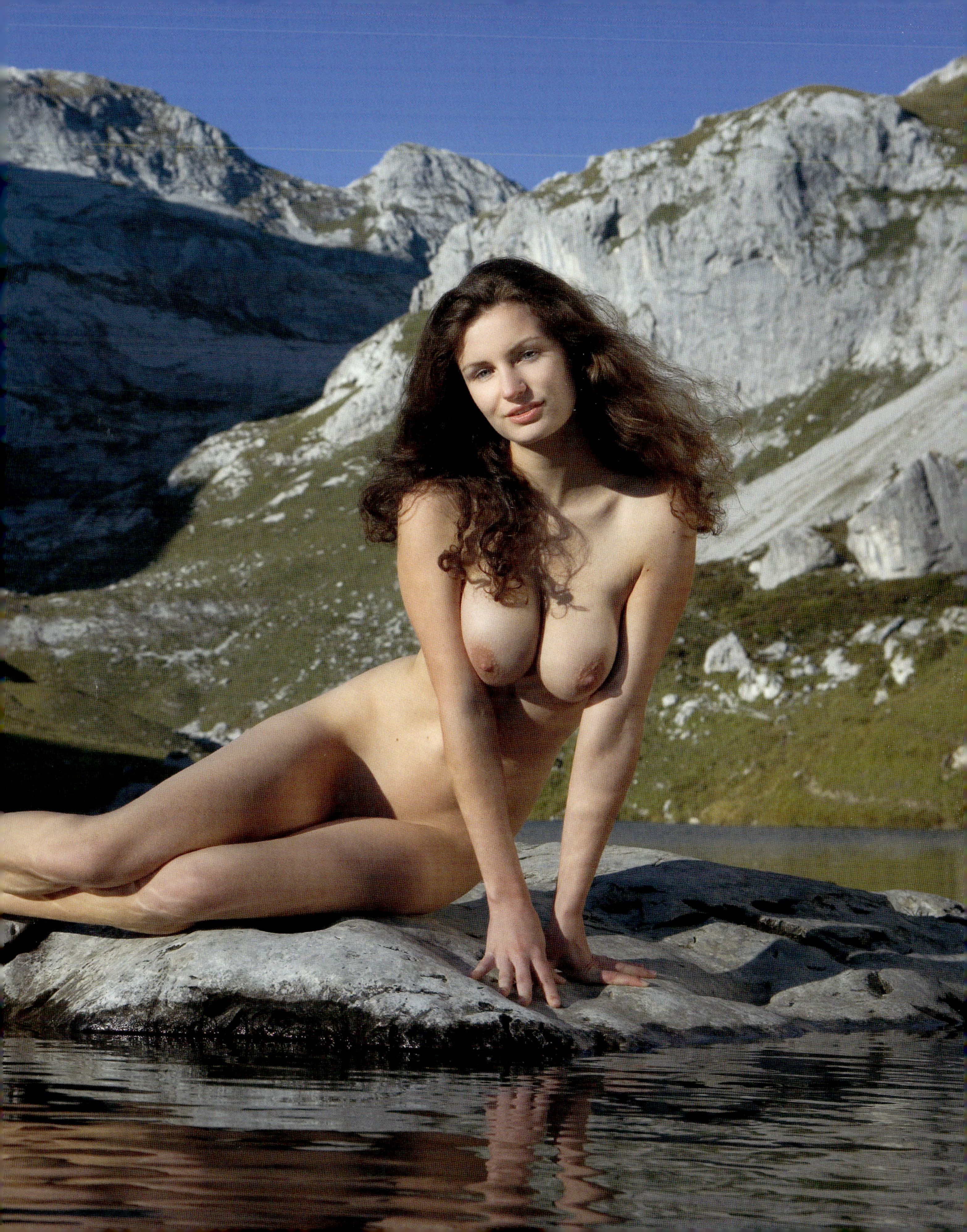

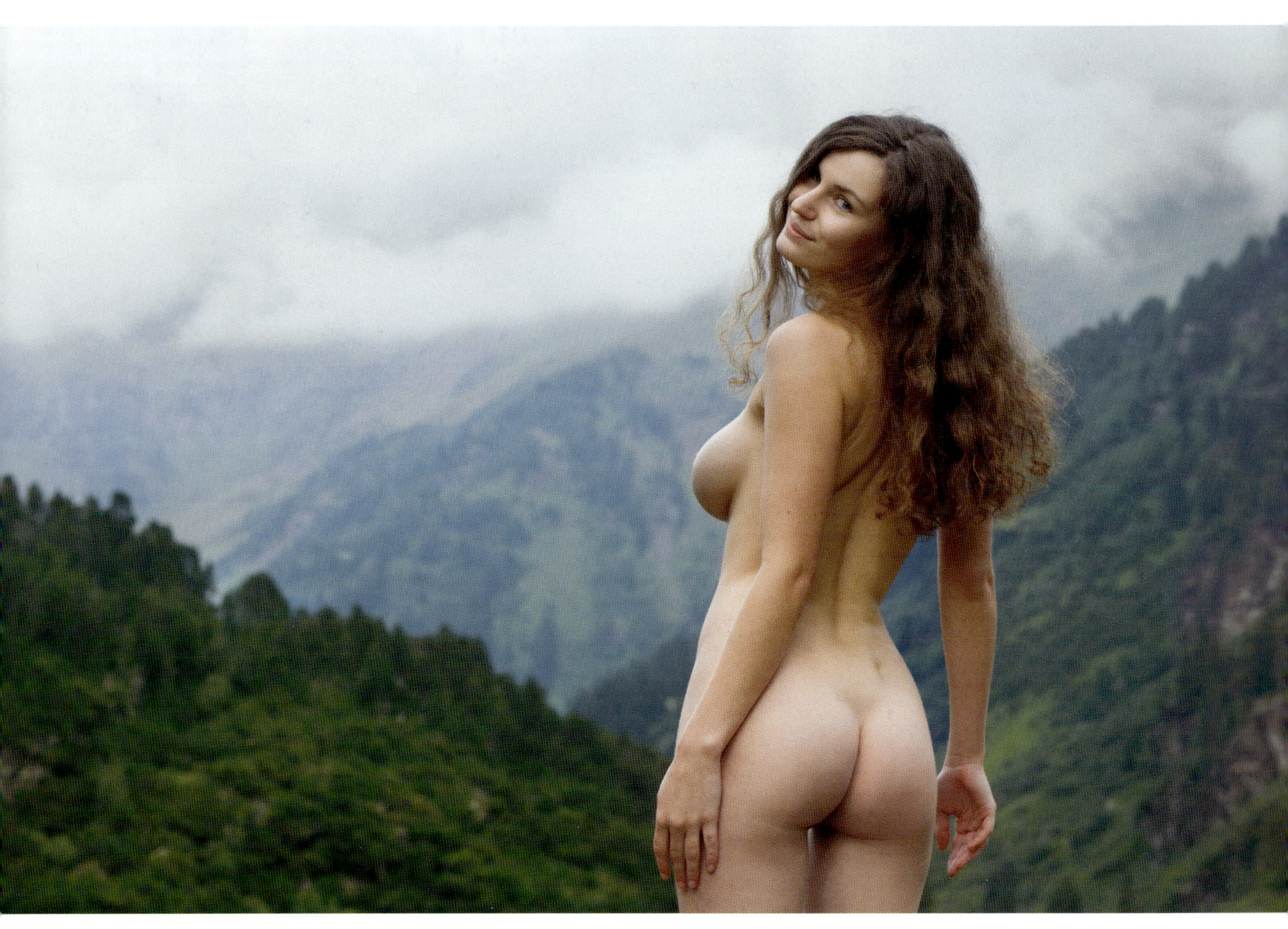

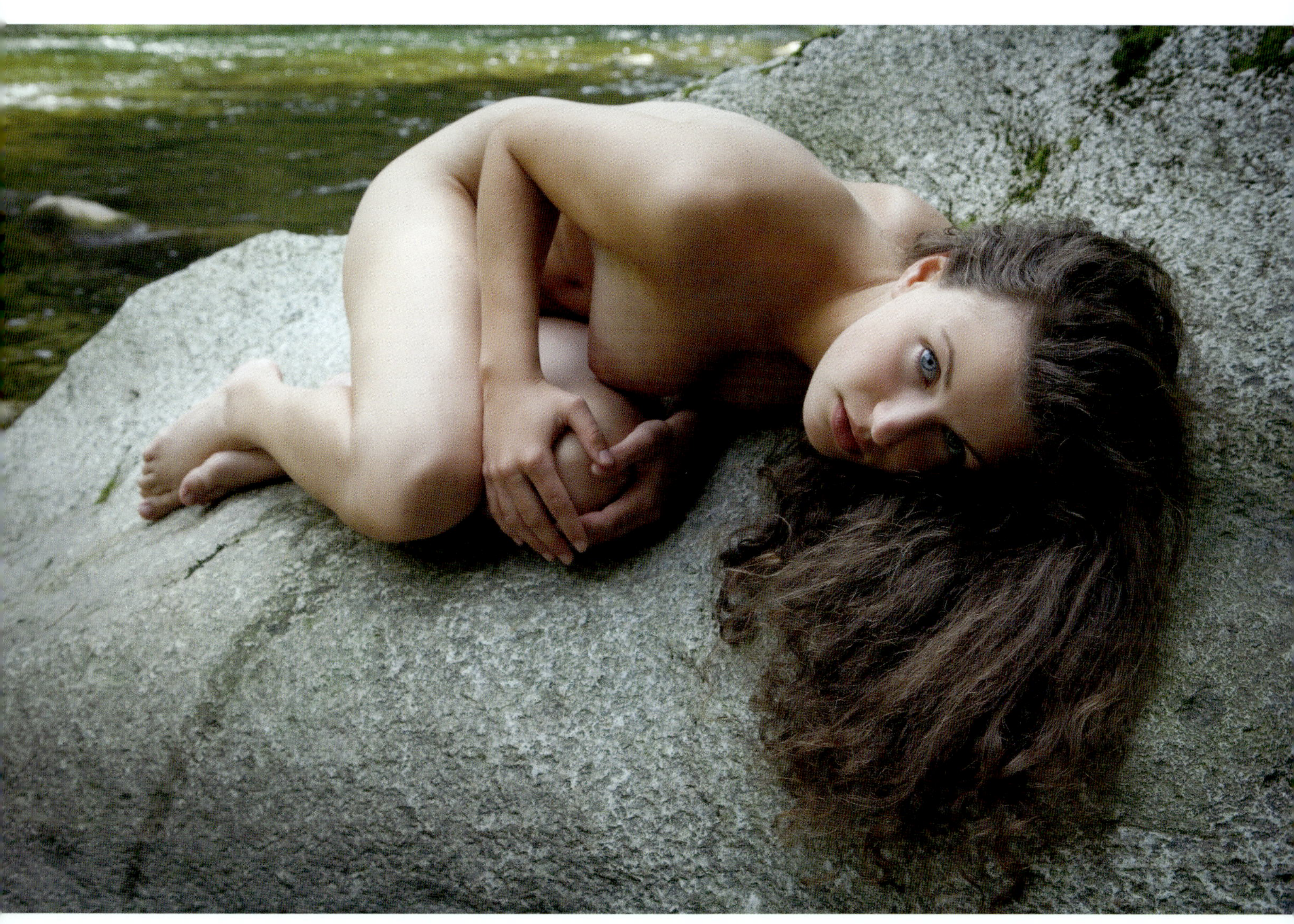

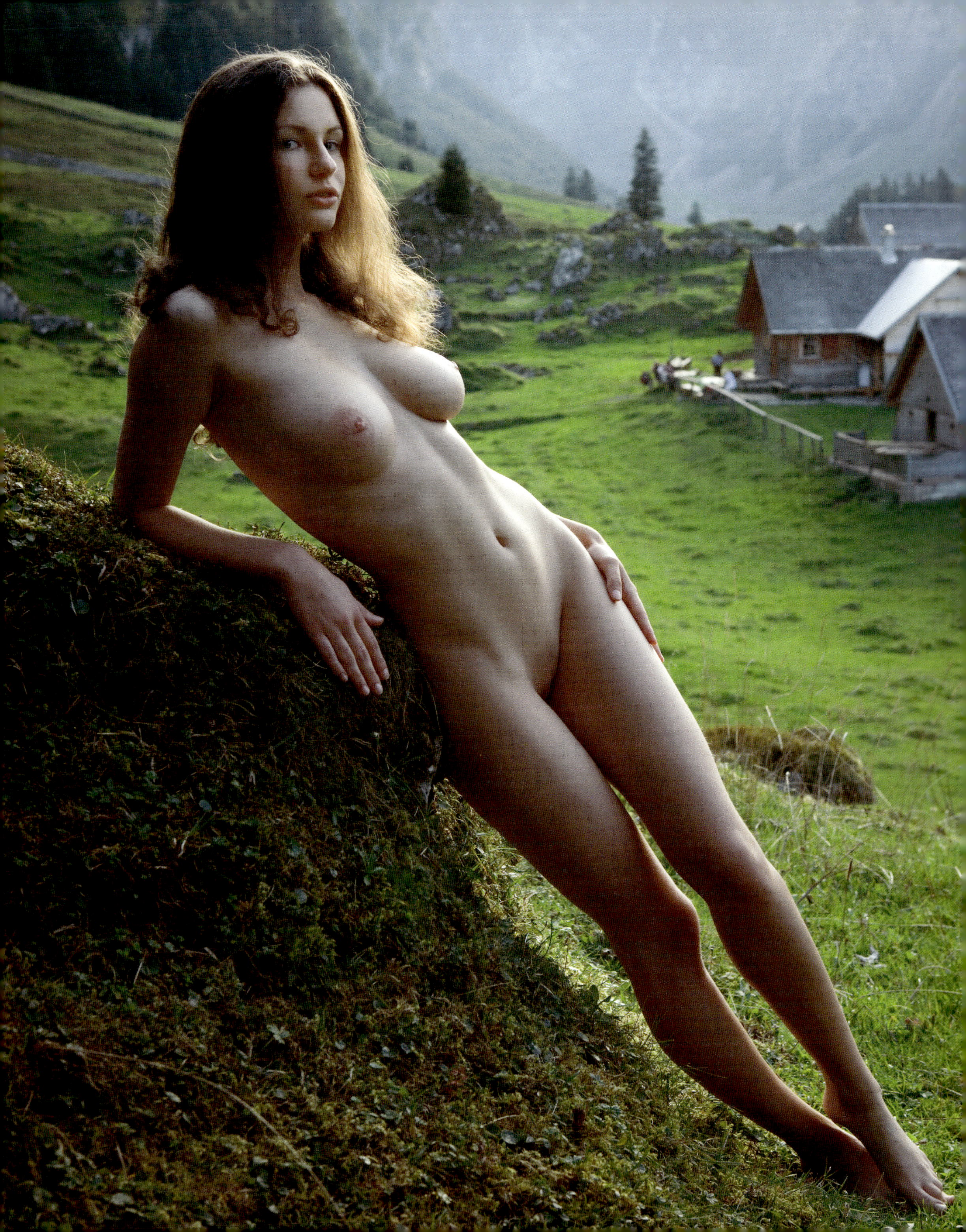

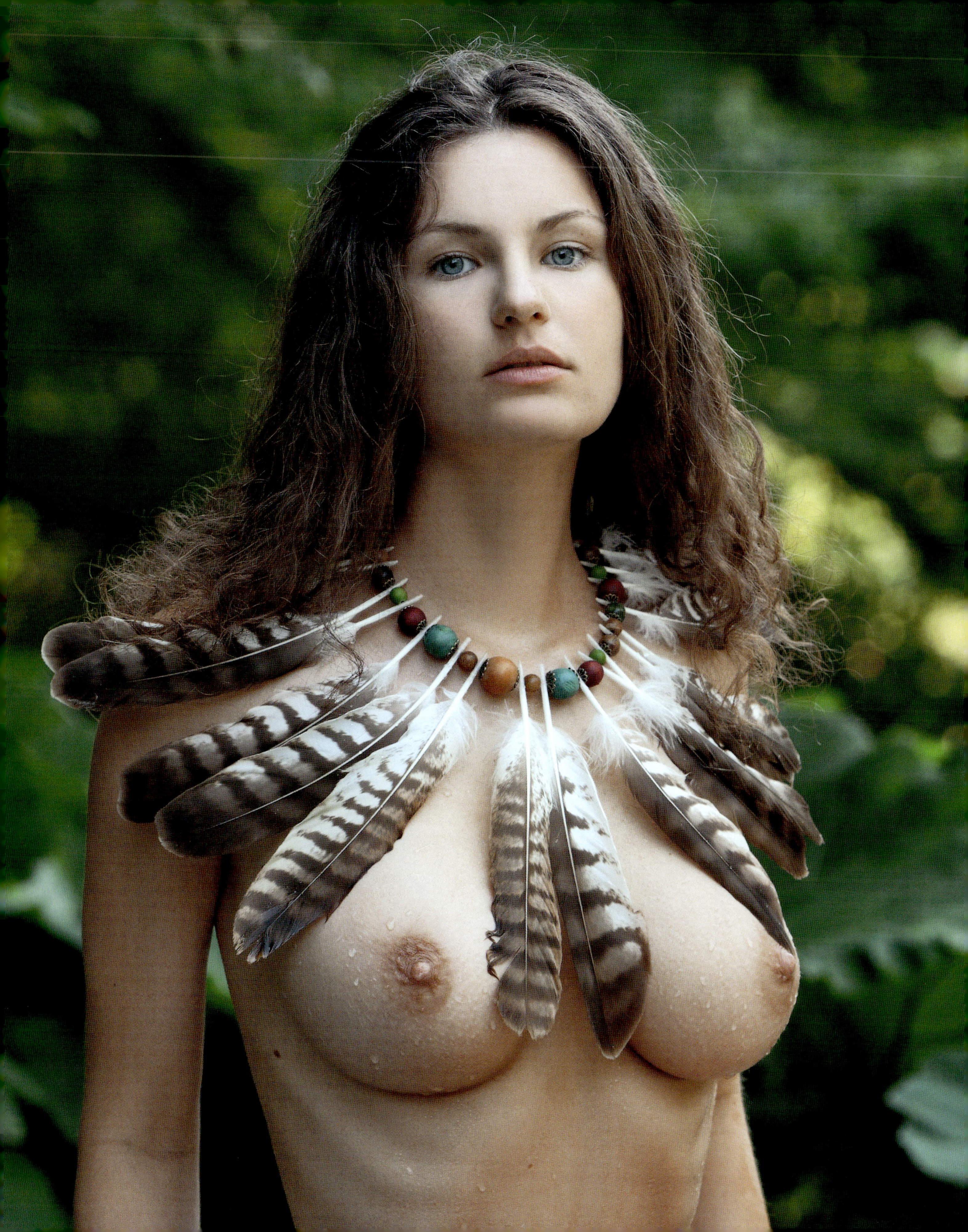

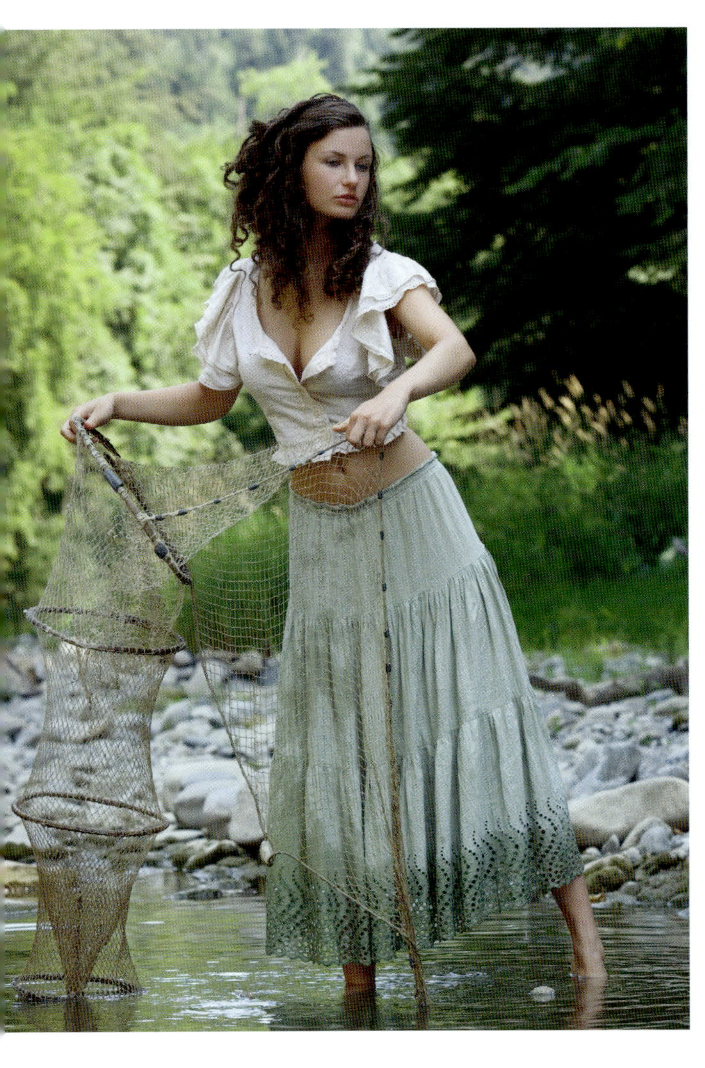

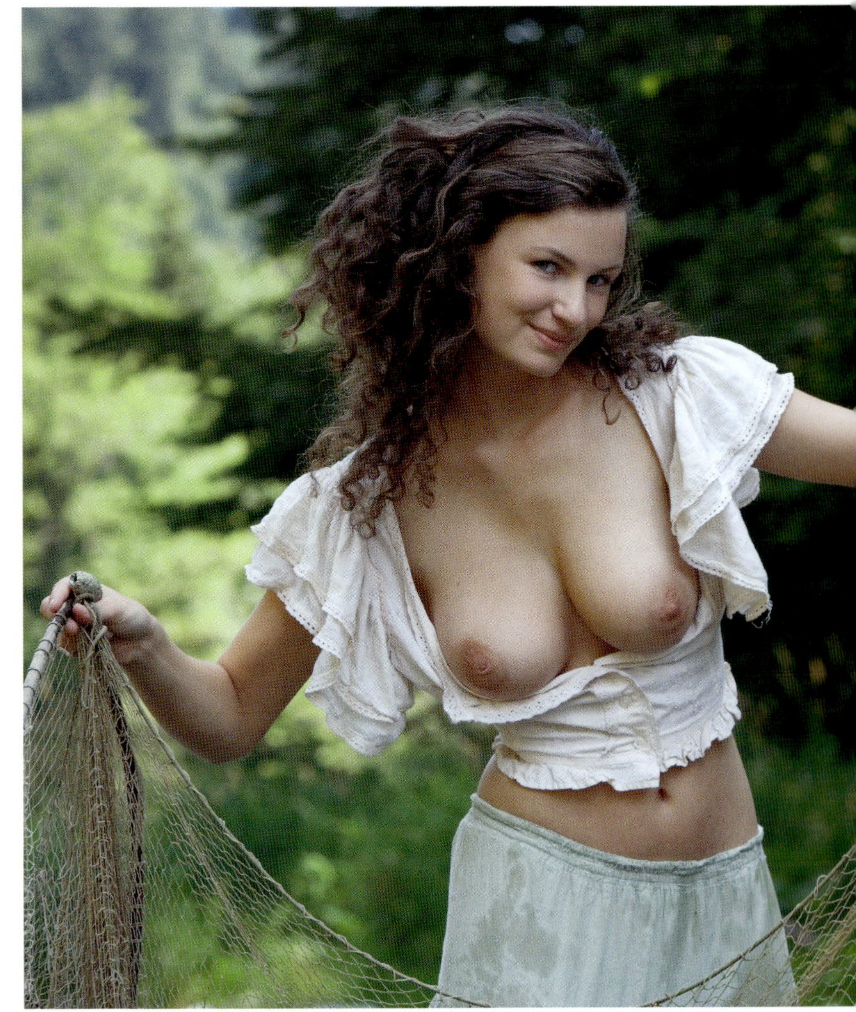

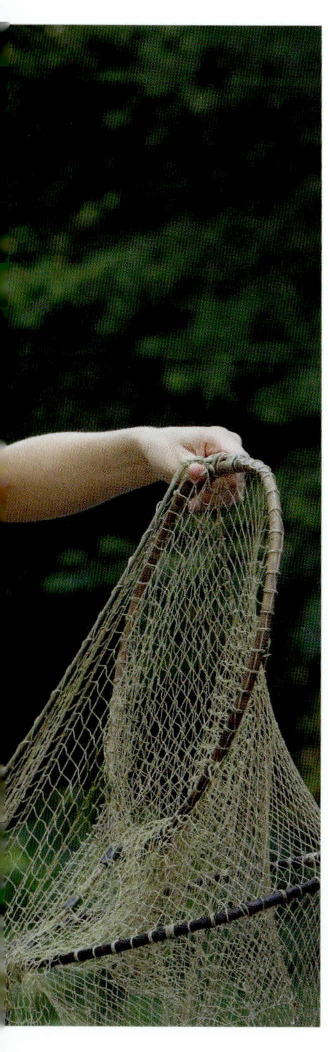

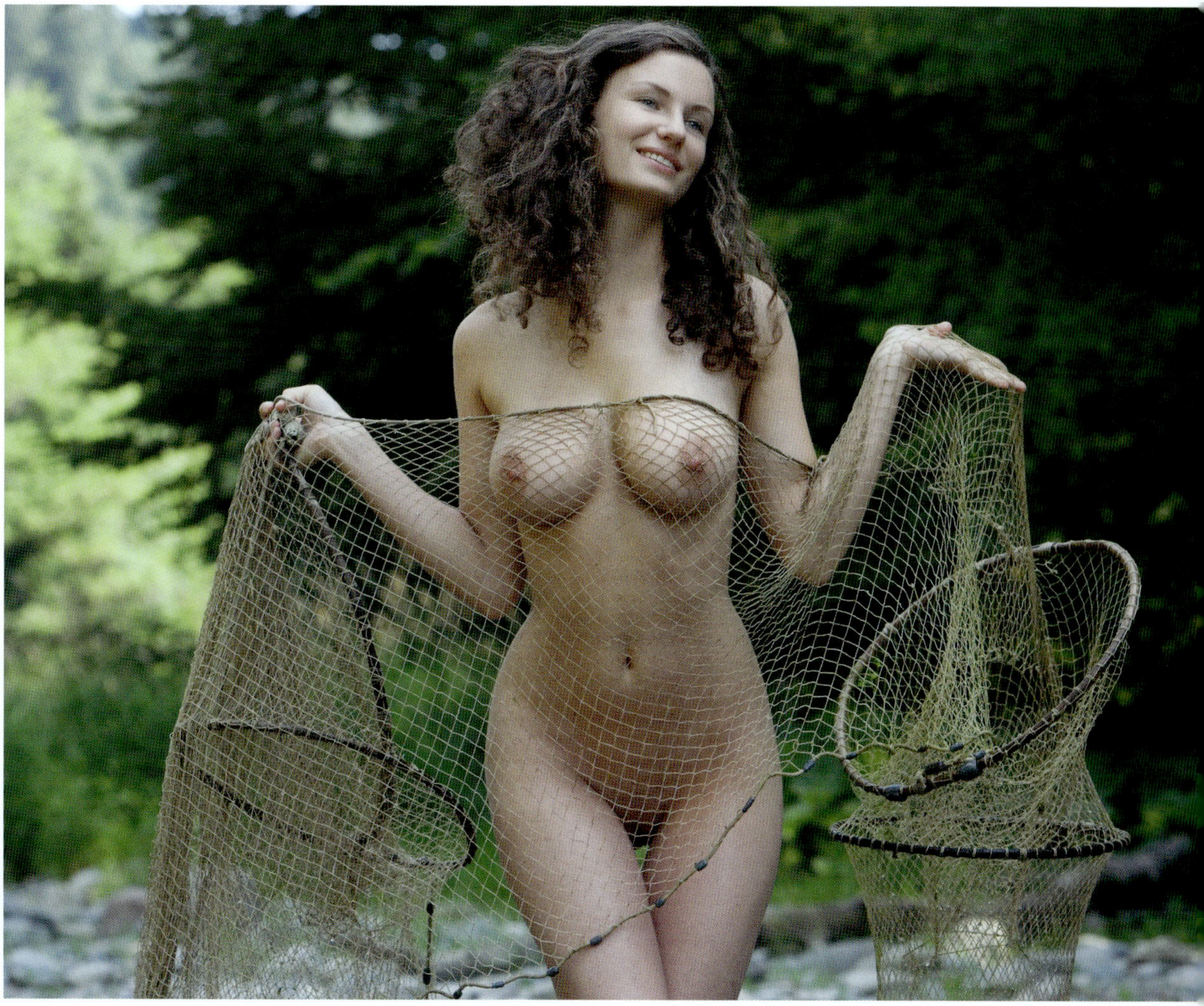

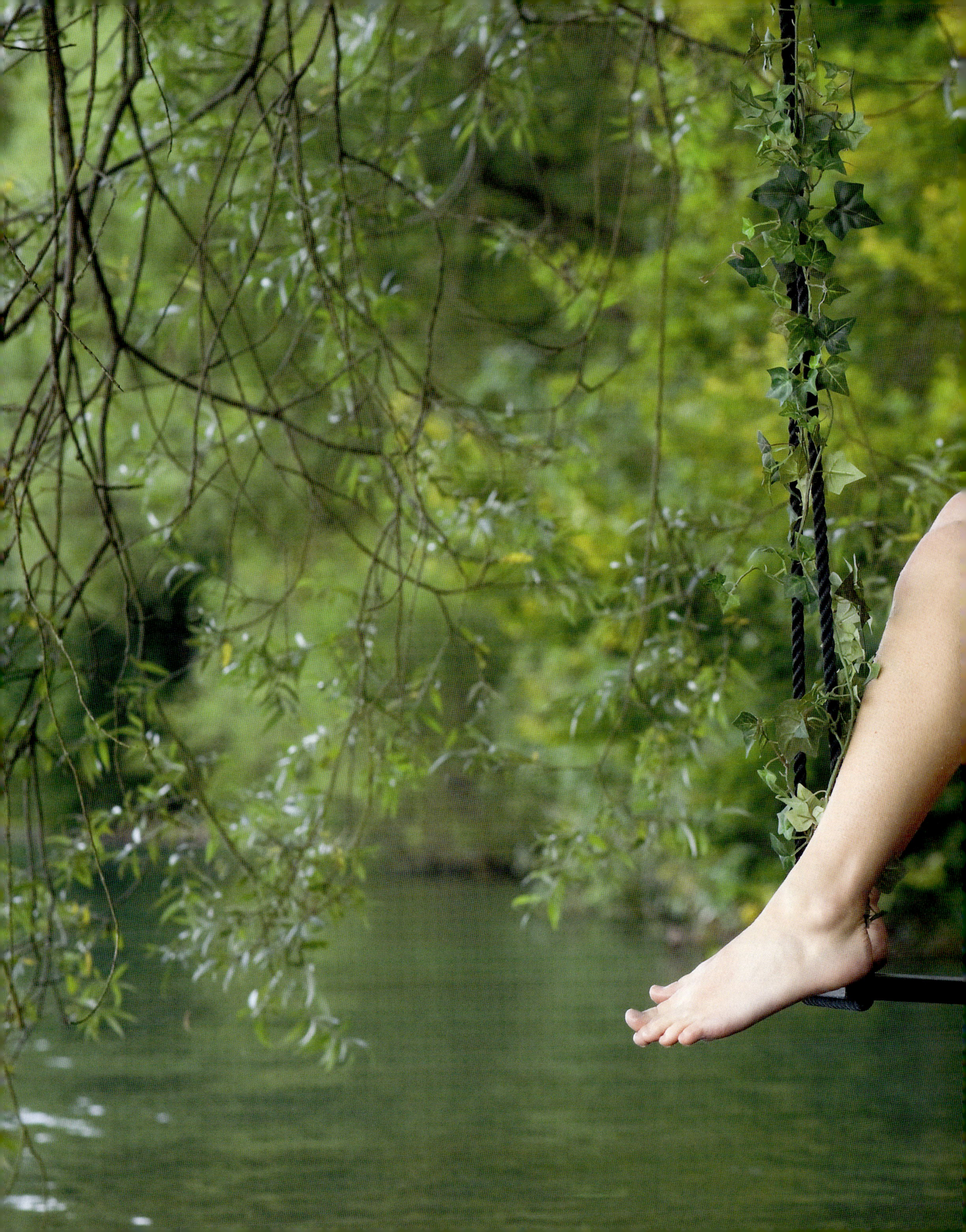

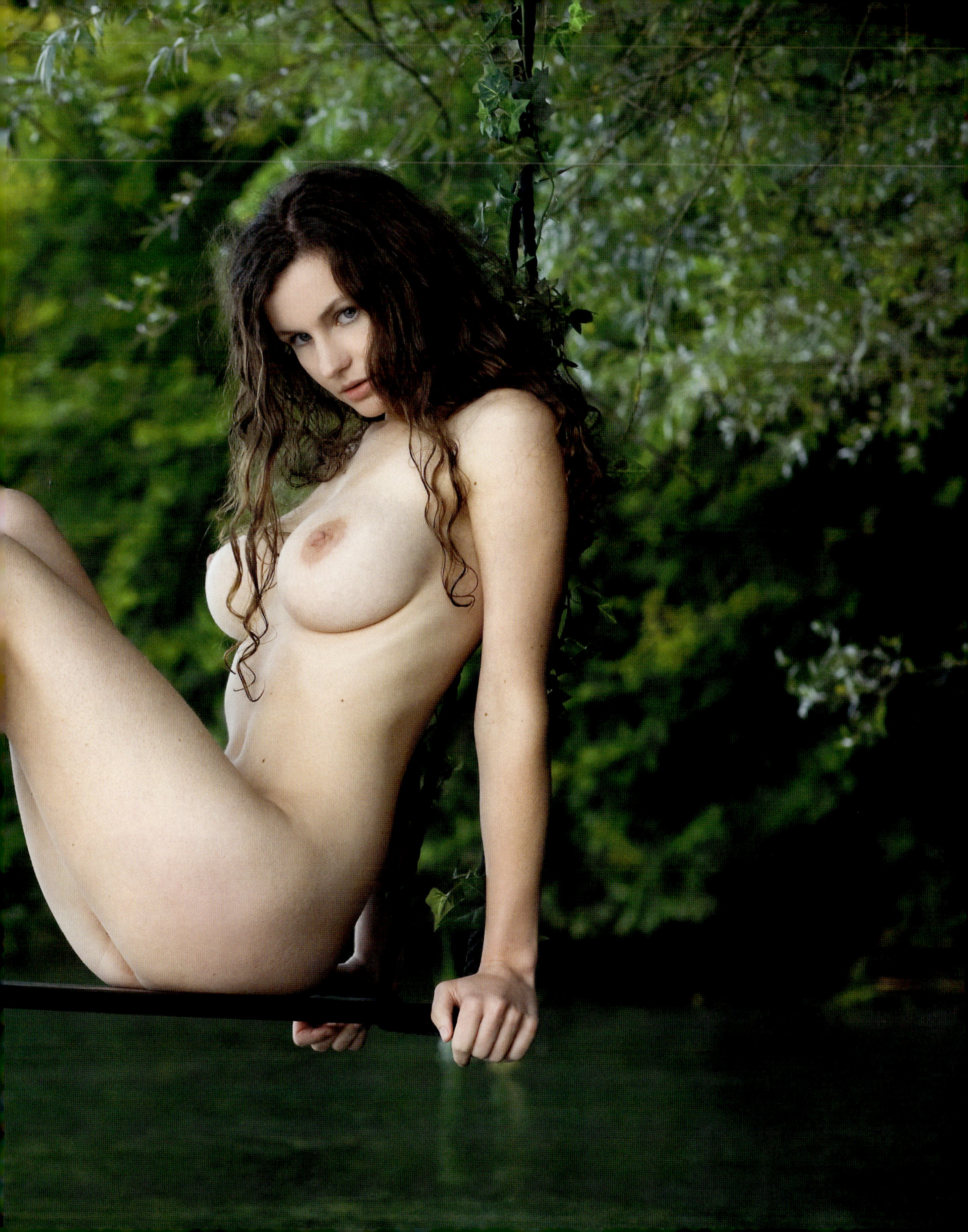

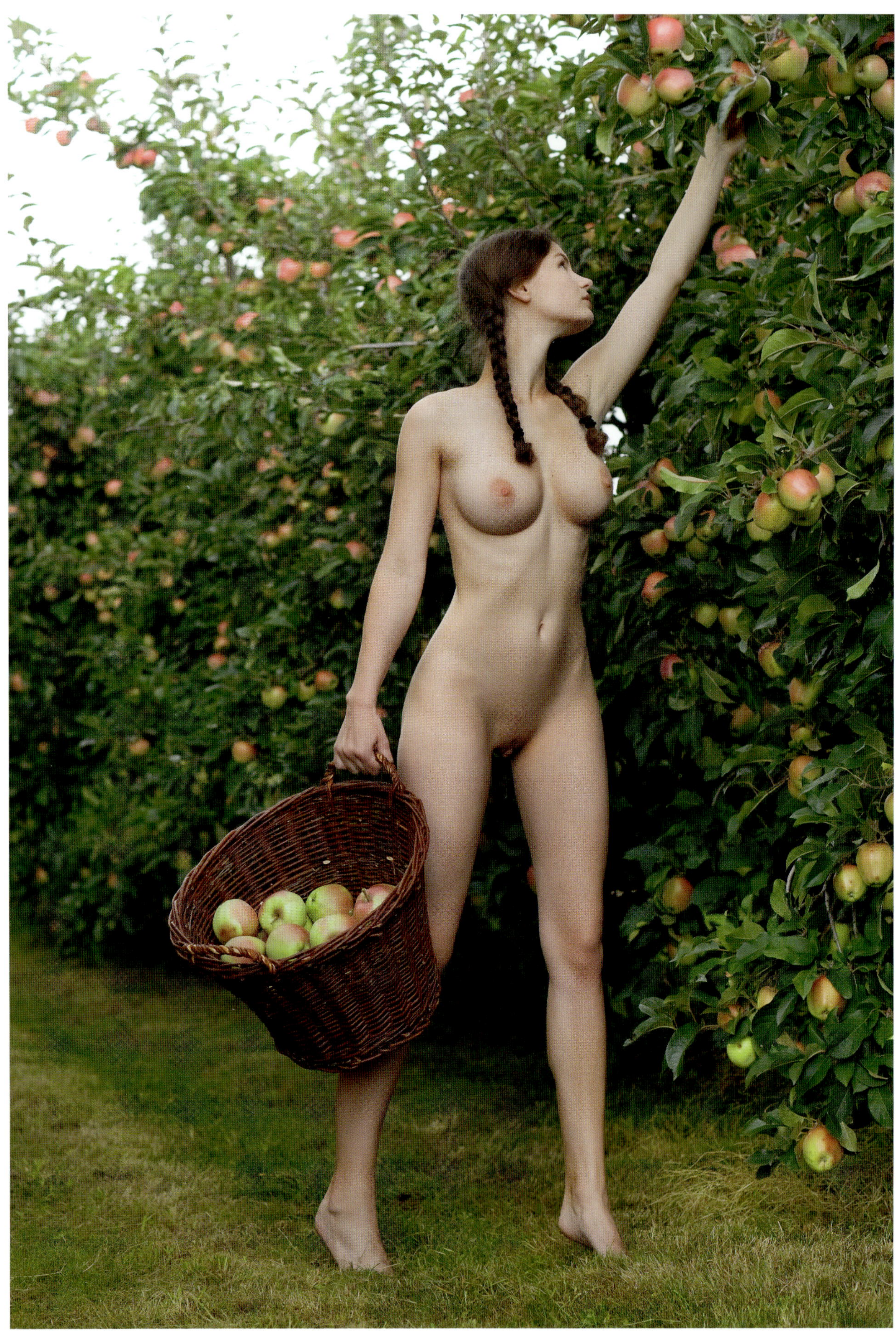

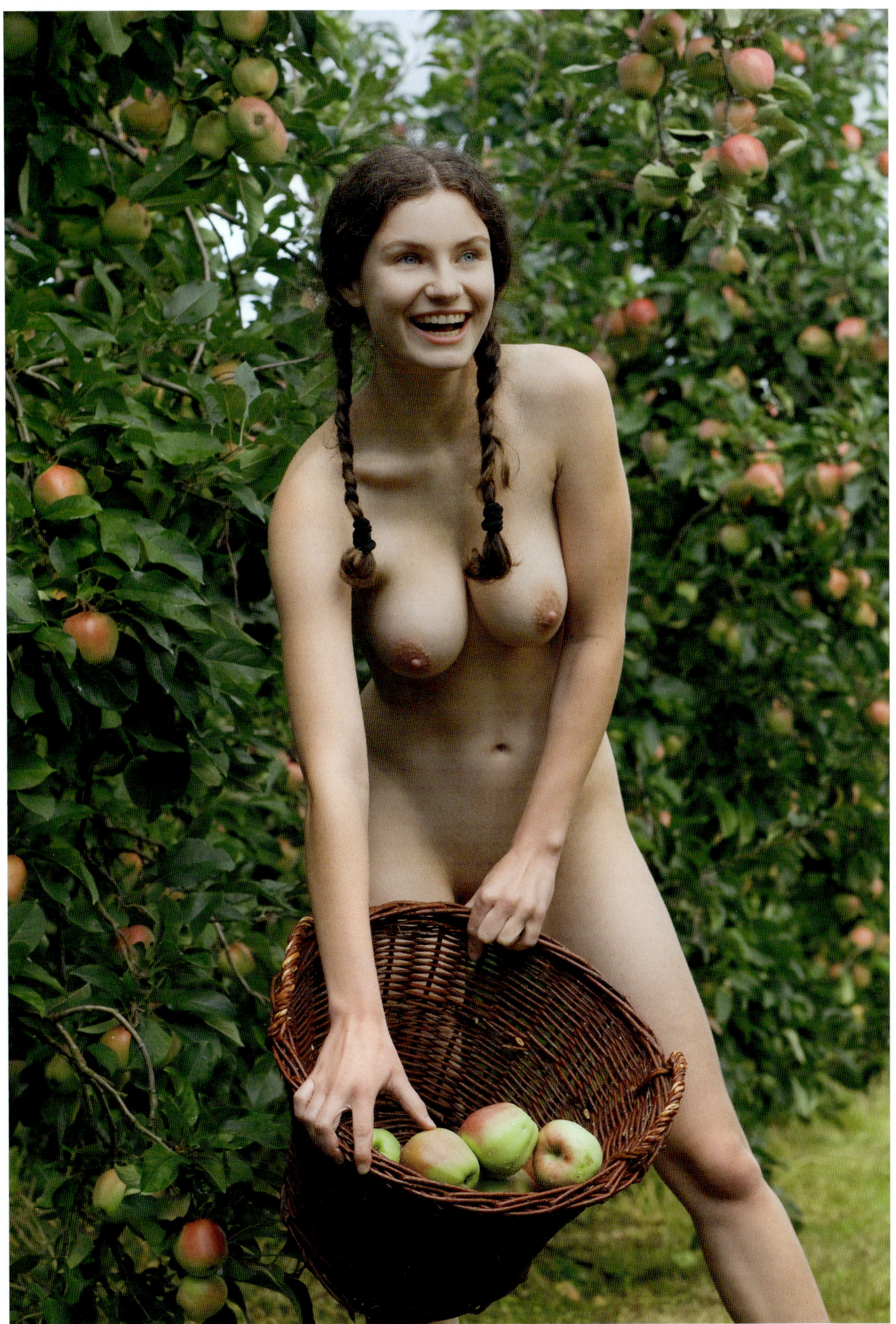

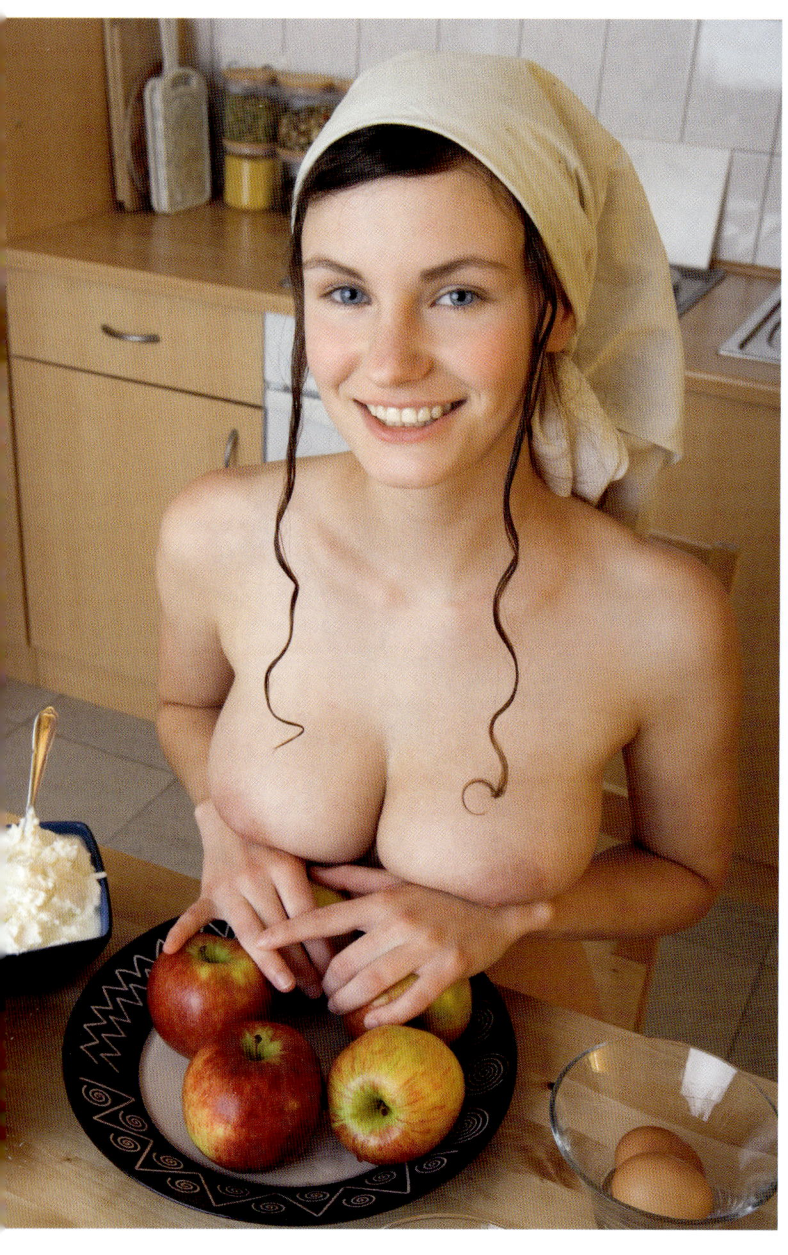

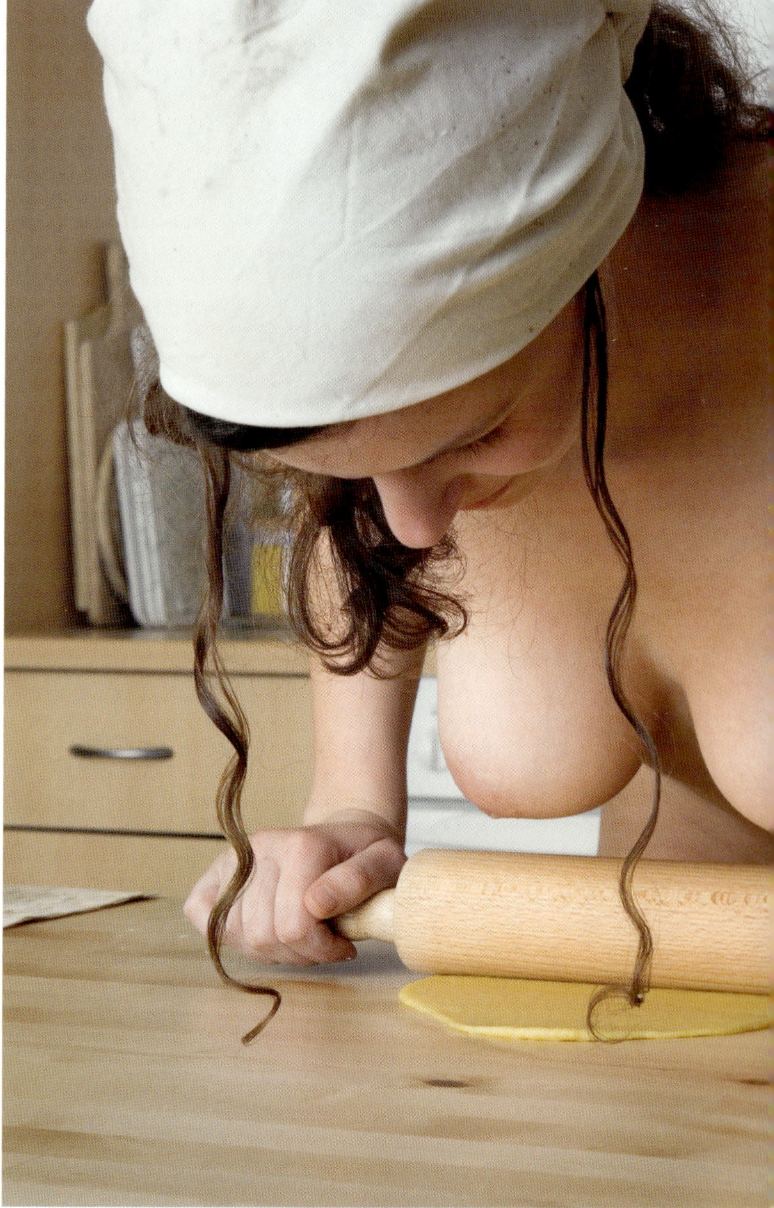

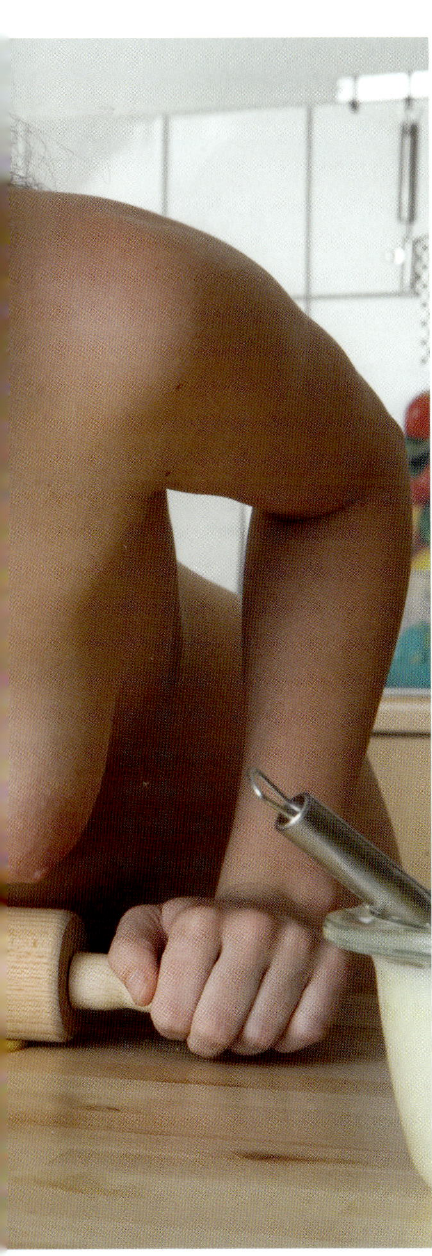

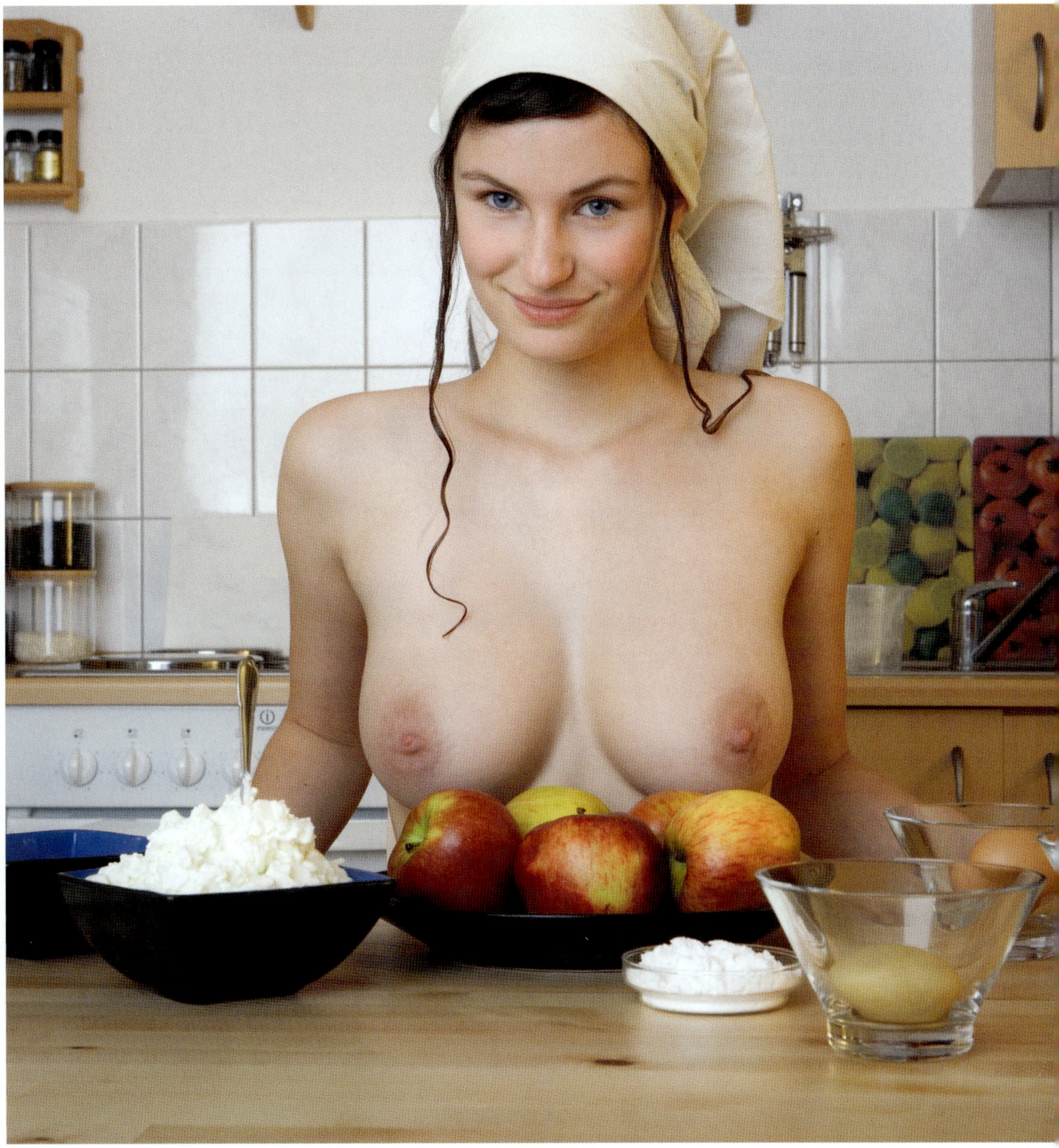

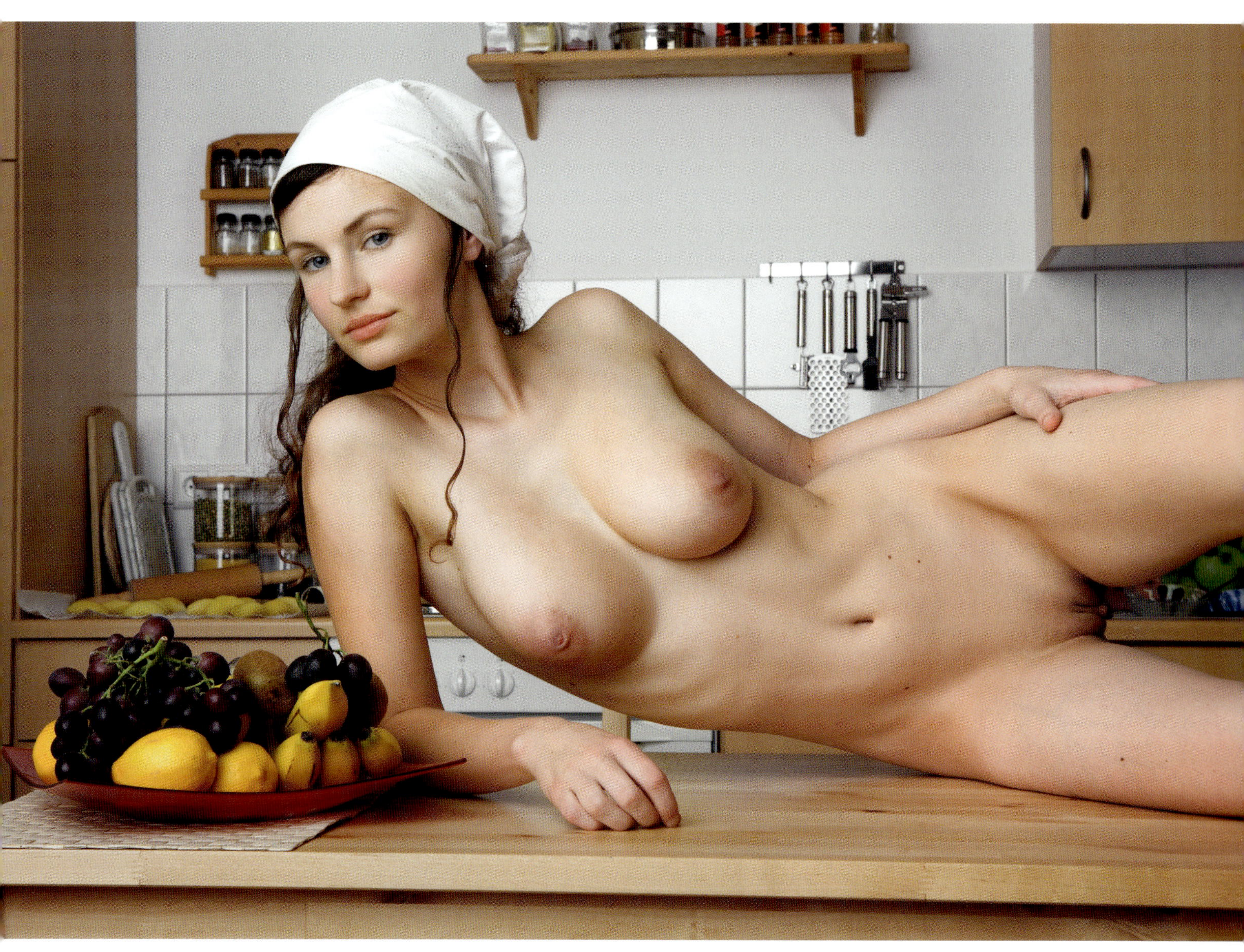

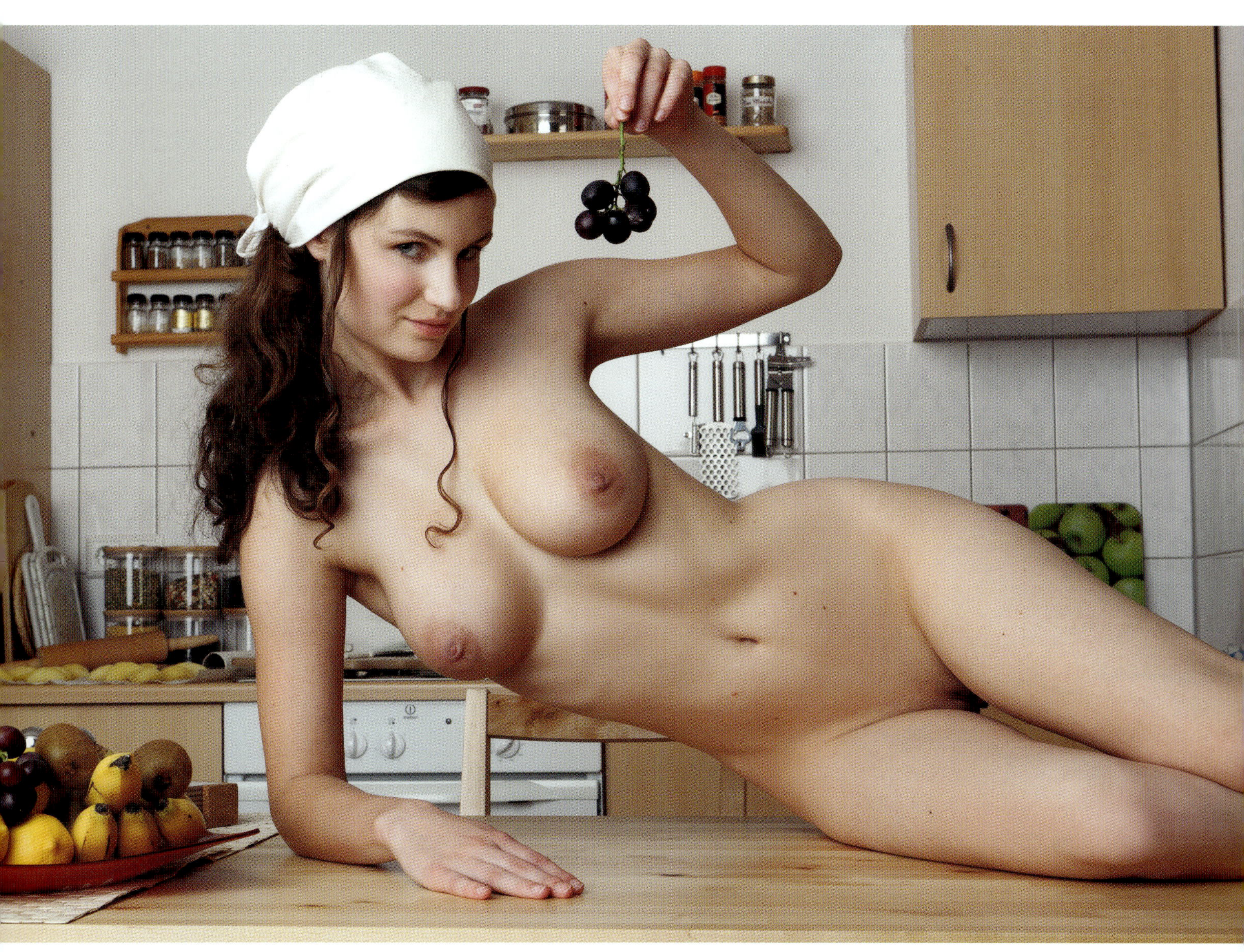

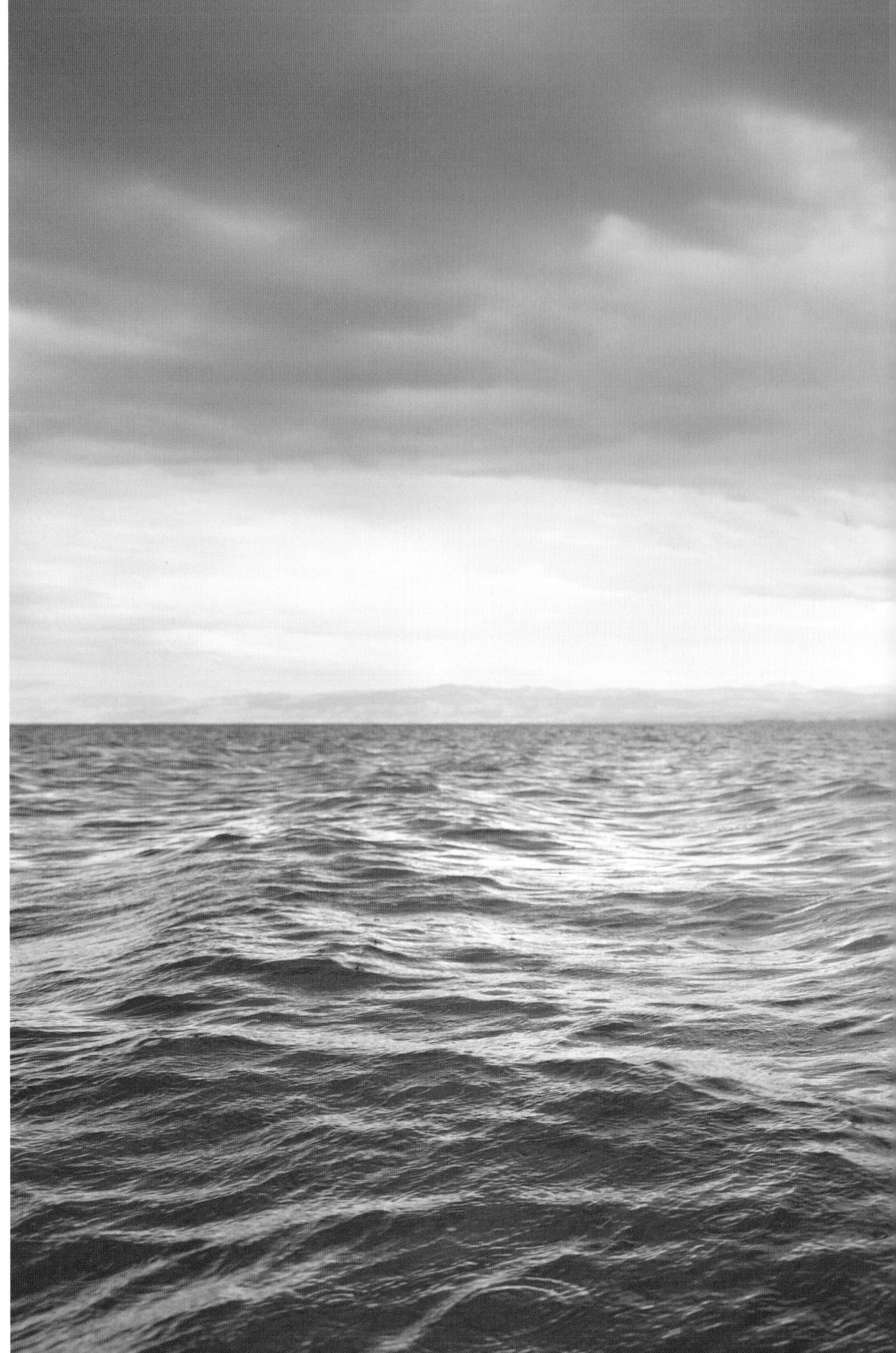

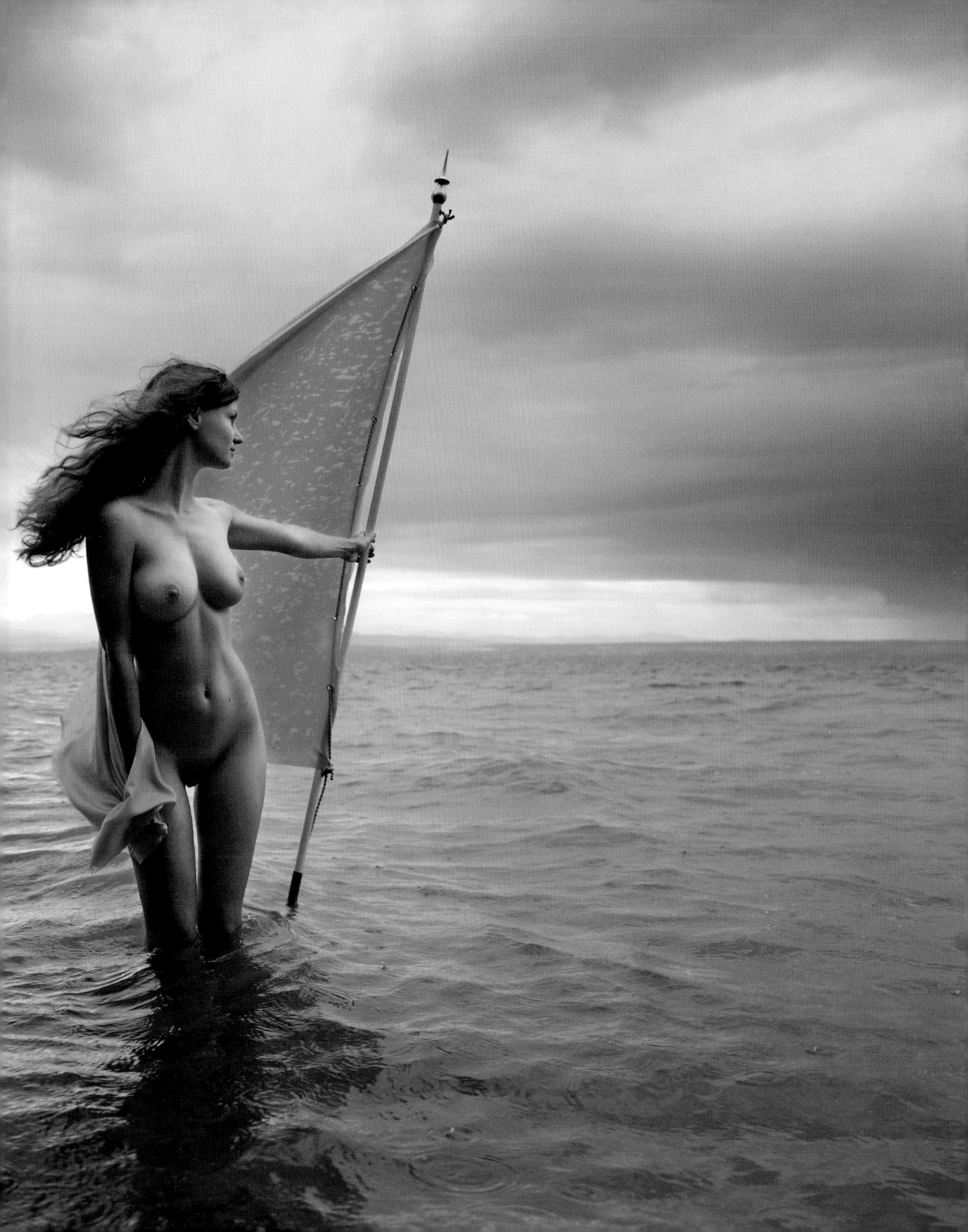

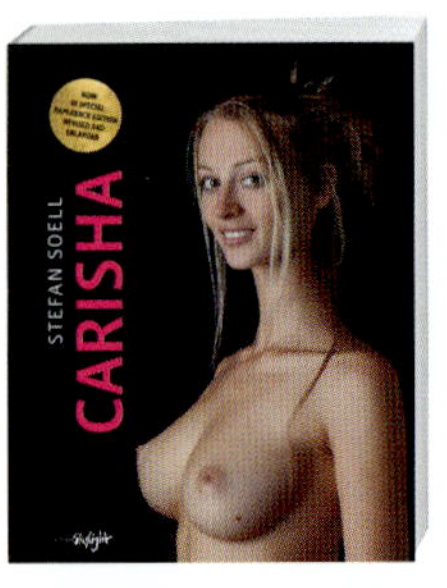

Stefan Soell
CARISHA
Aktualisierte und erweiterte Ausgabe in Paperback
Deutsch/Englische Originalausgabe
Special Paperback Edition revised and enlarged
Original English/German Edition
160 Seiten mit über 180 Fotos in Farbe
160 pp., with over 180 pictures in color
Paperback im Format 19 × 23,5 cm
ISBN 978-3-03766-685-2

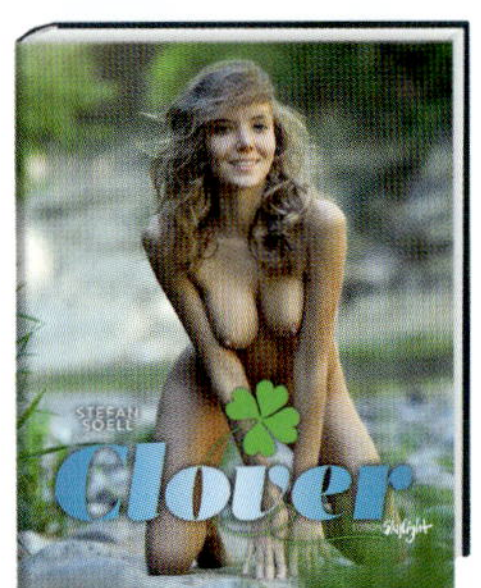

Stefan Soell
CLOVER
Deutsch/Englische Originalausgabe
Original English/German Edition
128 Seiten mit über 130 Fotos in Farbe
128 pp., with over 130 pictures in full color
Fester Einband mit extra starken Deckeln
im Format 21 × 26,4 cm
Hardcover with extra strong boards
ISBN 978-3-03766-690-6

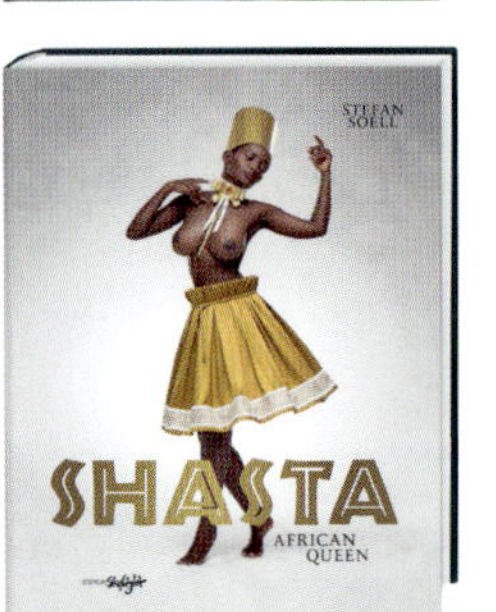

Stefan Soell
SHASTA – AFRICAN QUEEN
Deutsch/Englische Originalausgabe
Original English/German Edition
128 Seiten mit über 130 Fotos in Farbe
128 pp., with over 130 pictures in full color
Fester Einband mit extra starken Deckeln
im Format 21 × 26,4 cm
Hardcover with extra strong boards
ISBN 978-3-03766-682-1

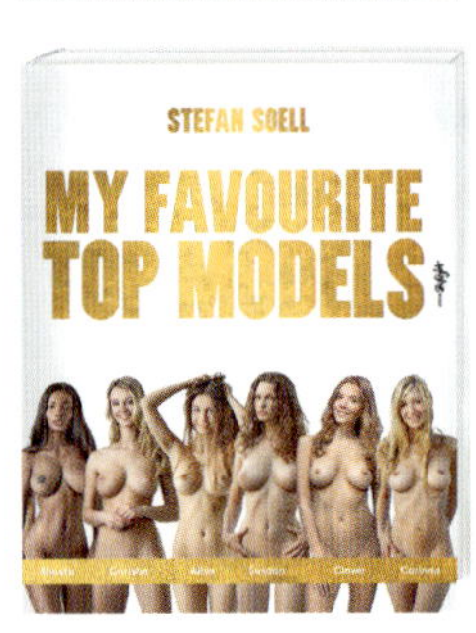

Stefan Soell
MY FAVOURITE TOP MODELS
2. Deutsch/Englische Ausgabe
Second English-German Edition
288 Seiten mit über 400 Fotos in Farbe
288 pp., with over 400 pictueres in full color
Fester Einband mit extra starken Deckeln
im Format 21 × 26,4 cm
Hardcover with extra strong boards
ISBN 978-3-03766-681-4

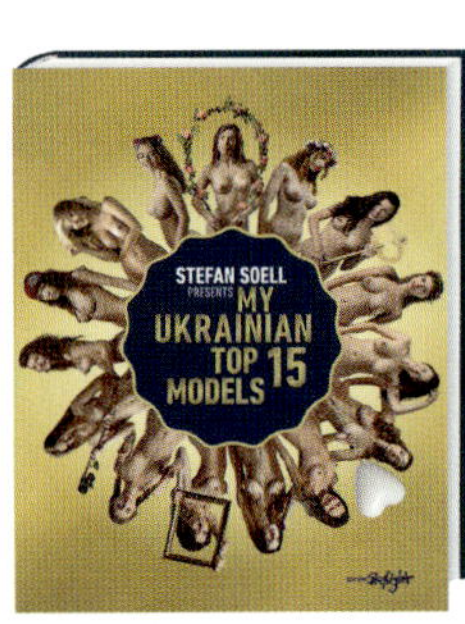

Stefan Soell
MY UKRAINIAN TOP 15 MODELS
2. Deutsch/Englische Ausgabe
Second English/German Edition
288 Seiten mit über 400 Fotos in Farbe
288 pp., with over 400 pictures in full color
Fester Einband mit extra starken Deckeln
im Format 21 x 26,4 cm
Hardcover with extra strong boards
ISBN 978-3-03766-686-9

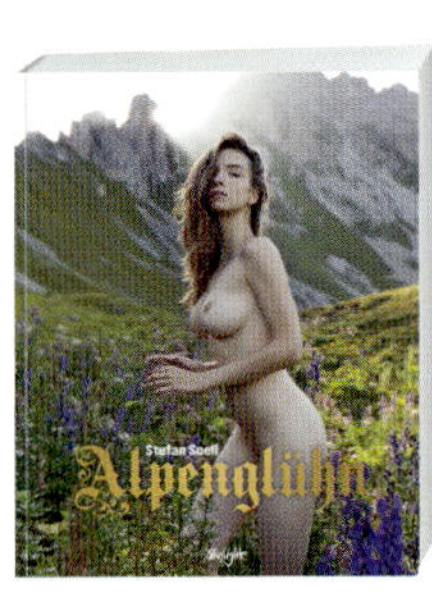

Stefan Soell
ALPENGLÜHN
Aktualisierte und erweiterte Ausgabe in Paperback
2. Deutsch/Englische Ausgabe
Special Paperback Edition revised and enlarged
Second English-German edition
192 Seiten mit über 220 farbigen Fotos
192 pp. with over 220 pictures in color
Paperback im Format 19 × 23,5 cm
ISBN 978-3-03766-673-9

www.edition-skylight.com

← COLLECT THEM ALL:

PHOTOBOOKS BY GENIUS PHOTOGRAPHER

STEFAN SOELL

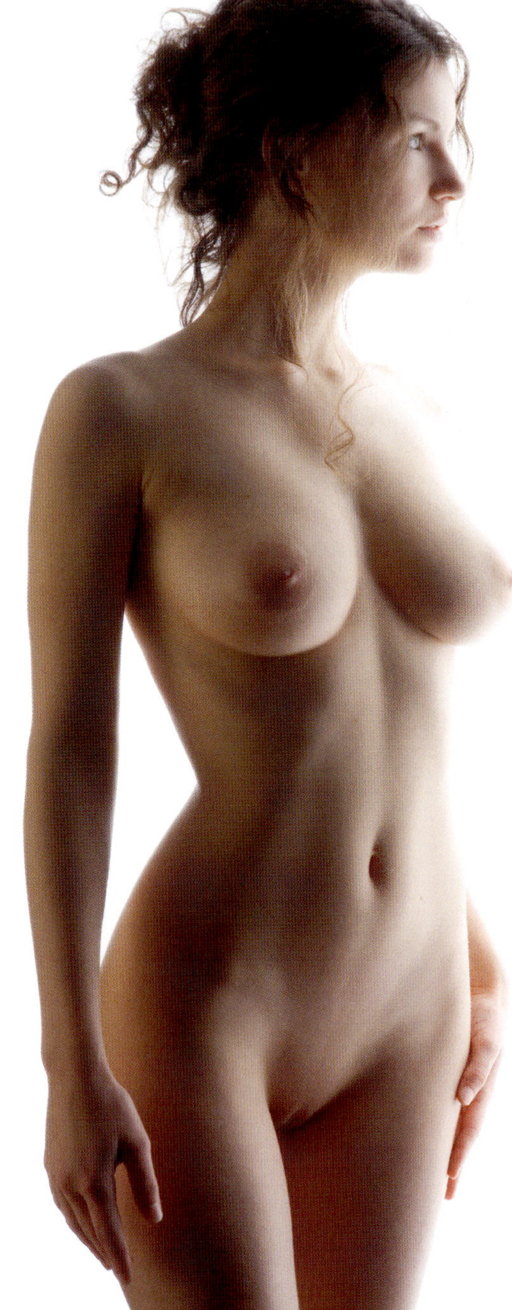